P9-CKU-774

Claude Taittinger

Jean Hugel

Jeffrey M. Pogash

Darrell Corti

Francisco Valle

Raymond Reynolds

Hubert Trimbach

Myron S. Nightingale

windows on the world
complete wine course

Kevin Zraly

STERLING PUBLISHING CO., INC. NEW YORK

designed by jim anderson
edited by felicia sherbert & robert hernandez

LIBRARY OF CONGRESS CATALOGING IN PUBLICATION DATA

ZRALY, KEVIN.
WINDOWS ON THE WORLD COMPLETE WINE COURSE.

INCLUDES INDEX.
1. WINE AND WINE MAKING. I. TITLE.
TP548.Z73 1985 641.2'22 84-26851
ISBN 0-8069-5582-1

PUBLISHED BY STERLING PUBLISHING CO., INC.
TWO PARK AVENUE, NEW YORK, N.Y. 10016
DISTRIBUTED IN AUSTRALIA BY CAPRICORN BOOK CO. PTY. LTD.
UNIT 5C1 LINCOLN ST., LANE COVE, N.S.W. 2066
DISTRIBUTED IN THE UNITED KINGDOM BY BLANDFORD PRESS
LINK HOUSE, WEST STREET, POOLE, DORSET BH15 1LL, ENGLAND
DISTRIBUTED IN CANADA BY OAK TREE PRESS LTD.
℅ CANADIAN MANDA GROUP, P.O. BOX 920, STATION U
TORONTO, ONTARIO, CANADA M8Z 5P9
MANUFACTURED IN THE UNITED STATES OF AMERICA

LITHOGRAPHY BY INTERSTATE LITHO CORP.

CONTENTS

dedication

First and foremost, to my parents and family, who have been a constant source of encouragement and understanding throughout my life.

To John Novi, for allowing me to learn about wines at the Depuy Canal House in High Falls, New York.

To Craig Claiborne, for giving the Depuy Canal House a four-star rating, which helped the restaurant's wine list grow to include 125 selections.

To Father Sam Matarazzo, who inspired me to take my study of wine to Europe.

To Peter Bienstock, who shared his older vintages with me.

To Herb Schutte, who gave me my first job in the wine business.

To Vincent Barcos, from whom I first heard about Windows on the World.

To Barbara Kafka, who recommended me for the job of cellarmaster at Windows on the World.

To Joe Baum, creator of Windows on the World, who had the original concept of hiring a young American as cellarmaster.

To Alan Lewis, director of Windows on the World, who hired me and has been instrumental in the wine program.

To Toni Aigner, president of Inhilco, who was the initial force behind this book.

To Mohonk Mountain House in New Paltz, New York, where ideas come easy.

To Raymond Wellington, for his editorial contributions and for writing the section about wine in restaurants.

To Kathy Talbert, whose conceptual ideas helped greatly in the writing of this book.

To Burton Hobson, president of Sterling Publishing Co., Inc., who had the faith to put "another wine book" on the market.

To Felicia Sherbert, my editor, without whom this book could not have been written.

To Ellen Kerr, who patiently typed and retyped the manuscript.

And most importantly, to my wife, Rosemary, who supported the writing of this book with her ideas, enthusiasm, and patience.

ACKNOWLEDGMENTS

I would like to express my deep appreciation to M. Shanken Communications, Inc. of New York City—publishers of *Impact* wine and spirits newsletter; *Market Watch* magazine; and *The Wine Spectator* for supplying information used in this book.

I am indebted to the winemakers in California and Europe who contributed their expertise and enthusiasm for this project. The signatures on the front and back pages represent some of the people whose help was invaluable to me.

I appreciate the editorial input provided by Stephen Topping.

Thanks to Michael Buller and Pan American Airlines.

Menu script by Philip Romeo.

All of the labels featured are wines recommended by the author.

FOREWORD

Did you know that there are 2,300 different Italian wine labels? And that Portugal produces as much wine as the United States? That the annual per capita consumption of wine in France and Italy is 22 to 24 gallons, but in the United States it is only two? Do you want to commit to memory the names of the more than 3,000 châteaus in the Bordeaux region of France, or are you seeking more useful knowledge?

Why is the subject of wine so complicated? For hundreds of years wine was consumed without fuss. Whatever was in your glass was what you drank. Sometimes it was good, but more often it was just palatable. You drank the wine that was produced in your area, and your main concern was whether it was red, white, or rosé. There was no great mystery about serving wine—no complex etiquette—until the last 50 years.

Today the maze of wine laws, regions, appellations, and grape varieties is a new twist in the ancient winemaking industry. The amount of information is staggering; the availability of wine is unsurpassed in history. New technology makes possible a wide variety of wines, and the consumer is dazzled by an array of styles, labels, and producers.

I had never planned on writing a wine book. For years different publishers contacted Windows on the World to persuade us to put our wine course into words. I had always declined because I felt there were too many wine books on the market. However, after much thought and a review of the wine books available, I saw the need for a *simpler* guide to wine. And so it began.

Where does one begin to explore this broad subject? As a wine educator I have discovered that the best way to teach people about wine is to answer their specific questions. Rather than lecture them, I listen and try to address their concerns.

The first step involved recording all eight classes of the wine course given by Windows on the World. Then the tapes were transcribed and edited in a question-and-answer format to make the facts more accessible. You do not have to sift through flowery descriptions to find answers to questions, which are arranged in order of complexity. Basic facts about a particular region or subject are covered at the beginning of each chapter—more specific details appear afterwards. To make the subject of wine fun, humorous anecdotes about wine are also featured. Maps and charts reinforce the information contained in the text.

This book won't answer every question—it addresses those most frequently asked, including how to choose, serve, taste, and enjoy wine. It provides easy-to-use information for both the novice and the more knowledgeable connoisseur.

The mystique of wine is very alluring, but it can also be intimidating. The enjoyment of wine should be denied no one, and we can all appreciate it in our own way. You may not wish to be a wine professional, but once you understand the basics you may want to learn much more about wine. It is an absorbing hobby that will give you a lifetime of pleasure.

For information regarding the Windows on the World correspondence course, write to:

Kevin Zraly
Windows on the World
One World Trade Center 107th Floor
New York, NY 10048

PREFACE

Not so many years ago, the average American travelling in Europe would remark with surprise on the custom of consuming wine with meals. It was unusual, even quaint, one of the European traditions worth bringing home.

Yet making wine a part of everyday American life took many years and much effort on the part of wine writers, wine merchants, and wine lovers all over the country. Among restaurants who contributed to the nation's oenological life, Windows on the World, atop New York's World Trade Center, is at the forefront.

Inhilco, the ten-year-old Hilton International subsidiary that manages the restaurant along with all others in the complex, operates Windows on the World with a very definite philosophy about wine and food. The menu draws on culinary traditions from France to China and the Windows on the World wine list is as global as the menu.

But marrying a spectacular wine list to a spectacular menu was only the beginning. It was imperative that every guest understood what we were offering. Our wines and our food had to be as accessible to the uninitiated as to connoisseurs. We needed a staff capable of explaining the many facets of our wine list in glorious detail.

And so, we set up a training program for our staff members. We schooled them in vintages and vineyards, taught them the differences between the wines of one region and those of another. Excited by this knowledge, our students became teachers themselves, and with every wine order transmitted their own enthusiasm to our guests—many of whom went on to become students at the Windows on the World Wine School, which was formed in 1978 as a natural extension of our staff wine-education program.

Kevin Zraly, who joined Inhilco in 1976, has been an integral part of the oenological activity at Windows on the World. He helped create our wine list, and was largely responsible for its winning *The Wine Spectator* magazine's

1981 Grand Award for having one of the best restaurant wine lists in America. In addition, Kevin Zraly set up both our staff wine-education program and our wine school. A native New Yorker who studied winemaking in California and has pursued his wine research in all the great wine regions of Europe, he loves to teach. His classes are informal and allow plenty of give and take. His own zest for wine shines through. The *Windows on the World Complete Wine Course* is imbued with this enthusiasm.

We hope that it simplifies your own understanding of wine—and makes studying it the adventure for you that it already is for him.

Curt R. Strand
President of Hilton International

INTRODUCTION

I first heard about Kevin from one of my European associates. Kevin had come to visit our winery during his self-training in Europe. He decided that the only way to learn about wine was to visit the wine country. For eight months he toured the vineyards of France, Italy, Germany, Spain, and Switzerland. Somehow he made an impression—in blue jeans, on a very small budget, but with the right questions and a passion to learn. Europeans encourage wandering students—they can tell the real student from the phony one. They know that Americans have an insatiable thirst for knowledge.

Kevin's interest in wine started during his student days in New Paltz, New York. He took a job as a part-time waiter at the Depuy Canal House in nearby High Falls, and ended up as the manager of the only four-star restaurant in the Catskills. Since his job included the ordering of wine, he decided to learn more on the subject.

He returned to New York City, knowing a lot about wine, and was hired by a wine and liquor wholesaler to sell accounts that were more interested in Wild Irish Rose than in Meursault and Château Lafite. Before you knew it, he was the wine buyer and sommelier at Windows on the World, which ultimately turned out to be the largest wine account in America, possibly in the whole world. The job title was cellarmaster, and he continued to expand the responsibilities of the position. He created what is probably the most innovative and most frequently revised wine list in the world. After all, with knowledge and a word processor and computer there is no longer any need to carve a wine list in stone. He trained a staff second to none to suggest and serve the wine, and, inevitably, he started a wine school. That wine school, being in the financial center of New York, has taught more top executives how to select and enjoy wine than any other.

The reward for success in America is promotion. Kevin was named Hilton International Wine Director in 1980, which enabled him to select some of the finest California wines for the Hilton International chain. Besides teaching the wine classes, he started an entirely new venture with *The Wine Spectator:* The California Wine Experience, a three-day spectacular whereby 700 people from across the country listen to lectures, attend tastings, seminars, happenings, and meet the people who make wine. To see Kevin supervise the mechanics of a tasting that has 700 people sample a dozen wines is to witness a person who could hold his own as the stage manager of the Metropolitan Opera. The task involves 8,400 glasses, and all 700 people are served twelve wines at precisely the same time without mix-up. And wonder upon wonder, he has trained others to organize such happenings as well as he does.

It was inevitable that Kevin would write a wine book sooner or later—and that it would be different from any other wine book. It is not written to impress the world with Kevin's knowledge or insight, both of which he has enough of and to spare. It was written to be *less* rather than *more*. It is reminiscent of that old saying: "If I had more time, I would have written a shorter book." Well, Kevin has written a shorter book. He has written the essential wine book, a succinct guide to the essentials—a basic guide that does not weigh you down with unnecessary information or erudition, which would only hamper you in your journey through the labyrinth of wine. And yet this no-nonsense guide is not lacking in the necessary trivia to make the material entertaining as well as informative—those little hooks of extraneous facts which are so essential for the mind to remember facts. The information is presented in a well-designed format, it is easy to use as a guide or reference book, and yet it is interesting enough to read at one sitting.

In addition, the section on how to create a wine list and stock a wine cellar in a restaurant is the best account I have ever read on the subject. It is both diverse and economical, and it will no doubt serve as a blueprint for many a wine list across the land. The section entitled "Wine in Restaurants," written by Raymond Wellington (director of wine services at Windows on the World), is a delightfully informative look at the ritual of ordering wine.

I have a feeling that this book is the first of a number of innovative, educational ventures by Kevin in the world of wines. He is not only a consultant to Hilton International, the program director for the California Wine Experience, and a winemaker himself in the Hudson Valley region of New York State, but he gains new ideas for "spreading the wine faith" in his extensive contacts with the neophyte and the connoisseur. There exists an enormous amount of information about wine, which most other writers seem to complicate. This first venture should gain Kevin an enthusiastic new following.

Peter M. F. Sichel

prelude to wine

You're in a wine shop looking for "that special wine" to serve at a dinner party. Before you walked in, you had at least an *idea* of what you wanted, but now as you scan the shelves, you are overwhelmed. "There are so many wines," you think to yourself, ". . . and so many prices." You take a deep breath, boldly pick up a bottle that looks impressive, and buy it. Then you hope that your guest will like your selection.

Does this sound a little farfetched? For some of you, yes. But the truth is that this is a very common occurrence for the wine beginner and even for the intermediate. And it doesn't have to be that way. Wine should be an enjoyable experience. By the time you finish this book, you'll be able to buy from a retailer with confidence, or even look in the eyes of a cellarmaster and ask for the selection of your choice with no hesitation. But first we must start with basics—the foundation of your wine knowledge. Read carefully, because you'll find this section invaluable as you relate it to the chapters that follow. You may even want to refer back to this Prelude to Wine occasionally to reinforce what you learn.

For the purpose of this book, wine is the fermented juice of grapes.

What is fermentation?

Fermentation is the process by which the grape juice turns into wine. The formula for fermentation is:

$$\text{Sugar} + \text{Yeast} = \text{Alcohol} + \text{Carbon Dioxide } (CO_2)$$

Sugar is present naturally in the ripe grape. *Yeast* also occurs naturally, as the white bloom on the grape skin. However, this natural yeast is not always used in today's winemaking. Instead, laboratory strains of pure yeast have been isolated, each strain contributing something unique to the style of wine. The fermentation process ends when all the sugar has been converted into *alcohol* or the alcohol level has reached 15 percent, which kills off the yeast. The *carbon dioxide* dissipates into the air, except in the case of Champagne and other sparkling wines where it is retained through a special process.

Why do the world's fine wines come only from certain areas?

A combination of factors are at work. The areas with a reputation for fine wines have the right soil and favorable weather conditions, of course. But, in addition, these areas look at winemaking as an important part of their history and culture.

Is all wine made from the same kind of grape?

The major wine grapes come from the genus *Vitis vinifera*. In fact, both European and California winemakers use the *Vitis vinifera*, which includes several different varieties of grapes—both red and white. However, there are other grapes used for winemaking. The native grape variety in America is the genus *Vitis labrusca*, which is grown widely in New York State. *Hybrids* are sometimes a cross between *Vitis vinifera* and *Vitis labrusca*, planted primarily on the East Coast of the United States.

The following are the three major categories of grapes and a sampling of the varieties found in each one:

VITIS VINIFERA	VITIS LABRUSCA	HYBRIDS
Cabernet Sauvignon	Concord	Baco Noir
Chardonnay	Catawba	Seyval Blanc

What are the three major types of wine?

Table Wine: 8 percent to 14 percent alcohol
Sparkling Wine: 8 percent to 14 percent alcohol + CO_2
Fortified Wine: 17 percent to 22 percent alcohol

All wine fits into one of these categories.

Winemaking begins in the vineyard, growing the grapes. This is crucial to the whole process.

Where are the best locations to plant grapes?

Grapes are an agricultural product that requires specific growing conditions. Just as you wouldn't try to grow oranges in New York State, you wouldn't try to grow grapes at the North Pole. *There are limitations* on where vines can be grown. Some of these limitations are the growing season; the number of days of sunlight; the angle of the sun; average temperature; and rainfall. Soil is of primary concern, and proper drainage is a requisite. The right amount of sun ripens the grapes properly to give them the sugar/acid balance that makes the difference between fair, good, and the best wine.

To sum up, there are five important factors in winemaking:

1. Geographic position 2. Soil 3. Weather 4. Grapes
5. Vinification (the actual winemaking process)

Does it matter what type of grapes are planted?

Yes, it does. Traditionally, many grape varieties produce better wines when planted in certain locations. For example, most red grapes need a longer growing season than white grapes and are usually planted in warmer (more southerly) locations. In the colder northern regions—in Germany and northern France, for instance—most vineyards are planted with white grapes. On the other hand, in the warmer regions of Italy, Spain, and Portugal, the red grape thrives.

Vines are planted during their dormant periods, usually in the months of April or May. A vine does not usually produce grapes suitable for winemaking until the third year. Most vines will continue to produce quality grapes for up to 40 years.

When is the harvest?

Grapes are picked when they reach the proper sugar/acid ratio for the style of wine the vintner wants to produce. Go to a vineyard in June and taste one of the small green grapes. Your mouth will pucker because it's so tart and acidic. Return to that same vineyard—even to that same vine—in September or October and the grapes will taste sweet. All those months of sun have given the grape sugar as a result of photosynthesis. "Brix" is the winemaker's measure of sugar in grapes.

What effect does weather have on the grapes?

Weather can interfere with the quality of the harvest, as well as its quantity. In the spring, as vines come out of dormancy, a sudden frost may stop the flowering, thereby reducing the yields. Even a strong windstorm can affect the grapes adversely at this crucial time. In 1983 in the French region of Burgundy, certain villages were pelted by a 15-minute hailstorm. Its effects will not soon be forgotten—it caused almost $2 million worth of damage. Not enough rain, too much rain, or rain at the wrong time can also wreak havoc.

Rain just before the harvest will swell the grapes with water, diluting the juice and making thin, watery wines. Lack of rain, as in the drought period in California (1975, 1976, and 1977), will affect the balance of wines for those years. A severe drop in temperature may affect the vines even outside the growing season. Case in point: The New York State Christmas Day Massacre of 1980, when the temperature dipped 50 degrees in one day. The result was a severe loss of production for the following year, and in some cases the vines were completely killed, necessitating costly replanting.

What can the vineyard owner do in the case of adverse weather?

A number of countermeasures are options for the grower. Some of these are used while the grapes are on the vine; others are part of the winemaking process.

Problem	**Results In**	**Solution**
Frost	Reduced yield	Various frost protection methods: giant flame throwers to warm vines
Not enough sun	Unripe grapes	Chaptalization (the addition of sugar to the must—fresh grape juice—during fermentation)
Too much rain	Thin, watery wines	Move vineyard to drier climate
Mildew	Rot	Spray with copper sulfate
Phylloxera	Dead vines	Graft vines onto resistant rootstock
Drought	Scorched grapes	Irrigate or pray for rain

What Is Phylloxera?

Phylloxera is one of the grapevine's worst enemies. This grape louse eventually kills the entire plant. An epidemic infestation in the 1870s came close to destroying all the vineyards of Europe. Luckily, the roots of the native American vines were immune to this louse. After this was discovered, all the vines were pulled up and grafted onto American rootstocks.

Can white wine be made from red grapes?

Yes. The color of wine comes entirely from the grape skins. By removing the skins immediately after picking, no color is imparted to the wine and it will be white. In the Champagne region of France, a large percentage of the grapes grown are red, yet most of the resulting wine is white.

What is tannin and is it desirable in wine?

Tannin is a natural compound that comes from the skins, stems, and pips of the grapes and even from the wooden barrels in which certain wines are aged. It acts as a preservative and, without it, certain wines could not be aged. In young wines, tannin can be very astringent and make the wine taste bitter. Red wines have a higher level of tannin than whites.

Is acidity desirable in wine?

All wine will have a certain amount of acidity. Winemakers try to have a balance of fruit and acidity. In general, white wines have more acidity than reds. An overly acidic wine is usually described as tart.

What is meant by "vintage"? Why is one year considered better than another?

A vintage indicates the year the grapes were harvested, so every year is a vintage year. A vintage chart reflects the weather conditions for the various years. Better weather results in a better rating for the vintage.

Are all wines meant to be aged?

No. It's a common misconception that all wines improve with age. In fact, over 90 percent of all the wines made in the world are meant to be consumed within one year.

How is wine production regulated worldwide?

Each major wine-producing country has a government organization which regulates all aspects of wine production and sets certain minimum standards which must be observed.

FRANCE: Appellation d'Origine Contrôlée (A.O.C.)
ITALY: Denominazione di Origine Controllata (D.O.C.)
UNITED STATES: Bureau of Alcohol, Tobacco, and Firearms (B.A.T.F.)
GERMANY: Ministry of Agriculture

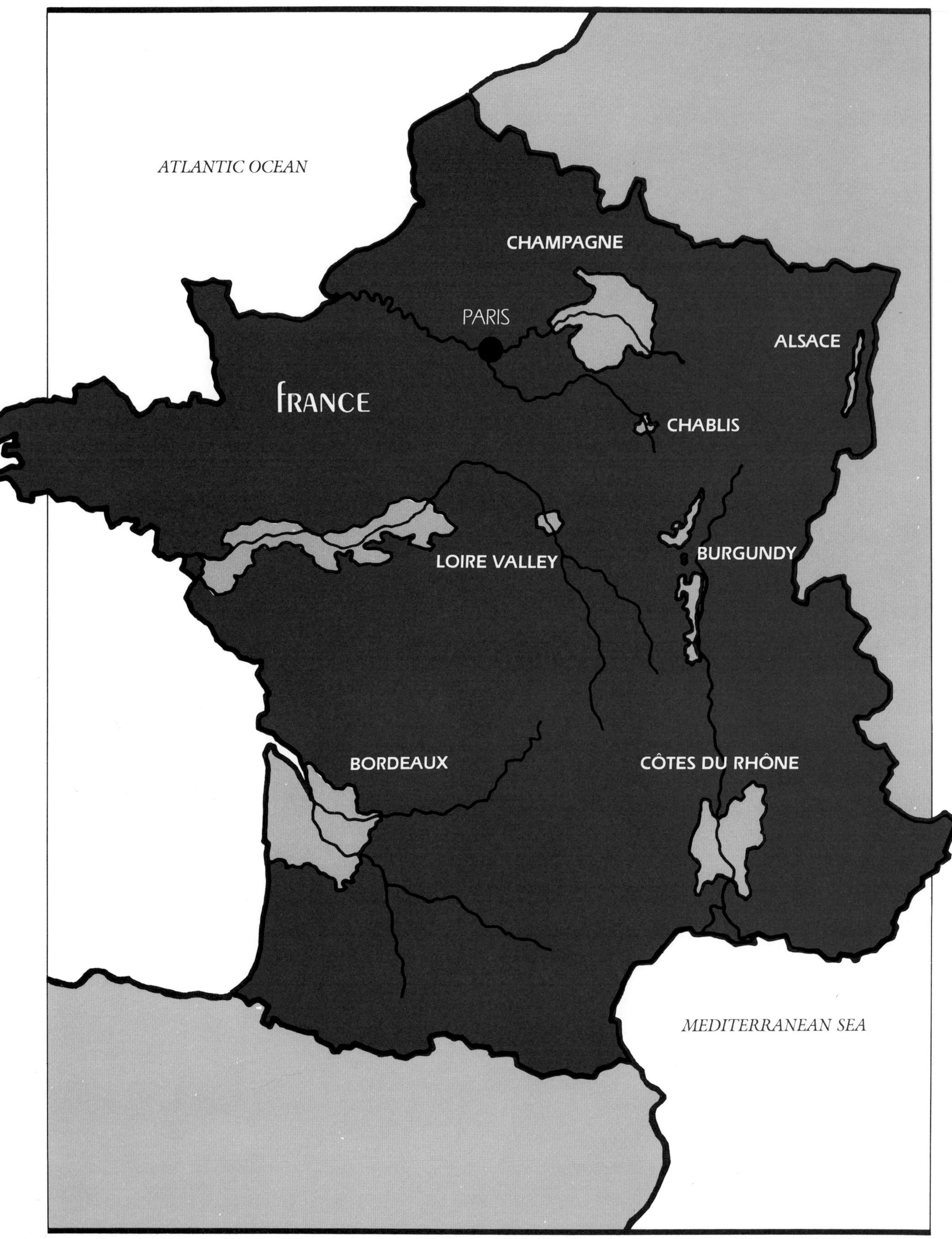

ATLANTIC OCEAN
CHAMPAGNE
PARIS
ALSACE
FRANCE
CHABLIS
BURGUNDY
LOIRE VALLEY
BORDEAUX
CÔTES DU RHÔNE
MEDITERRANEAN SEA

The White Wines of France

Understanding French Wine

Before we begin our first "class," "The White Wines of France," I think you should know a few important points about *all* French wines. Let's take a look at a map of France to get familiar with the main wine-producing areas. As we get further along, you'll understand why geography is so important.

Here's a quick rundown of which areas produce what kinds of wine:

Champagne—sparkling wine
Loire Valley—mostly whites
Alsace—mostly whites
Burgundy—red and white
Bordeaux—red and white
Côtes du Rhône—mostly red

I'm sure that you've had a French wine at one time or another. Why? Because French wines have the reputation of being among the best. There's a reason for this, and it goes back to quality control.

French winemaking is regulated by strict government laws that are set up by the *Appellation d'Origine Contrôlée*. If you don't want to say "Appellation d'Origine Contrôlée" all the time, you can simply say the "A.O.C." This is the first of many wine "lingo" abbreviations you'll learn in this book.

Only 15% of all French wines are worthy of A.O.C. designation.

A.O.C.

Established in the 1930s, the Appellation Contrôlée laws set *minimum* requirements for each wine-producing area in France. The A.O.C. laws also help in deciphering French wine labels. This is because the A.O.C. controls the following:

	Example	Example
1. Geographical place of origin.	Chablis	Pommard
2. Grape variety: What grapes can be planted where.	Chardonnay only	Pinot Noir only
3. Minimum alcohol content: This varies depending upon the particular area where the grapes are grown.	10%	10.5%
4. Vinegrowing practices: For example, a vintner can produce only so much wine per acre.	40 hectoliters/ hectare	35 hectoliters/ hectare

Hectare—metric measure; 1 hectare = 2.471 acres.

Hectoliter—metric measure; 1 hectoliter = 26.42 U.S. gallons.

There are more than 250 A.O.C. wines.

There are, however, other classifications for French wine.

Vins Delimités de Qualité Supérieure—Known more simply as V.D.Q.S., this is a step below A.O.C. wines.

Vins de Pays—This is a new category that regulates the origin and production of the wine, but it is less strict than A.O.C. and V.D.Q.S.

Vins de Table—These are ordinary, simple table wines and represent almost 75 percent of all wines produced in France.

Basically, 75 percent of all French wine is meant to be consumed as a simple beverage. Many of these wines are marketed under proprietary names and are the French equivalent of California jug wines. Don't be surprised if you go into a grocery store in France to buy wine and find it in a plastic wine container with no label on it! You can see the color through the plastic—either red, white or rosé—but the only marking on the container is the alcohol content, ranging from 9 to 14 percent. You choose your wine depending on what you have to do the rest of the day.

When you purchase wines, keep these distinctions in mind, because there is not only a difference in quality, but also in price.

The four major white-wine-producing regions of France are:

Alsace
Loire Valley
Bordeaux
Burgundy

Let's start with Alsace and the Loire Valley, because these are the two French regions truly known for white wines. As you can see from the map, Alsace, the Loire Valley, and Chablis (a white-wine-producing region of Burgundy) have one thing in common. They are all located in the northern region of France. These areas produce white wines predominantly, because of the shorter growing season and the cooler climate, both of which are best suited for growing white grapes.

Famous non-A.O.C. French wines that are available in the United States include: Partager, Valbon, Moreau, Pere Patriarch, Boucheron, and Chantefleur.

Champagne is another major white-wine producer, but that's a chapter in itself.

ALSACE

I often find that people are confused about the differences between wines from Alsace and those from Germany. Why do you suppose this is?

First of all, Alsace and Germany grow the same grape varieties. When you think of Riesling, what are your associations? You'll probably answer Germany and sweetness. That's a very typical response. However, after the winemaker from Alsace harvests his Riesling, he makes the wine much differently from his German counterpart. The winemaker from Alsace ferments every bit of the sugar in the grape, while in Germany, the winemaker adds a small amount of the naturally sweet unfermented grape juice back into the wine, which creates the typical German style. Of all Alsace wines, 99 percent are totally dry.

Another fundamental difference between wine from Alsace and Germany is the alcohol content. Wine from Alsace has 11 to 12 percent alcohol, while German wine has a mere 8 to 9 percent.

With the Statue of Liberty now over 100 years old, it's interesting to note that she was designed and built in the Alsace region.

Before World War I, Alsace was part of Germany.

All wines produced in Alsace are A.O.C.-designated wines, and represent some 20% of all A.O.C. white wines in France.

Just to confuse you a bit more, both wines are bottled in a similarly shaped bottle that is tall with a tapering neck.

Alsace produces 6% red wines. These generally are consumed in the region and are rarely exported.

What are the white grapes grown in Alsace?

The big three that you should know are:

Riesling—accounts for 20 percent
Gewürztraminer—accounts for 20 percent
Pinot Blanc—accounts for 18 percent

Wine labelling in Alsace is different from other regions administered by the A.O.C., because Alsace is the only region that labels its wine by specific grape variety. All Alsace wines that put the name of the grape on the label must contain 100% of that grape.

What type of wine is produced in Alsace?

As we mentioned earlier, virtually all the Alsace wines are dry. Riesling is, without question, the major grape planted in Alsace and is responsible for the highest-quality wines of the region. The other wine Alsace is known for is Gewürztraminer, which is in a class by itself. Most people either love it or hate it, because Gewürztraminer has a very distinctive style. "Gewürz" is the word for "spice," which aptly describes the wine.

Pinot Blanc is a "new-style" wine for the region and is becoming increasingly popular with the growers of Alsace.

In the last ten years, there have been more Pinot Blanc and Riesling grapes planted in Alsace than any other variety.

How should I select an Alsace wine?

Two factors are important in choosing a wine from Alsace: the grape variety and the reputation and style of the shipper. Some of the most reliable shippers are:

Hugel & Fils
F. E. Trimbach
Léon Beyer
Dopff "Au Moulin"

There are 30,000 acres of grapes planted in Alsace, but the average plot of land for each grower is only three acres.

Why are shippers so important?

Because the majority of the landholders in Alsace don't grow enough grapes for it to be economically feasible to produce and market their own wine. Instead, they sell their grapes to a shipper who produces, bottles, and markets the wine under his name. The art of making high-quality wine lies in the selection of grapes made by each shipper.

Sometimes you'll see "Grand Cru" on an Alsace label. This wine can be made only from the best grape varieties of Alsace, and it will have a higher degree of alcohol than the standard shipper's varietal.

What are the different quality levels of Alsace wine?

The vast majority of the wine is a shipper's varietal: A very small percentage is labelled with a specific vineyard's name. Some wines are also labelled "Réserve" or "Réserve Personelle." These terms are not legally defined, and their importance is determined by the shipper's reputation.

Should I lay down my wines for long aging?

In general, most Alsace wines are made to be consumed young—that is, three to five years after they're bottled. As in any fine wine area, there is a small percentage of great wines produced in Alsace that may be aged for ten years or more.

What are the best values in Alsace wine?

One of the nicest aspects of buying Alsace wine is the price. There is a good price/value relationship—in other words, you get your money's worth. The majority of Alsace wines are very affordable, of good quality, and available in most markets.

In 1983, 60,000 cases of Alsace wine were sold in the United States.

The Alsace region has little rainfall, especially during the harvest, and the town of Colmar, the Alsace wine center, is the second-driest city in France. That's why they say a "one-shirt harvest" will be a good vintage.

Best Bets for Recent Vintages of Alsace

The two best vintages in the last ten years: 1976 1983

Other very good recent years: 1979 1981

WINE AND FOOD

When I was recently in Alsace, I spoke with two of the region's most well-known producers to find out what type of food they enjoy with the wines from Alsace. Here's what they prefer:

Jean Hugel—"With Riesling, fish in a white sauce or butter sauce. With Gewürztraminer, smoked salmon, turkey, or Chinese food."

Mr. Hugel described Pinot Blanc as, "round, soft, not aggressive . . . an all-purpose wine . . . can be used as an apéritif, with all kinds of paté and charcuterie, and also with hamburgers. Perfect for brunch—not too sweet or flowery."

Hubert Trimbach—"Riesling with fish—blue trout with a light sauce." He recommends Gewürztraminer as an apéritif, or with *foie gras* or any paté at the end of the meal; with Muenster cheese, or a stronger cheese such as Roquefort.

Alsace is also known for its fruit brandies—"eaux-de-vie:"
Framboise—raspberries
Kirsch—cherries
Mirabelle—yellow plums
Fraise—strawberries

For the Gourmet:
There are four restaurants with one or more stars in Alsace.

For the Tourist:
Visit the beautiful wine village of Riquewihr, circa fifteenth–sixteenth century.

For further reading:
Alsace, S. F. Hallgarten
Alsace, Pamela Van Dyke Price

loire valley

In the Loire Valley, 75% of the wines produced are white, and the majority of those are dry.

The Loire Valley is famous not only for its wines, but also as a summer retreat of royalty. Elegant and sometimes enormous châteaus enhance the countryside.

Starting at the town of Nantes on the Atlantic Ocean, the Loire Valley stretches inland for 600 miles along the Loire River.

There are two grape varieties you should be familiar with:

Sauvignon Blanc
Chenin Blanc

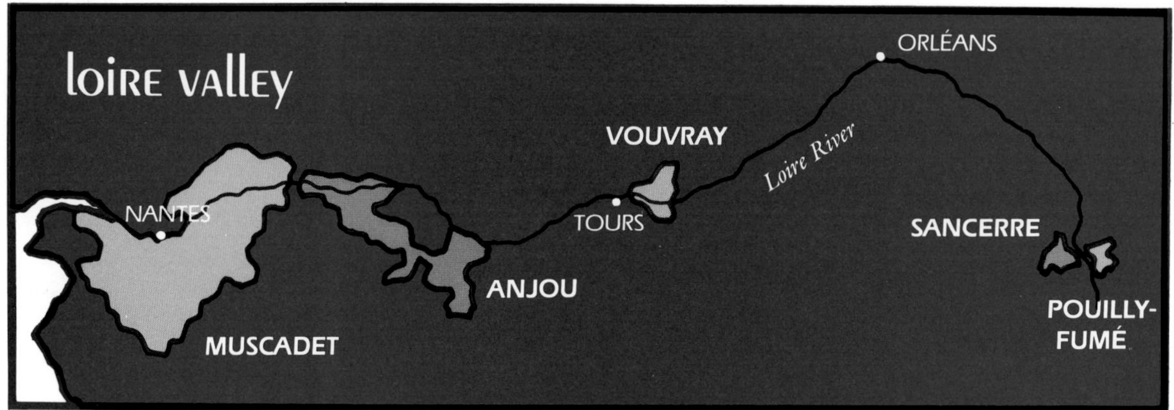

Rather than select by grape variety and shipper, as in Alsace, you should choose a Loire Valley wine by style and vintage. Here are the main styles:

Pouilly-Fumé—A dry wine that has the most body and concentration of all the Loire Valley wines; it is made with 100 percent Sauvignon Blanc.
Muscadet—A light, dry wine , made from 100 percent Melon grape.
Sancerre—Striking a balance between the Pouilly-Fumé and the Muscadet, it is made with 100 percent Sauvignon Blanc.
Vouvray—The "chameleon"; it can be dry, semi-sweet, or sweet, and it is made from 100 percent Chenin Blanc.

In the last 10 years, production of Pouilly-Fumé has doubled.

How did Pouilly-Fumé get its name and what does "Fumé" mean?

Many people ask me if Pouilly-Fumé is smoked, because they automatically associate the word "Fumé" with smoke. That's not the case. The word "fumé" comes from the white morning mist that blankets the area. As the sun burns off the mist, it looks as though smoke is rising.

The distinct nose (bouquet) of Pouilly-Fumé comes from a combination of the Sauvignon Blanc grape and the soil of the Loire Valley.

When are the wines ready to drink?

Generally, Loire Valley wines are meant to be consumed young. The exception is a sweet Vouvray, which can be laid down for a longer time.

Here are more specific guidelines:

Pouilly-Fumé—three to five years
Sancerre—two to three years
Muscadet—one to two years

The Loire Valley also produces the world-famous Anjou Rosé.

Are the wines of the Loire expensive?

All the wines of the Loire are reasonably priced. They are considered the summer wines of the Parisians and may be found on the wine lists of most restaurants in Paris.

Best Bets for Recent Vintages of Loire Valley

1979 1981 1983

WINE AND food

Baron Patrick Ladoucette—Owner of Ladoucette Pouilly-Fumé (and incidentally the largest producer of Pouilly-Fumé)—recommends the following wine and food combinations:

Pouilly-Fumé—"Smoked salmon, turbot with hollandaise; white meat chicken; veal with cream sauce."

Sancerre—"Shellfish, simple food of the sea, because Sancerre is drier than Pouilly-Fumé."

Muscadet—"All you have to do is look at the map to see where Muscadet is made: by the sea where the main fare is shellfish, clams, and oysters."

Vouvray—"A nice semi-dry wine to have with fruit and cheese."

The best value in terms of price/quality relationship is found in the wines of Sancerre.

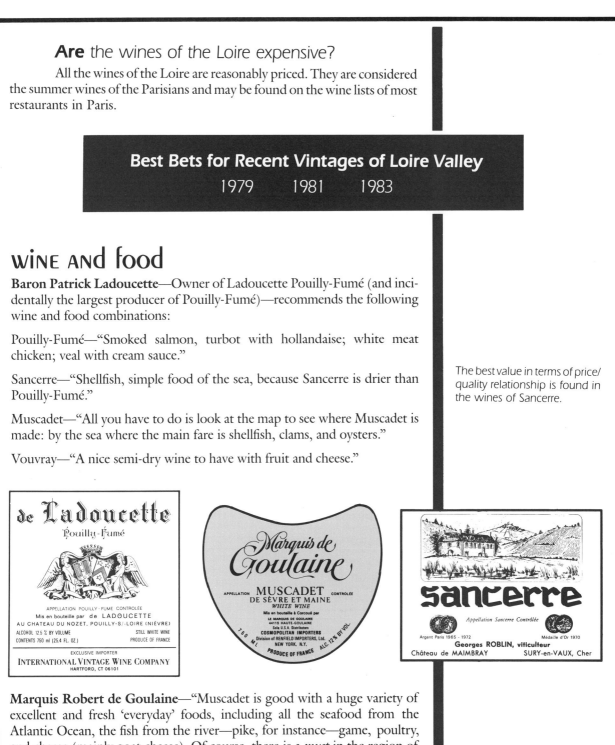

Marquis Robert de Goulaine—"Muscadet is good with a huge variety of excellent and fresh 'everyday' foods, including all the seafood from the Atlantic Ocean, the fish from the river—pike, for instance—game, poultry, and cheese (mainly goat cheese). Of course, there is a *must* in the region of Nantes: freshwater fish with the world-famous butter sauce, the *beurre blanc*, invented at the turn of the century by Clemence, who happened to be the chef at Goulaine. Finally, remember that most of the Loire wines, and specifically Muscadet, can be drunk on their own, as an apéritif or during a party. Muscadet with a dash of crème de cassis (black currant) is a wonderful way to welcome friends!"

THE WHITE WINES OF BORDEAUX

Doesn't Bordeaux always mean red wine?

That's a misconception. Actually, two of the five major areas of Bordeaux are known for their excellent white wines—Graves and Sauternes. Sauternes is world famous for its sweet white wine.

The major white grape varieties used in both areas are: **Sauvignon Blanc**
Sémillon

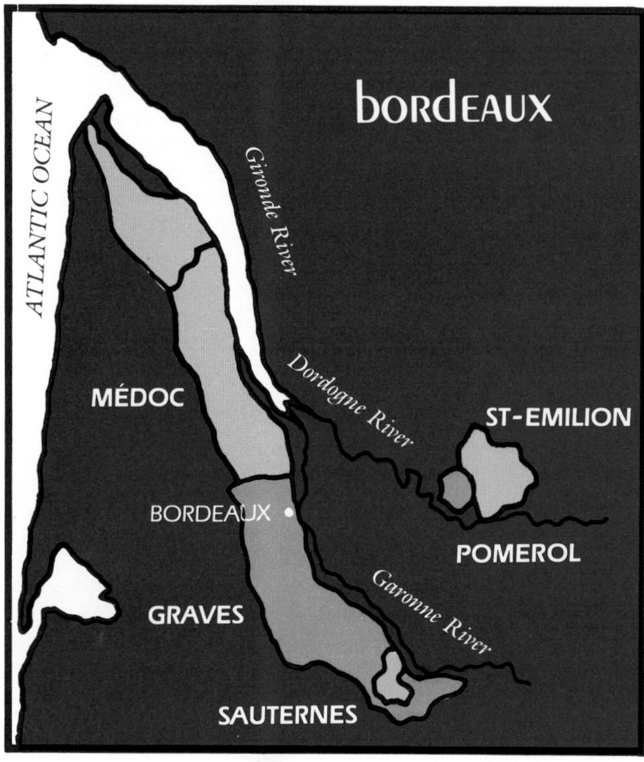

GRAVES

How are the white Graves wines classified?

There are three levels of quality distinction: **Graves**
Graves Supérieures
Classified Châteaus

The wine production of Graves is divided evenly between red and white.

The most basic Graves is simply called "Graves." One step above is "Graves Supérieures." Both are regional wines that may come from anywhere in the area of Graves. The best wines are known by the name of a particular château, a special vineyard that produces the best-quality grapes. The classified château wines are ranked better for many reasons. The grapes grown for these wines enjoy better soil and growing conditions overall. Also, the château wines and the regional wines of Graves are always dry, whereas Graves Supérieures are always semi-dry.

Graves Supérieures has slightly more alcohol content than the A.O.C. Graves.

How should I select a Graves wine?

My best recommendation would be to purchase a classified château wine. Here they are:

Classified white château wines are hard to find, since they make up only 3% of total white Graves production.

Château Bouscaut
Château Carbonnieux*
Domaine de Chevalier
Château Couhins
Château La Tour-Martillac
Château Laville-Haut-Brion
Château Malartic-Lagravière
Château Olivier*

*The largest producers of white Graves and the easiest to find.

The style of classified white château wines varies with the ratio of Sauvignon Blanc and Sémillon used. Château Olivier, for example, is made with 65% Sémillon, and Château Carbonnieux with 65% Sauvignon Blanc.

Best Bets for Recent Vintages of White Graves

1981 1982 1983

WINE AND FOOD

Alexis Lichine (Château Prieuré-Lichine)—He recommends shad from the Garonne River (April to June only) in a sauce *ravigote* (chopped egg, onion, oil and vinegar) with a full-bodied Graves, preferably one that has been aged, which will not be overpowerd by the oily fish.

Denise Lurton Moulle (Château La Louviere, Château Clos Fourtet)—With a young Graves: *Oysters Feuillete* in a light sauce of oyster juice, wine and butter. With an older Graves: baked salmon or striped bass in a rich sauce.

Jean Kressman (Château La Tour-Martillac)—Oysters, fish, cheese and nuts are excellent complements to a fine Graves.

Wendy Hodges (Château de France)—She recommends fish dishes—especially grilled fish—not in rich sauces.

Jean-Jacques de Bethmann (Château Olivier)—Oysters, lobster, *Rouget du Bassin d'Archon.*

The word "Graves" means gravel—the type of soil found in the region.

SAUTERNES

All French Sauternes are sweet, meaning that not all the grape sugar has turned into alcohol during fermentation. There is no such thing as a dry French Sauternes.

What are the main grape varieties in Sauternes?

Sauvignon Blanc
Sémillon

If the same grapes are used for both the dry Graves and the sweet Sauternes, how do you explain the extreme difference in styles?

First and most important, the best Sauternes is made primarily with the Sémillon grape. Secondly, to make Sauternes, the winemaker leaves the grapes on the vine longer. He waits for a mould to form called *Botrytis cinerea* (noble rot). When this "noble rot" forms on the grapes, the water within them evaporates and they shrivel. Sugar becomes concentrated as the grapes raisinate. Then, during the winemaking process, not all of the sugar is allowed to ferment into alcohol: hence, the high-residual sugar.

Sauternes is expensive to produce, because several pickings must be completed before the crop is entirely harvested. The harvest can last into November.

How do I buy Sauternes?

It's similar to buying the wines of Graves. You may buy a regional or a château wine. A regional wine, simply labelled Sauternes, may be a good buy, but it will not have the same intensity of flavor as a classified château wine. One other very important consideration is the vintage: In Sauternes, only buy the best years.

The Barsac district is adjacent to Sauternes and has the option of choosing between Barsac or Sauternes as its appellation.

How are Sauternes classified?

First Great Growth—Grand Premier Cru
Château d'Yquem*

First Growths—Premier Crus
Château La Tour Blanche*
Château Lafaurie-Peyraguey*
Clos Haut-Peyraguey*
Château de Rayne-Vigneau*
Château Suduiraut*
Château Coutet* (Barsac)
Château Climens* (Barsac)
Château Guiraud*
Château Rieussec*
Château Rabaud-Promis
Château Sigalas-Rabaud*

Second Growths—Deuxièmes Crus
Château Myrat (Barsac)
Château Doisy-Daëne (Barsac)
Château Doisy-Védrines* (Barsac)
Château Doisy-Dubroca
Château D'Arche
Château Filhot
Château Broustet (Barsac)
Château Nairac* (Barsac)
Château Caillou (Barsac)
Château Suau (Barsac)
Château de Malle*
Château Romer*
Château Lamothe

*These are the wines that are most readily available in the United States and are of consistent high quality. Many of the other châteaus are very small and do not export wine to the United States.

Best Bets for Vintages of Sauternes

1967 1970 1971 1975 1976 1979
1980 1981

What are the best values in Sauternes?

Most classified châteaus can be purchased at a reasonable price and would be a better choice than a Sauternes with only a regional appellation. These wines represent a good value for your money, considering the labor involved in production.

Sauternes is a wine you can age—in fact, most classified château wines in good vintages can age easily for ten to twenty years.

Just Desserts

My students always ask me, "What do you serve with Sauternes?" Here's a little lesson I learned when I first encountered the wines of Sauternes.

Many years ago when I was visiting the Sauternes region, I was invited to one of the châteaus for dinner. Upon arrival, my group was offered appetizers of *foie gras*, and to my surprise, they served Sauternes with it. All of the books that I had ever read said you should serve drier wines first and sweeter wines later. But since I was a guest, I thought it best not to question my host's selection.

When we sat down for the first dinner course, we were once again served a Sauternes. This continued through the main course—which happened to be rack of lamb—when another Sauternes was served.

I thought for sure our host would serve a great old red Bordeaux with the cheese course, but I was wrong again. With the Roquefort cheese was served a very old Sauternes.

With dessert soon on its way, I got used to the idea of having a dinner with Sauternes, and waited with anticipation for the final choice. You can imagine my surprise when a red Bordeaux—Château Lafite-Rothschild—was served with dessert!

My point is that Sauternes does not have to be served *only* with dessert. Actually, all of the Sauternes went well with the courses, because all of the sauces complemented the wine and food.

By the way, the only wine that didn't go well with the dinner was the Château Lafite-Rothschild with the dessert, but we drank it anyway.

Perhaps this anecdote will inspire you to serve Sauternes with everything. Personally, I prefer to enjoy Sauternes by itself; I'm not a believer in the dessert wine category. At Cellar in the Sky, we serve Sauternes ten minutes before dessert to prepare you for the final course. This dessert wine is dessert in itself.

WINE AND FOOD

I spoke with some of the château owners in Bordeaux to find out what they prefer to serve with Sauternes. Here's what they said:

Alexis Lichine (Château Prieuré-Lichine)—He recommends a fine old Sauternes or Barsac, pungent in quality, with a dessert of *Oeufs à la Neige*.

Wendy Hodges (Château de France)—Sauternes can be served as apéritifs. They also go well with *foie gras*, Roquefort and Stilton cheeses, and shellfish.

Brigitte Lurton (Château Brane-Cantenac, Château Durfort-Vivens, Château La Louviere, Château Clos Fourtet)—As an apéritif, with grilled fish, white meats, cheeses (especially blue cheese), and *foie gras*.

Christine Schyler (Château Kirwan)—She recommends Sauternes as apéritifs or with *foie gras*.

The White Wines of Burgundy

Where is Burgundy?

Burgundy is a region located in central eastern France. Its true fame is as a wine-producing area.

What is Burgundy?

This may sound like a silly question, but many people are confused about what a Burgundy really is because the name is often misused on the market.

For our purposes, Burgundy is one of the major wine-producing regions that holds an A.O.C. designation in France. *Burgundy is not a synonym for red wine, even though many red wines are simply labelled "Burgundy."* Many of these Burgundy wines are ordinary table wines that are rough, dark red and heavy. They may come from California, South Africa, Australia, or Chile, and bear little resemblance to the styles of authentic French Burgundy wines.

The exact breakdown in production of red to white wines in Burgundy is four-fifths red to one-fifth white.

"You mean France makes burgundy, too?"

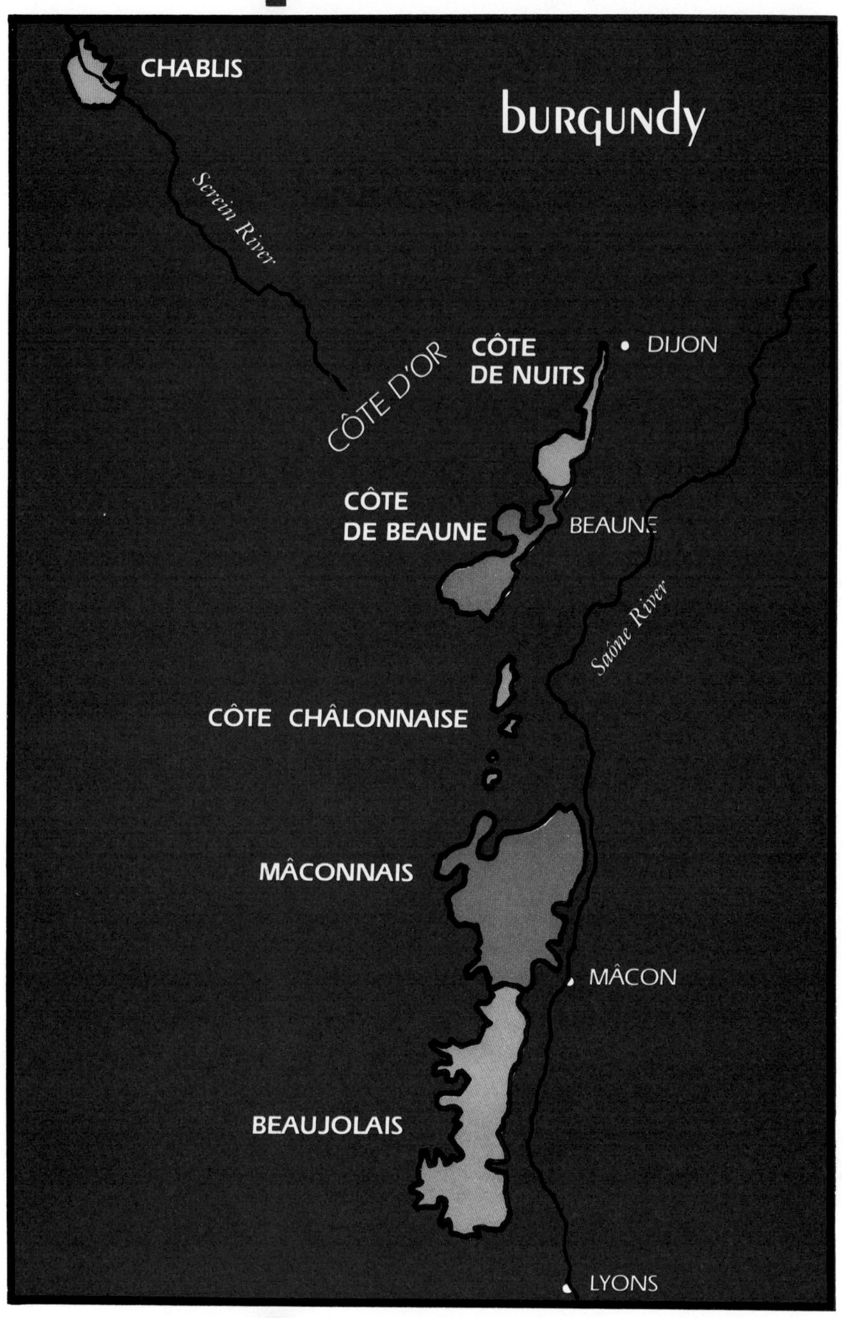

Although Chablis is a part of the Burgundy region, it is a three-hour drive south to the area of Mâconnais.

What are the main areas of Burgundy?

Chablis

Côte d'Or { **Côte de Nuits**, **Côte de Beaune** }

Côte Châlonnaise

Mâconnais

Beaujolais

Before we go into Burgundy, region by region, it is important to know the types of wines that are produced there. Take a look at the chart below: It breaks down the types of wine and tells you the percentage of reds to whites.

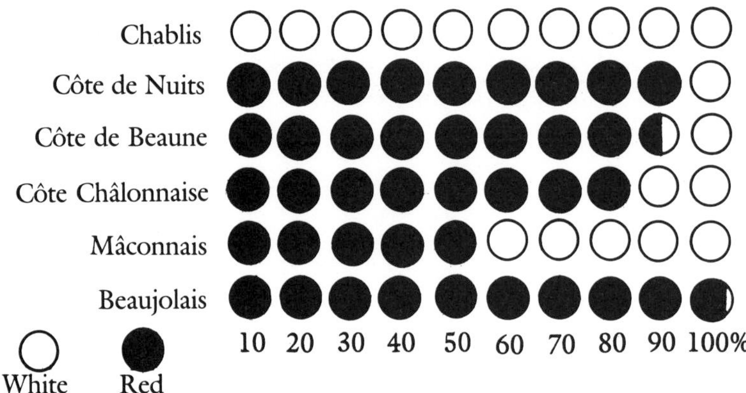

Burgundy is another one of those regions that is so famous for its red wines that people sometimes forget that some of the finest white wines of France are also produced there. The three areas in Burgundy which produce world-famous white wines are:

Chablis **Côte de Beaune** **Mâconnais**

If it's any comfort to you, you need to know only one white grape variety—Chardonnay. All of the great white Burgundian wine is made from 100 percent Chardonnay.

Is there only one type of white Burgundy?

Even though Chardonnay is used to make all the best white French Burgundy wines, the different areas produce many different styles. Much of this has to do with where the grapes are grown and the vinification procedures. In the areas of Chablis and Mâconnais, the grapes are harvested, mostly fermented, and aged in stainless-steel tanks. In the Côte de Beaune, after the grapes are harvested, a good percentage of the wines are fermented in wood. Then the wines are transferred to small oak barrels where they age. The wood adds depth, body, flavor, and longevity to the wines.

White Burgundies have one trait in common: They are dry.

Another white grape found in the Burgundy region is the Aligoté. It is a lesser grape variety and usually the grape name appears on the label.

The Story of Kir

Over the last few years, the apéritif "Kir" has become very popular. It is a mixture of white wine and cassis (made from black currants). It was the favorite drink of the former mayor of Dijon, Canon Kir, who originally mixed the sweet cassis to balance the acidity of the Burgundy white wine made from the Aligoté grape.

A Note on the Use of Wood

Every wine region in the world has its own way of producing wines. Wine was always fermented and aged in wood—until the introduction of cement tanks, glass-lined tanks, and most recently, stainless-steel tanks. Despite these technological improvements, many winemakers prefer to use the more traditional methods. For example, wines from the firm of Louis Jadot are fermented in wood as follows:

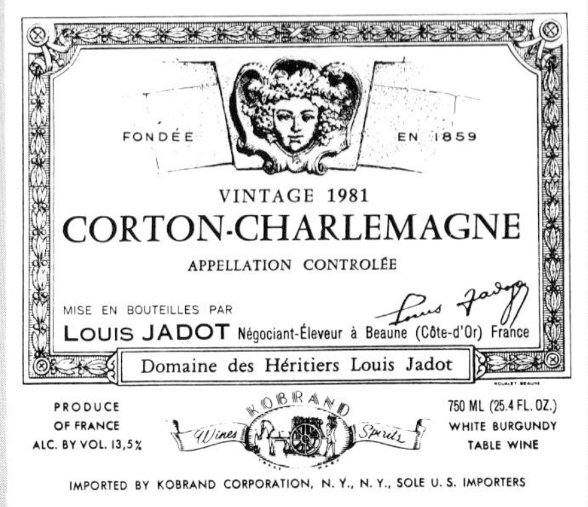

one-third of the wine is fermented in new wood

one-third of the wine is fermented in one-year-old wood

one-third of the wine is fermented in older wood

Jadot's philosophy is the better the vintage, the more the wood aging; the lesser the vintage, the less the wood aging. A lesser vintage wine will usually not be aged in new wood because of the likelihood of the wine being overpowered by it. The younger the wood, the more flavor and tannin it gives to the wine.

There are 250 grape growers in Chablis but only five age their wine in wood.

Most Premier Cru wines give you the name of the vineyard on the label, but others are simply called "Premier Cru," which is a blend of different "Cru" vineyards.

The average yield for a village wine in Burgundy is 360 gallons per acre. For the Grand Cru wines it is 290 gallons per acre, a noticeably larger concentration, which produces a more flavorful wine.

How are the white wines of Burgundy classified?

The type of soil and the angle and direction of the slope are the primary factors determining quality. Here are the levels of quality:

1. **Village Wine**—Bears the name of a specific village. ($ = good)
2. **Premier Cru**—From a specific vineyard with special characteristics, within one of the named villages. Usually a Premier Cru wine will list the village first and the vineyard second. ($$ = better)
3. **Grand Cru**— From a specific vineyard which possesses the best soil and slope in the area and meets or exceeds all other requirements. In certain areas of Burgundy, the village will not appear on the label—only the vineyard name is used. ($$$$ = best)

Chablis

Chablis is the northernmost area in Burgundy that produces only white wine.

Isn't Chablis just a general term for white wine?

The name "Chablis" suffers from the same misinterpretation and overuse as does the name "Burgundy." Because the French did not take the necessary precautions to protect the use of the name "Chablis," it is now randomly applied to many ordinary bulk wines from other countries. Chablis has come to be associated with some very undistinguished wine, *but this is not the case with French Chablis.* In fact, the French take their Chablis very seriously. There is a special classification of Chablis.

What are the quality levels of Chablis?

Petit Chablis—The most ordinary Chablis; rarely seen in the United States.

Chablis—A wine that comes from Chardonnay grapes grown anywhere in the Chablis district.

Chablis Premier Cru—A very good quality of Chablis that comes from specific high-quality vineyards.

Chablis Grand Cru—The highest classification of Chablis, and the most expensive because of its limited production. There are seven vineyards in Chablis entitled to be called Grand Cru.

The best price/value wine is a Chablis Premier Cru.

There are only 220 acres planted in Grand Cru vineyards.

If you're interested in buying only the best Chablis, here are the seven Grand Cru and the most important Premier Cru vineyards:

THE GRAND CRUS OF CHABLIS

Les Clos
Vaudésir
Valmur
Blanchots
Preuses
Grenouilles
Bougros

THE TOP PREMIER CRU VINEYARDS OF CHABLIS

Vaillons
Montée de Tonnerre
Monts de Milieu
Fourchaume
Montmains
Côte de Lechet
Vaulorent

The winter temperatures in some parts of Chablis can match those of Norway.

Has Chablis changed over the last twenty years?

The cold, northerly climate of Chablis poses a threat to the vines. Back in the late 1950s, Chablis almost went out of business because the crops were ruined by frost. Through modern technology, vintners have learned to control this problem. The biggest change in the region of Chablis, then, has occurred as a result of improved methods of frost protection, with more and better wine being produced.

Over the last ten years, the number of vineyards in Chablis has increased fivefold.

How should I buy Chablis?

The two major aspects to look for in Chablis are the shipper and the vintage. Here is a list of the most important shippers of Chablis to the United States:

Albert Pic & Fils
A Regnard & Fils
Domaine de la Maladière
Joseph Drouhin
J. Moreau & Fils
Guy Robin
Simonnet-Febvre & Fils
Robert Vocoret
Louis Jadot

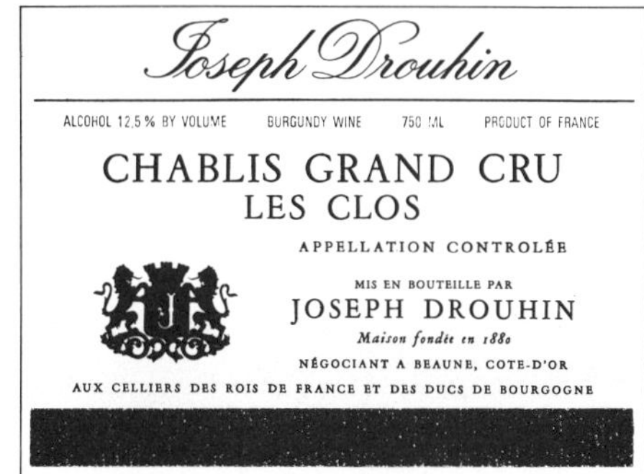

Joseph Drouhin
ALCOHOL 12.5 % BY VOLUME
BURGUNDY WINE
750 ML
PRODUCT OF FRANCE
CHABLIS GRAND CRU
LES CLOS
APPELLATION CONTROLÉE
MIS EN BOUTEILLE PAR
JOSEPH DROUHIN
Maison fondée en 1880
NÉGOCIANT A BEAUNE, COTE-D'OR
AUX CELLIERS DES ROIS DE FRANCE ET DES DUCS DE BOURGOGNE

Best Bets for Recent Vintages of Chablis

1982 1983

Your best value will be found in the 1983 vintage. It was the largest harvest they've had in the last five years, with perhaps even more body than you would expect of a normal Chablis. My advice, however, is to drink the 1982 now because the 1983 is a more full-bodied wine and will last longer.

Two important white wines of Burgundy made in limited quantity from the Côte de Nuits are Musigny Blanc and Clos Blanc de Vougeot.

When should I drink my Chablis?

Chablis—within two years from the vintage
Premier Cru—two to four years
Grand Cru—three to five years

CÔTE DE BEAUNE

This is one of the two major areas of the Côte d'Or. Very few of the wines from this area are white, but they are some of the finest examples of dry white wine produced in the world and are considered a benchmark for winemakers everywhere.

Côte de Beaune

Here is a list of the most *important* villages and vineyards in the Côte de Beaune that produce white wines.

Village	**Premier Cru Vineyards**	**Grand Cru Vineyards**
Aloxe-Corton		Corton-Charlemagne Charlemagne
Beaune	Clos des Mouches	None
Meursault	Les Perrières Les Genevrières La Goutte d'Or Les Charmes Blagny Poruzots	None
Puligny-Montrachet	Les Combettes Les Caillerets Les Pucelles Les Folatières Clavoillons Les Referts	Montrachet* Bâtard-Montrachet* Chevalier-Montrachet Bienvenue-Bâtard-Montrachet
Chassagne-Montrachet	Les Ruchottes Morgeot	Montrachet* Bâtard-Montrachet* Criots-Bâtard-Montrachet

*The vineyards of Bâtard-Montrachet and Montrachet overlap between the villages of Puligny-Montrachet and Chassagne-Montrachet.

The three most important white-winemaking villages are:

Meursault
Puligny-Montrachet
Chassagne-Montrachet

Puligny-Montrachet
APPELLATION CONTROLÉE
Louis Latour
MIS EN BOUTEILLE PAR LOUIS LATOUR
NÉGOCIANT A BEAUNE (COTE-D'OR)

Puligny-Montrachet
LES REFERTS
APPELLATION CONTROLÉE
Louis Latour
MIS EN BOUTEILLE PAR LOUIS LATOUR
NÉGOCIANT A BEAUNE (COTE-D'OR)

Montrachet
APPELLATION CONTROLÉE
Louis Latour
MIS EN BOUTEILLE PAR LOUIS LATOUR
NÉGOCIANT A BEAUNE (COTE-D'OR)

All three villages produce their wine from the same grape—100 percent Chardonnay.

As Robert Drouhin, premier winemaker in Burgundy, says: "The difference between the Village wine, Puligny-Montrachet, and the Grand Cru Montrachet, is not in the type of wood used in aging or how long the wine is aged in wood. The primary difference is in the location of the vineyards, i.e., the soil and the slope of the land."

Then what makes each wine different?

In Burgundy, one of the most important factors in making a good wine is *soil*. Soil makes the difference between a Village, a Premier Cru, and a Grand Cru wine. Another major factor that makes the wines different in style is the vinification procedure the winemaker uses—the recipe. It's the same as if you were to compare the chefs at three gourmet restaurants. They may start out with the same ingredients, but it's what they do with those ingredients that matters.

Best Bets of Côte de Beaune White

1978 1979 1982 1983

CÔTE CHÂLONNAISE

The Côte Châlonnaise is the least known of the major wine districts of Burgundy. Not many wines are exported from this area. Even though the Châlonnaise is best known for such red wines as Givry and Mercurey (see the chapter on the red wines of Burgundy), it *does* produce some very good white wines that not many people know about, which means value for you. I'm referring to the wines of Montagny and Rully , made from Chardonnay and Pinot Blanc grapes. These wines are of the highest quality produced in the area, similar to the white wines of the Côte d'Or.

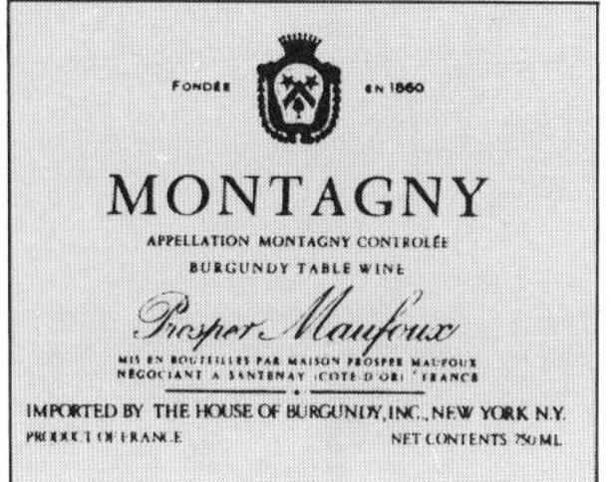

MÂCONNAIS

The southernmost white-wine-producing area in Burgundy, the Mâconnais, has a warmer climate than the Côte d'Or and Chablis. Mâcon wines, in general, are pleasant, light, uncomplicated, reliable table wines, which represent a very good value.

Over two-thirds of the wines from the Mâconnais are white.

What are the quality levels of Mâconnais wines?

From basic to best:

Mâcon Blanc
Mâcon Supérieur
Mâcon-Villages
St-Véran
Pouilly-Vinzelles
Pouilly-Fuissé

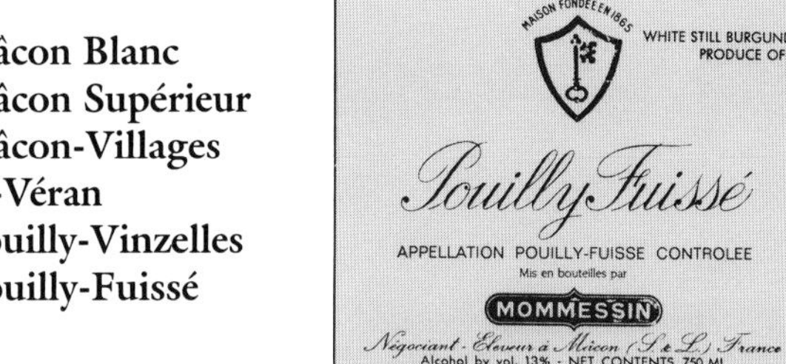

There is a village named Chardonnay in the Mâconnais area where it is said the grape's name originated.

Of all Mâcon wines, Pouilly-Fuissé is without question one of the most popular. It is the highest-quality Mâconnais wine, fashionable to drink in the United States long before most Americans discovered the splendors of wine. As wine consumption increased in America, Pouilly-Fuissé and other famous areas such as Pommard, Nuits-St-Georges, and Chablis became synonymous with the best wines of France, and could always be found on any restaurant's wine list. The price of Pouilly-Fuissé has risen dramatically over the last few years solely because of the laws of supply and demand.

Pouilly-Fuissé prices in 1983 ended up 30% higher than wines such as Puligny-Montrachet and Meursault. Expect even higher prices over the next two years.

In an average year, 300,000 cases of Pouilly-Fuissé are produced—not nearly enough to supply all of the restaurants and retail shops for worldwide consumption.

"If you start talking to him about 'Pooly-Foossy,' I'll walk right out."

In my opinion, the Mâcon-Villages is the best value. Why pay more for Pouilly-Fuissé (sometimes three times as much) when a simple Mâcon or St-Véran will do just as nicely?

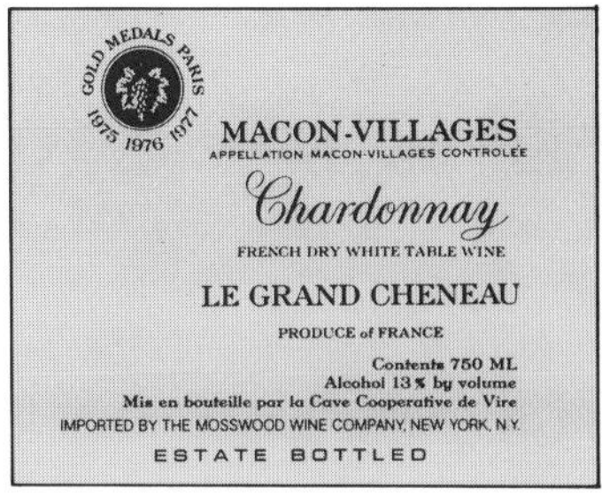

Best Bets of Recent Vintages of Mâcon White

1981 1982 1983

OVERVIEW

Now that you're familiar with the many different white wines of Burgundy:

How do you choose the right one for you?

The first requirement to look for is the vintage year. With Burgundy, it is especially important to buy a good year. Then it becomes a question of taste and the cost. If price is no object, aren't you the lucky one?

First of all, decide if you prefer a light or full-bodied wine. Also, after some trial and error, you may find that you prefer the wines of one shipper over another. Here are some of the shippers to look for when buying white Burgundy:

Bouchard Père & Fils
Joseph Drouhin
Louis Jadot
Louis Latour
Ropiteau Frères
Mommessin
Prosper Maufoux

Estate-bottled wines: The wine is made, produced, and bottled by the owner of the vineyards.

Although 80 percent of Burgundy wines are sold through shippers, some fine estate-bottled wines are available in limited quantities in the United States. They are produced by:

Domaine Leflaive (Meursault, Puligny-Montrachet)
Domaine Bachelet-Ramonet (Chassagne-Montrachet)
Domaine Bonneau du Martray (Corton-Charlemagne)
Domaine Matrot (Meursault)
Domaine Etienne Sauzet (Chassagne-Montrachet, Puligny-Montrachet)

WINE AND FOOD

When you choose a white Burgundian wine, you have a whole gamut of wonderful food possibilities. Let's say that you decide upon a wine from the Mâconnais area. Very reasonably priced, Mâconnais wines are suitable for picnics as well as more formal dinners. Or you may select one of the fuller-bodied Côte de Beaune wines that can even stand up to a hearty steak, or if you prefer, the all-purpose wine, Chablis. Here are some tempting combinations offered by the winemakers.

Robert Drouhin—Has Chablis with any fish—seafood, oysters—but, "No cream sauce, please."

Côte de Beaune wines go well with "any fish except oysters, but without a heavy sauce." Some of the dishes Mr. Drouhin enjoys with these wines are "a richer fish, sweetbreads, veal—but not red meat."

André Gagey (Louis Jadot)—Says that Chablis is a great match for oysters, snails, and shellfish, but a "Grand Cru Chablis should be had with trout."

On white wines of the Côte de Beaune, Mr. Gagey gets a bit more specific. "With Village wines, which should be had at the beginning of the meal, try a light fish or quenelles (light dumplings)."

"Premier Cru and Grand Cru wines can stand up to heavier fish and shellfish such as lobster—but with a wine such as Corton-Charlemagne, smoked Scottish salmon is a tasty choice."

Mr. Gagey's parting words on the subject: "Never with meat."

Jean-Francois Bouchard—Enjoys Chablis as an apéritif or with the first course of a meal; it's nice with shellfish and light fish "that is not too fleshy," and also with fish terrine.

Louis Latour—Believes that one should have Chablis with oysters and fish. Mr. Latour's favorite recent vintages for Burgundian wines are 1979 and 1982. Unlike most of the other experts in the trade, Mr. Latour says the white wines of Burgundy go well with meat because of the wine's body. His recommendation for Corton-Charlemagne: "Have it in the middle of the afternoon with *foie gras*."

Jean-Jacques Moreau—Likes to have his Chablis with oysters and other seafood and says, "Chablis is not for red meat, but it is fine for all white meats with cream sauce. It also goes well with all cheeses such as goat cheese, Gruyère, and Emmentaler.

One of Mr. Moreau's favorite combinations is Premier Cru Chablis with *escargots à la bourguignonne*. For him, the garlic does not overpower the wine—so enjoy!

For further reading on Burgundy wines, I recommend *The Wines of Burgundy* by H. W. Yoxall and *Burgundy* by Anthony Hanson.

If you're taking a client out on a limited expense account, a safe wine to order is a Mâcon. If the sky's the limit, go with the Meursault!

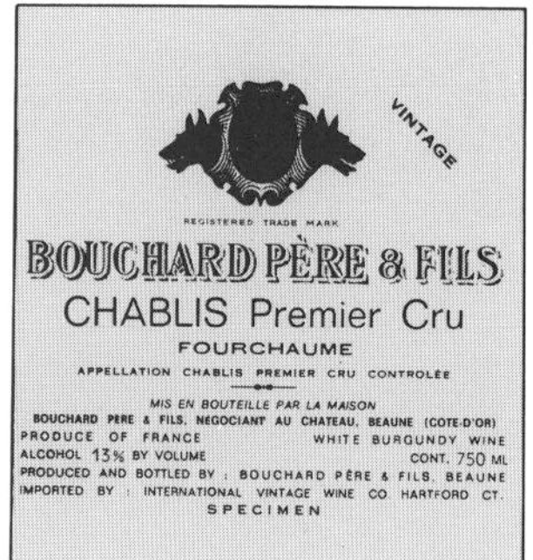

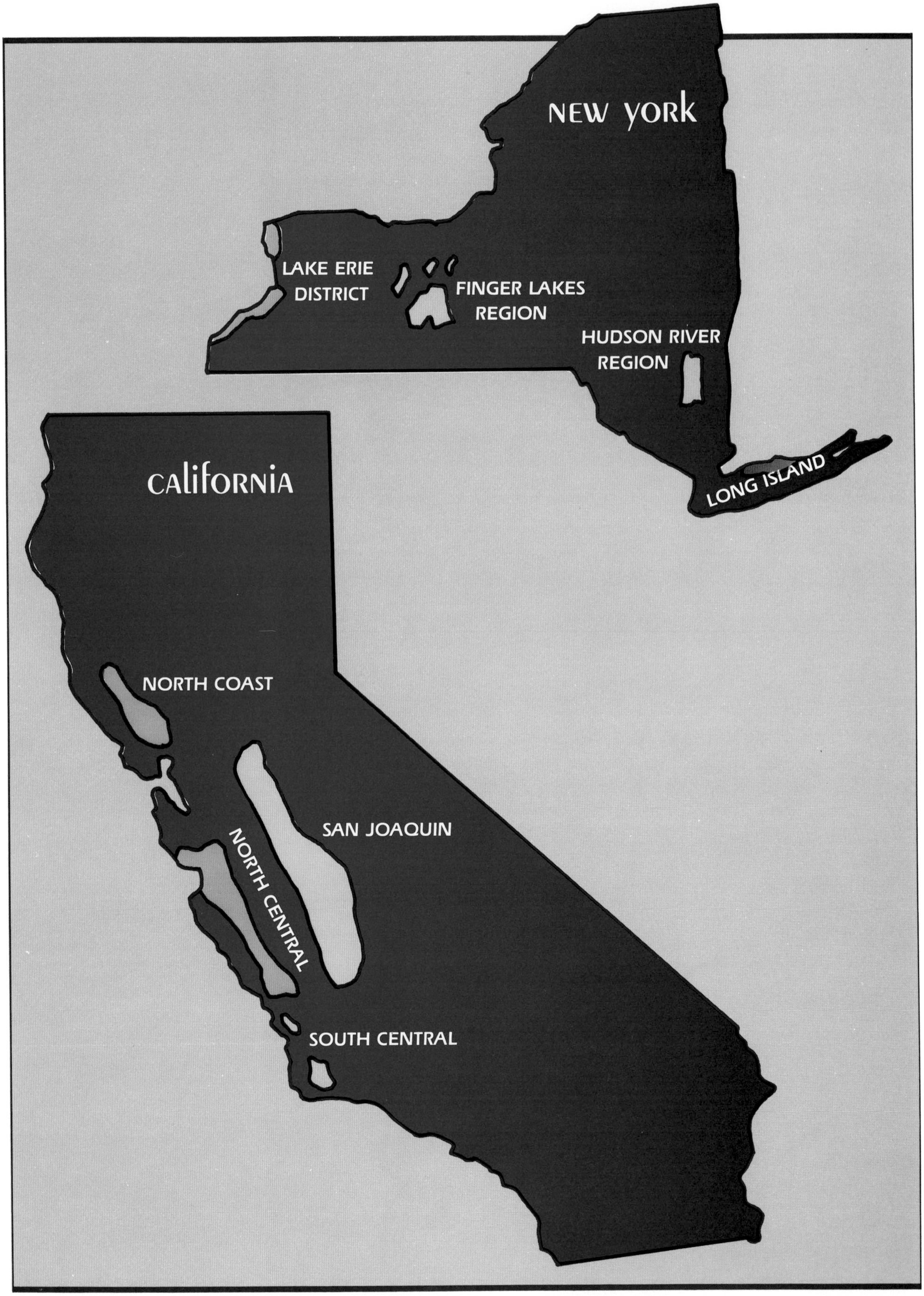

NEW YORK
LAKE ERIE DISTRICT
FINGER LAKES REGION
HUDSON RIVER REGION
LONG ISLAND
CALIFORNIA
NORTH COAST
SAN JOAQUIN
NORTH CENTRAL
SOUTH CENTRAL

THE WHITE WINES OF CALIFORNIA AND NEW YORK

Before discussing the wines of California and New York, let's take a look at American drinking habits. You may wonder why it took so long for wine to become popular in the United States. You only have to look at the largest-selling beverage in the United States in 1960—milk! In 1960, Americans consumed less than one gallon of wine per person each year—quite a difference from 38 gallons per year for milk.

Let's bring this up to date: In 1984, Americans consumed an average of 36 gallons of soft drinks (that means Coca-Cola, Dr. Pepper, Pepsi, Seven-Up—all of them). Does that mean you should sell your shares in the dairy industry?

We can make a projection here, as we would in any other industry. What do you think the leading drink will be in 1990? Yes, once again it's soft drinks, which are expected to take a staggering lead at 50 gallons per person per year. Beer takes second place, and milk gets pushed into third. As for wine, while consumption will more than double, Americans will drink less than five gallons each year on the average.

As you can see, every year wine becomes more and more a part of American culture. What began as a "light" white wine interlude before lunch or dinner is turning into a full-fledged love affair with wine. We have not yet begun to see the full potential of wine as part of American daily life—because it has not yet become part of daily meals.

Before turning to the exciting world of California wines, I'd like to talk about the other major winemaking regions in the United States—New York and Washington State.

Wine has never been America's favorite beverage. In fact, 30% of all Americans don't drink alcoholic beverages of any kind, and another 30% do not drink wine. This leaves only 40% of Americans who drink wine at all—and, in the final analysis, only 5% of the population drink 75% of all the wine.

The World's Top 10 Wine-Drinking Countries*

Rank	Country	Gallons Per Person
1	Italy	24
2	France	23
3	Portugal	21
4	Argentina	19
5	Spain	15
6	Chile	14
7	Luxembourg	13
8	Switzerland	13
9	Greece	12
10	Austria	9

**Impact* (trade magazine)

In the United States, a "wine drinker" is a person who drinks one glass of wine each week.

NEW YORK STATE

New York State is by far the second-largest wine-producing state in America. While New York produces less than one-tenth of California's volume, its wine production is 15 times greater than the third-largest wine-producing state, Washington.

The four major wine regions in New York are:

Finger Lakes—with the largest wine production east of California

Hudson River Region—with a great concentration of premium farm wineries

Lake Erie District—the largest grape-growing district east of California

Long Island—New York's fastest-growing wine region

New York's Hudson Valley boasts the oldest active winery in the United States—Brotherhood, which recorded its first vintage in 1839.

Of the American wines, 90% are produced in California and 7% in New York State.

Grapes are grown and wine is produced in 40 of the 50 states.

The United States ranks 30th in wine consumption—but 12th in beer and 10th in spirits.

The Beginning of Winemaking in the United States

When colonists came to America, many of them settled in New England. They were very pleased to find vines already growing wild, so they didn't have to worry about importing their own.

The first thing they did was prune the existing vines and plant more of the same. Three years later—the time it takes before a mature grape crop can produce wine—they harvested the grapes and made the wine. After they tasted the first vintage, they were disappointed to learn that the wine didn't taste the same as the wine they drank in Europe.

The only way to make their own style of wine was to bring their own grapes—actually, cuttings of the vines. Once again, ships from Europe landed on the East Coast and the colonists took the *Vitis vinifera* vines and planted them.

What happened? Nothing. The vines didn't grow. The cold was blamed, but actually the European vines lacked immunity to local plant diseases and pests. (If the colonists had had access to today's methods to control these problems, the *vinifera* grapes would have thrived on the East Coast just as they do today.)

What grapes grow in New York State?

These fall into three main categories:

Native American (*Vitis labrusca*)
French American (French-American hybrids)
European (*Vitis vinifera*)

Of the New York grapes crushed for wine (73,000 tons in 1983), 72% were Native American, 22% French-American, and 6% European.

Thomas Jefferson, America's first wine connoisseur, had 200 acres of vineyards planted in Virginia.

Native American Varieties

The *Vitis labrusca*, or Native American, varieties are very popular among grape-growers in New York State, because they are hearty grapes that can withstand the cold winters. Among the most familiar grapes of the *Vitis labrusca* family are Concord, Catawba, and Delaware. Traditionally, until the last decade, these are the grapes that have been used to make most New York State wines. In describing these wines, the words "foxy," "grapy," "Welch's," and "Manischewitz" are often used. These words are a sure sign of *labrusca*.

The average American consumes one-tenth the wine that the average Italian or French person drinks.

Foxy Wine

When you read about traditional New York wines in most books, they call the bouquet and the aroma of the wine "foxy." The big question is, what exactly does "foxy" mean?

To answer this, I conducted a survey. Yes, I went around New York State and talked to all of the winemakers who grow *Vitis labrusca*. Finally, I found a winemaker who told me quite simply: "It's obvious. It smells like a wet fox."

Your assignment before you go on to the next chapter is to go out and find a wet fox—and smell it. It's obvious to the winemaker, and it will be obvious to you.

But is that what "foxy" means? Not really. The translation of *labrusca* is the "fox grape"—meaning foxes (and deer, for that matter) like to eat it off the vine.

European Varieties

Thirty years ago, some New York wineries began to experiment with the traditional European (*Vitis vinifera*) grapes. Dr. Konstantin Frank, a Russian viticulturist skilled in cold-climate grape-growing, came to the United States and catalyzed efforts to grow *Vitis vinifera* in New York. This was unheard of—and laughed at—years ago. Other vintners predicted that he'd fail, that it was impossible to grow *vinifera* in New York's cold and capricious climate.

"What do you mean?" Dr. Frank replied. "I'm from Russia—it's even colder there."

Most people still laughed, but Charles Fournier of Gold Seal Vineyards was intrigued enough to give Konstantin Frank a chance to prove his theory.

Sure enough, Dr. Frank was successful with the *vinifera* and has produced some world-class wines, especially his Riesling and Chardonnay. So have several other New York wineries, thanks to the vision and courage of Dr. Frank and Charles Fournier.

1982
Glenora
JOHANNISBERG RIESLING
FINGER LAKES
PRODUCED AND BOTTLED BY
GLENORA WINE CELLARS, DUNDEE, NEW YORK 14837
Alcohol 10.6% by volume

Among 213 wines entered in the 1984 New York State Fair Wine Competition, 29 were Native American, 110 were French-American, and 75 were European—reflecting a pronounced trend away from Native American varieties and towards European varieties.

French-American Varieties

In an effort to hedge their bets, some New York winemakers have chosen the compromise of planting French-American hybrid varieties. These combine European taste characteristics with vine hardiness to withstand New York's cold winters. These varieties were originally developed by French viticulturists in the nineteenth century. Seyval Blanc and Ravat are the most promising white wine varieties; Baco Noir and Chancellor are the best reds.

Some of the most promising table wines from New York today are made from the European grape varieties and some of the French-American varieties.

What trends should I look for in New York wines?

Long Island has seen the largest growth of new vineyards. In the last three years, Long Island has grown from 100 acres to over 700 acres, with faster expansion expected in the future.

Since 1976—because of the Farm Winery Act—more than 50 new wineries have opened in New York. Primarily, these new vineyards specialize in wine made from either European or French-American grape varieties. The Hargrave Vineyard in Cutchogue (northeastern Long Island), for example, specializes in European varietal wines and produces some 8,000 cases per year. And several wineries in the Finger Lakes have already established themselves as consistent producers of high-quality wines. Three well-known examples are Glenora, Heron Hill, and Wagner.

However, most of New York's many new wineries are only beginning to discover and develop their own styles, which makes New York a very exciting region to watch. Essentially, New York is in the midst of a winemaking renaissance combining over a century of tradition with new experimentation in grape-growing and winemaking. More and more wineries, including several new ones in the Hudson Valley, will be producing world-class wines in the next few years.

WEST · PARK
1983
ESTATE BOTTLED
Hudson River Region
CHARDONNAY
GROWN PRODUCED & BOTTLED BY WEST PARK WINE CELLARS
WEST PARK-ON-HUDSON, NEW YORK ALCOHOL 12.5% BY VOLUME

1982

Hargrave Vineyard
North Fork
Long Island New York
Chardonnay

The major wine-producing area in Washington State is the Yakima Valley.

Chateau Ste Michelle
WASHINGTON
FUMÉ BLANC
SAUVIGNON BLANC

Château Ste. Michelle is owned by the U.S. Tobacco Company.

WASHINGTON STATE

In terms of national distribution, Washington State is a relative newcomer to the winemaking industry. Its major winery, Château Ste. Michelle, accounts for 75 percent of the state's wine production—and some very good wine at that. They market a wide range of varietal wines, such as Sauvignon Blanc and Cabernet Sauvignon. Other Washington State labels to look for: Associated Vintners (Columbia Cellars) and Preston Wine Cellar.

Of course, very good wines are produced throughout the United States, such as Idaho, Michigan, Oregon, and Texas, but a discussion of each is beyond the scope of this book. For further reading, I recommend *The Wines of America* by Leon D. Adams.

California

What are the main viticultural areas of California?

The map should help familiarize you with the winemaking regions. It's easier to remember them if you put them into four groups:

North Coast—Napa Valley
Sonoma County
Mendocino County
Lake County

North Central Coast—Monterey County
Santa Clara
Livermore

South Central Coast—San Luis Obispo
Santa Barbara

San Joaquin Valley

Even though you may be most familiar with the Napa and Sonoma valleys, the fact is that only 9 percent of all California wine comes from these two regions combined. In fact, the bulk of California wine is from the San Joaquin Valley, where they produce mostly "jug" wines. This region accounts for 62 percent of the wine grapes planted. Maybe that doesn't seem too exciting—that the production of jug wine dominates the California winemaking industry—but Americans are not atypical in this respect. For example, the A.O.C. (Appellation d'Origine Contrôlée) wines account for only 15 percent of all French wines, while 85 percent are everyday table wines.

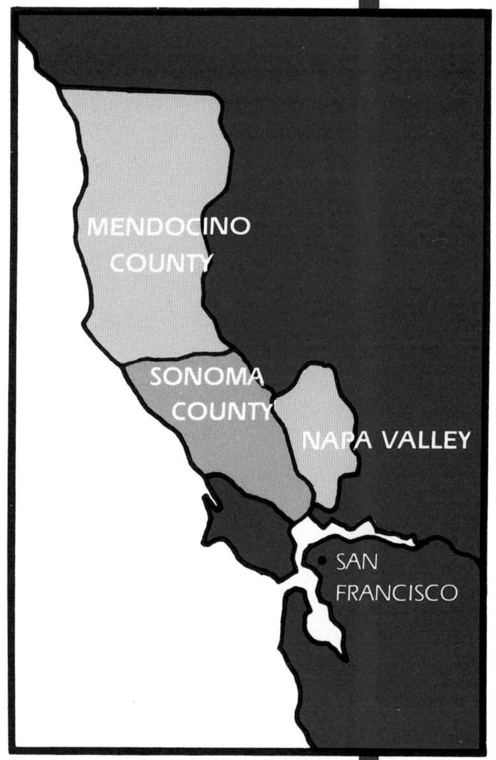

Traditionally, the areas known for producing fine varietal wines in California are the counties along the North Coast: Napa, Sonoma, and Mendocino.

The top five California wineries' Table Wine 1983 (in production):
Ernest & Julio Gallo
Almaden
Heublein (Inglenook, Beaulieu, Italian Swiss Colony)
Monterey Vineyards
Paul Masson

Gallo sells one out of every four bottles of American wine. They produce more than 52 million cases per year—over a million cases per week. They can also change the blend of a wine with a mere touch through a computerized winemaking process.

The best-known wineries of California in the 1950s:
Wente
Martini
Inglenook
Beaulieu
Korbel
Concannon
Beringer
Krug
Paul Masson
Almaden

Sonoma is where winemaking north of San Francisco began.

A Note on Jug Wines

The phrase "jug wine" refers to simple, uncomplicated, everyday drinking wine. You're probably familiar with these types of wine: they're usually labeled with a generic name, such as "Chablis" or "Burgundy." Inexpensive and well-made, these wines were originally bottled in jugs, rather than in conventional wine bottles, hence, the name "jug wine." They are very popular, and account for the largest volume of California wine sold in the United States.

Ernest & Julio Gallo is the major producer of jug wines in California. In fact, many people credit the Gallo brothers with converting American drinking habits from whiskey to wine. Several other wineries also produce their own jug wine, among them, Almaden, Paul Masson, and Taylor California Cellars.

In my opinion, the best-made jug wines in the world are from California. They maintain both consistency and quality from year to year.

1984 was the earliest harvest ever recorded in California. At least one winery began picking grapes on July 31.

The Napa Valley attracts 1–1.5 million visitors each year.

The Napa Valley was officially recognized as a viticultural area in 1982.

Acres of wine grapes planted in Napa: 29,689.
Number of wineries: 150.

Acres of wine grapes planted in Sonoma: 30,187.
Number of wineries: 105.

Acres of wine grapes planted in Mendocino: 10,921.
Number of wineries: 29.

One of the reasons California produces such a wide variety of wines is that it has so many different climates. Some areas are as cool as Burgundy, Champagne, and the Rhine, while others are as warm as the Rhône Valley, Italy, Spain, and Portugal. If that's not diverse enough, these winegrowing areas have inner districts with "microclimates," or climates within climates. One of the microclimates in Sonoma County, for example, is the Alexander Valley; Dry Creek in Sonoma and Los Carneros in Napa are two others that appear on wine labels. Incidentally, these microclimates are often recognized officially as "appellations of origin" by the American government.

To better understand this concept, let's take a close look at the Château St. Jean label.

State: California

County: Sonoma

Viticultural Area: Alexander Valley

Vineyard: Robert Young

Winery: Château St. Jean

What is California's winemaking history?

Although California wines have come into national and international prominence only recently—within the past twenty years—the winemaking industry in the state is more than 200 years old.

The Gold Rush in 1849 started a mass migration to the West Coast. While many were following the call, "Go west, young man," not so many were getting rich panning for gold. What did they do? The same thing any businessman would do to survive—change businesses.

Since the land was free and open, many chose farming as the most logical option, and one of the most popular crops was grapes. This led to the real beginning of the California wine industry.

Now, don't get the idea that frustrated gold miners created the whole California winemaking industry. In fact, many Europeans who settled in California brought their grapes and winemaking tradition with them.

In 1919 something terrible happened, at least for the wine industry—Prohibition! Prohibition lasted for fourteen miserable years, until 1933.

In 1861, Mrs. Lincoln served American wines in the White House.

When Robert Louis Stevenson honeymooned in the Napa Valley in 1880, he described the efforts of local vintners to match soil and climate with the best possible varietals: "One corner of land after another . . . this is a failure; that is better; this is best. So bit by bit, they grope about for their Clos de Vougeot and Lafite . . . and the wine is bottled poetry."

1769: Padre Junipero Serra came to California from Mexico with the *vinifera* grape to plant for his missions.
1831: Jean Louis Vignes brought the first European grape cuttings of classic wine varieties to California.
1861: Count Agoston Haraszthy brought 100,000 *vinifera* vine cuttings from Europe. The story goes that it was the governor of California who selected Haraszthy to take the trip to Europe to buy the cuttings. Even at this early date, California saw the potential for a wine industry.

What effect did Prohibition have on the California wine industry?

By the end of prohibition, most wineries were out of business. The only wineries to survive legitimately were those that produced table grapes for home winemaking and, of course, sacramental wine.

Beringer, Beaulieu, and the Christian Brothers are a few of the wineries that survived this dry time by supplying sacramental wine. Since these wineries didn't have to interrupt production during Prohibition, they had a jump on those that had to start all over again after the law was repealed. But once again, we're getting ahead of our story.

In the late 1800s, California wines were winning medals in international competition.

In 1927 there were 635,000 acres of vineyards in California. In fact, in 1923 there were more grapes planted in California than today.

One Way to Get Around Prohibition . . .

During Prohibition, people used to buy grape concentrate from California and have it shipped back to the East Coast. The top of the container was stamped in big, bold letters—CAUTION: DO NOT ADD SUGAR OR YEAST OR ELSE FERMENTATION WILL TAKE PLACE!

Of course, we know the formula: Sugar + Yeast = Alcohol. Do you want to guess how many people had the sugar and yeast ready the very moment the concentrate arrived!

A varietal wine is labelled with the predominant grape variety used in making the wine. Federal regulations as of 1983 specify that at least 75% of the grapes used must be of the variety cited.

Robert Mondavi was a great promoter for the California wine industry. "He was able to prove to the public what the people within the industry already knew—that California could produce world-class wine," said Eric Wente.

When did California begin to make better-quality wines?

Frank Schoonmaker, one of the first American wine experts who worked as an importer and a writer, convinced many California winery owners to market their best wines using varietal labels as early as the 1940s.

Robert Mondavi may be one of the best examples of a winemaker who concentrated solely on varietal wine production. In 1966, Mondavi left the Charles Krug Winery and started the Robert Mondavi Winery. His role was important to the evolution of varietals in California because even though he wasn't the first, he was among the first major winemakers to make the switch and concentrate on the new venture.

Today these better-quality wines are the benchmark of the new California wine industry.

From the Corporate Ladder to the Vine

The new California grape "farmers":

"Farmer"	Winery	Profession
Robert Travers	Mayacamas	Investment banker
David Stare	Dry Creek	Civil engineer
Tom Jordan	Jordan	Geologist
Rodney Strong	Rodney Strong	Dancer/choreographer
Michael Robbins	Spring Mountain (Falcon Crest)	Engineer
Jack Davies	Schramsberg	Management consultant
James Barrett	Chateau Montelena	Attorney
Tom Burgess	Burgess	Air Force pilot
Joseph Phelps	Phelps	Construction
Donn Chappellet	Chappellet	Food vending
Warren Winiarski	Stag's Leap Wine Cellars	College lecturer
Richard Graff	Chalone	Harvard music graduate
Ely Callaway	Callaway	Former President of Burlington Industries
Joe Heitz	Heitz	Air Force pilot
Eugene Trefethen	Trefethen	Industrialist
David Benion	Ridge	Electronics scientist
Brooks Firestone	Firestone	Take a guess!

How did California come so far so fast in the wine industry?

Gallo spent $32 million advertising their products in 1983.

First and foremost, Americans became "wine conscious." Without that interest there would have been no need to develop the product and no economic basis for its existence. And it is, of course, the American way to create a product and go as far with it as possible: "We'll beat out the competition; we'll show that we're the best and can compete with the best."

Location—Napa and Sonoma, the two major quality wine regions, are 1½ hours from San Francisco by car. Their closeness to the city encourages people to visit the region often, taste the wines, and participate—for business or pleasure, or both.

Weather—Plenty of sunshine, warm temperatures, and a long growing season all add up to good conditions for growing many varieties of grapes. Sure, California is subject to sudden changes in weather—the same as any other wine-growing region in the world—but climate is not a major worry to Californians.

Money and Marketing Strategy—This factor simply cannot be overemphasized. Perhaps marketing does not *make* the wine, but it certainly helps *sell* it. In California, the Coca-Cola Company (Atlanta) put its marketing ability to work and created Taylor California Cellars. You didn't see Taylor of California six years ago—it didn't exist—but within a few years it became a leading brand because of astute marketing.

The University of California at Davis and Fresno State University—These schools have been the training grounds for many young California winemakers. They learn new techniques from a truly scientific study of wine: The soil, the different strains of yeast, stainless steel fermentation, and other winemaking and viticulture techniques.

1978
SMOTHERS
CALIFORNIA
WHITE RIESLING
This wine is 85% White Riesling, 10% Gewurztraminer and 5% Sylvaner. The addition of small quantities of Traminer and Sylvaner to this White Riesling has resulted in a well-balanced, dry wine especially suited for consumption with meals.
Alcohol 10% by volume.
Produced and Bottled by Vine Hill Wines, Inc. Santa Cruz, Ca. 95065

What do Lillian Disney, the Smothers Brothers, Christina Crawford, Wayne Rogers, Francis Ford Coppola, and Pat Paulsen have in common? They all own vineyards in California.

The Corporate Players in the California Wine Game

1942: Joseph E. Seagram buys Paul Masson.
1967: National Distillers buys Almaden.
1969: Heublein buys United Vintners (Italian Swiss Colony, Beaulieu, and Inglenook Vineyards).
1972: Pillsbury buys Souverain.
1972: Joseph Schlitz Brewery buys Geyser Peak Winery.
1973: Coca-Cola (New York) buys Franzia Brothers.
1973: Moët-Hennessy plants 700 acres in Napa for Domaine Chandon.
1978: Coca-Cola (Atlanta) buys Sterling and Monterey Vineyards and creates Taylor of California Cellars.
1983: Seagram's becomes the number-two wine marketer of California wines through its acquisition of all of the Coca-Cola (Atlanta) wineries.
1984: Suntory International buys Château St. Jean Winery of Sonoma for $40 million.

How is California winemaking different from the technique in Europe?

European winemaking has established traditions that have remained essentially unchanged for hundreds of years. This involves the ways in which grapes are grown and harvested, and in some cases includes winemaking procedures.

"There is more potential for style variation in California than Europe because of the greater generosity of the fruit."—*Warren Winiarski, winemaker/owner, Stag's Leap Wine Cellars, Napa Valley.*

In California, there are few traditions, and the winemakers are able to take full advantage of modern technology. Furthermore, there is freedom to experiment and create new products. Some of the experimenting the California winemakers do, such as combining different grape varieties to make new styles of wine, is prohibited by some European wine control laws. So Californians have opportunities to try many new ideas—opportunities sometimes forbidden to European winemakers.

"You are never going to stylize the California wines the same way that European wines have been stylized because we have more freedom to experiment. I value my freedom to make the style of wine I want more than the security of the A.O.C. laws. Laws discourage experimentation."—*Louis Martini.*

Eurowinemaking in California

Many well-known and highly respected European winemakers are investing in California vineyards to make their own wine. For example:

- A joint venture of Baron Philippe de Rothschild, owner of Château Mouton-Rothschild in Bordeaux, and Robert Mondavi, of the Napa Valley, has been formed to produce a wine called Opus One.
- The owners of Château Pétrus in Bordeaux, the Moueix family, now have vineyards in California. Their first wine will be released soon and will be called Dominus.
- Moët & Chandon, which is part of Moët/Hennessy, owns Domaine Chandon in the Napa Valley. They also own the New York importing firm Schieffelin & Company, which owns Simi, a well-known winery in Sonoma.
- Other Champagne and sparkling wine houses with operations in California:
  —Piper Heidsieck (France) owns 50 percent of Piper-Sonoma.
  —Laurent-Perrier is working with Almaden Vineyards.
  —Roederer has grapes planted in Mendocino County.
  —Mumm is planning to produce a sparkling wine at Sterling Vineyards, owned by Joseph E. Seagram & Sons.
  —The Spanish Champagne house Codorniu owns land near San Luis Obispo and the Santa Ynez Valley. Freixenet owns land in Sonoma County.
- The Torres family of Spain owns land in Sonoma County.
- Georges Duboeuf, famous producer/exporter of Beaujolais, makes a fine wine from the Gamay grape in Sonoma County.
- Rémy Martin recently formed a joint venture with Jack Davies of Schramsberg, maker of one of California's finest sparkling wines, to produce premium brandy. The first case went for $21,000.

Another way in which California winemaking is different from European winemaking is that many Californians carry an entire line of wine. Almaden, for example, produces more than 25 different labels. Château Lafite-Rothschild in Bordeaux, on the other hand, produces only one wine.

In addition to modern technology and experimentation, you can't ignore the fundamentals of winegrowing: California's rainfall, weather patterns, and soils are very different from those of Europe.

"Surprisingly good, isn't it? It's Gallo. Mort and I simply got tired of being snobs."

The Gallo "University"

The Ernest & Julio Gallo Winery celebrated its 50th year in the wine industry in 1983. The two brothers were in business long before California wines became popular in the United States and internationally. Not only is theirs the largest winery in the United States, but it also has a reputation for maintaining the highest standards in the production of its wines. Many of the famous winemakers of today's smaller California wineries learned their trade under the guidance of Ernest & Julio Gallo.

Here is a small list of some of the "graduates":

Winemakers	**Winery**
Bill Bonetti	Sonoma Cutrer
Jerry Luper	formerly with Chateau Montelena; now with Chateau Bouchaine
Dick Peterson	Monterey Vineyards
Philip Togni	Cuvaison
Walter Schug	Joseph Phelps

Others who worked at Gallo, but went into management positions:

Leigh Knowles	Chairman of the Board of Beaulieu Vineyards
Richard Maher	President of Seagram's Wine Co.
Terence Clancy	President of Callaway Winery and Frederick Wildman & Sons Importers

THE WINE CELLARS OF
ERNEST & JULIO GALLO
ERNEST & JULIO GALLO VINTED & CELLARED THIS WINE & BOTTLED IT IN MODESTO CALIF.
ALCOHOL 12.5% BY VOLUME

Should California wines be compared to European wines?

Why not? We compare our cars and our cheeses to those of Europe. Besides, California *wanted* to put its wines next to the Europeans' so people would recognize the quality of the California wines. And it worked!

In 1976, Château Montelena Chardonnay won first place in a blind tasting with French white Burgundies held in Paris. (Also, at the same tasting, Stag's Leap Cabernet Sauvignon placed above the top French Bordeaux.)

It's important to remember that fine European vintages are traceable as far back as a century, if not more, but California only began producing fine varietals in any quantity during the last 20 years. There's no track record in California yet, although it is being established.

More interaction is sure to take place between California and Europe in the wine industry, since so many prominent Europeans, who were somewhat skeptical at first, have begun to reach for a piece of the California action.

In 1972, the Baron Philippe de Rothschild said, "All American wines taste the same. They all taste like Coca-Cola." In 1979, the Baron and Robert Mondavi formed a joint venture to produce a Cabernet-style wine in the Napa Valley called Opus One.

What is meant by "style"? How are different styles of wine actually created?

Style refers to the characteristics of the grapes and wine. It is the trademark of the individual winemaker—an "artist" who tries different techniques to explore the fullest potential of the grapes.

Most winemakers will tell you that 95 percent of winemaking is in the quality of the grapes they begin with. The other 5 percent can be traced to the "personal touch" of the winemaker. Here are just a few of the hundreds of decisions a winemaker must make in developing his style of wine:

- When should the grapes be harvested?
- Should the juice be fermented in stainless-steel tanks or oak barrels? How long should it be fermented? At what temperature?
- Should the wine be aged at all? How long? If so, should it be aged in oak? What kind of oak—American, French, Yugoslavian?
- What varieties of grapes should be blended, and in what proportion?
- How long should the wine be aged in the bottle before it is sold?

The list goes on. Because there are so many variables in the making of a wine, producers can create many styles of wine from the same grape variety—so you can choose the style that suits *your* taste.

The point of all this is that California, unlike Europe, is still looking for its own style, and because of the relative winemaking freedom in the United States, the "style" of California may continue to be *diversity*.

"How the hell can you compare 200 years to 2,000."—*A California winemaker.*

"The French make the best French wines. California makes the best California wine made in the world."—*Maynard Amerine, noted oenologist.*

The first case of Opus One sold for $24,000 at the 1984 Napa Auction. It was purchased by Charles Mara, a retailer from Syracuse, New York.

I've mentioned stainless-steel fermentation tanks so often by now that I'll give you a definition, in case you need one. These tanks are temperature controlled: They allow the winemaker to ferment the wines slowly at a low temperature to retain their fruitiness and delicacy, while preventing browning and oxidation.

Ambassador Zellerbach, who created Hanzell Winery, was one of the first California winemakers to use small French oak aging barrels because he wanted to create a Burgundian style.

"A winemaker's task is to bring to perfection the natural potential that is in the fruit itself."—*Warren Winiarski, winemaker/owner, Stag's Leap Wine Cellars, Napa Valley.*

Why is California wine so confusing?

Many students ask me this, and I can only tell them that I'm glad I learned all about the wines of France, Italy, Germany, Spain, and the rest of Europe before I tackled California—because the European wines were so much easier to understand. There are many more details to learn about California wines than about any of the others. We've already covered most of the reasons that California wines are so confusing: Price differences are reflected in the styles (you can get a Chardonnay wine in any price range from $2 to $25—so how do you choose?); constant changes in the wine industry; experimentation which keeps the California wine industry in a state of flux; and the labels, another source of mega-information.

California wine has no classification system that resembles the European equivalent.

Château St. Jean of Sonoma may make six different Chardonnays and seven different Rieslings every vintage!

Another note on winemakers and style: In California many winemakers move around from one winery to another just as a good chef may move from one restaurant to the next. This is not uncommon! They may choose to carry and use the same "recipe" from place to place, if it is particularly successful, and sometimes they will experiment and create new styles.

"If it's a California wine you wish, Mr. Larry will assist you."

What about the prices of California varietal wines?

You can't necessarily equate quality with price. Some excellent varietal wines that are produced in California are well within the budget of the average consumer. On the other hand, some varietals (primarily Chardonnay and Cabernet Sauvignon) may be quite expensive.

As in any market, it is mainly supply and demand that determines price. However, new wineries are affected by start-up costs, which sometimes are reflected in the price of the wine. Older, established wineries, which have long ago amortized their investments, are able to keep their prices low when the supply/demand ratio calls for it.

Remember, when you're buying California wine, price does not always reflect quality.

So, you want to buy a vineyard in California . . .? Today, one acre in Napa Valley costs $20,000 to $30,000 unplanted, and it takes an additional $6,000 per acre to plant. This per-acre investment sees no return for three to five years. To this, add the cost of building the winery, buying the equipment, and hiring the winemaker!

Creative Financing—Overheard at "The Diner" in Yountville, Napa:
"How do you make a small fortune in the wine business?"
"Start with a large fortune and buy a winery."

How do I choose a good California wine?

One way is to look at the label. California labels tell you everything you need to know about the wine—and more. Here are some quick tips you can use when you scan the shelves at your favorite retailer.

- The most important piece of information on the label is the producer's name. In this case the producer is Beringer.
- As of January 1983, if the grape variety is on the label, a minimum of 75 percent of the wine must be derived from that grape variety. If the wine was made before 1983, it must contain at least 51 percent of the labelled variety. The label below shows that the wine is made from the Sauvignon Blanc grape.
- If the wine bears a vintage date, 95 percent of the grapes must have been harvested that year.
- If a wine is designated "California," then 100 percent of the grapes must have been derived from grapes grown in California.
- If the label designates a certain federally recognized viticultural area, such as Sonoma (on this label), then at least 85 percent of the grapes used to make that wine must have been grown in that location.
- The alcohol content is given in percentages. Usually, the higher the percentage of alcohol the fuller the wine will be.
- "Produced and bottled by" means that at least 75 percent of the wine was fermented by the winery named on the label.
- Some wineries will tell you the exact varietal content of the wine, and/or the sugar content of the grapes when they were picked, and/or the amount of residual sugar (to let you know how sweet or dry the wine is).

"Reserve" on the label has no legal meaning. In other words, there is no law that defines it. Some wineries, such as Beaulieu Vineyards and Robert Mondavi Winery, still mark some of their wines "Reserve." BV's "Reserve" is from a particular vineyard; Mondavi's "Reserve" is made from a special blend of grapes, presumably his best. Others include "cask" wines from Inglenook and "special selections" from Louis Martini.

Why do some Chardonnays and Cabernet Sauvignons cost more than other varietals?

In addition to everything we've mentioned before, many wineries age these wines in wood—sometimes for more than a year. Oak barrels have doubled in price over the last five years, averaging $300 per barrel. Add to this the cost of the grapes and the length of time before the wine is actually sold.

Over 500 different California wineries market Chardonnay.

What are the white grape varieties grown in California?

One of them is **Chardonnay**, sometimes labelled Pinot Chardonnay. This green-skinned European (*vinifera*) grape is considered the finest grape variety in the world. It is responsible for all the great French white Burgundies such as Meursault, Chablis, and Puligny-Montrachet. In California, it has been the most successful white grape, yielding a wine of tremendous character and magnificent flavor. The wines are often aged in small oak barrels, increasing their complexity. In the vineyard, yields are fairly low and the grapes command high prices. Chardonnay is always dry, and benefits more than any other American white wine from aging. Superior examples can keep and develop well in the bottle for ten years or longer.

Is there any Chardonnay in a California Chablis?

Probably not. This is because Chardonnay is the most expensive grape used to make some of the best-quality wines in California (that's *one* reason to remember the varietal name "Chardonnay").

"Why," you ask, "did you say, in the last chapter, that Chablis must have 100 percent Chardonnay?"

Good observation. That's because in France the standards set by the Appellation d'Origine Contrôlée (A.O.C.) regulations require it. Early California winemakers, however, "borrowed" the names of famous European

Chardonnay grapes are very expensive, costing up to $1,500 per ton. Even though French Chablis is made from 100% Chardonnay, no California "Chablis" jug wines are made from this grape.

winemaking regions such as Chablis, and applied them to their own wines, regardless of the grape variety used to produce them. In the United States, the standards set by the Bureau of Alcohol, Tobacco and Firearms (B.A.T.F.) still permit this practice. As mentioned earlier, each viticultural region in the world has its own set of rules that follow from the planting of the grapes through the actual winemaking process.

A typical California jug wine, "Chablis," contains 60% Thompson seedless and 40% French Colombard grapes.

What makes one Chardonnay different from another?

Put it this way: There are many brands of ice cream on the market. They use similar ingredients, but there is only one Häagen-Dazs. The same is true for wine. We need to consider whether a wine is aged in wood or stainless steel; how long it remains in the barrel (part of the style of the winemaker); and, of course, where the grapes come from.

What are the other major California white wine grapes?

Sauvignon Blanc—sometimes labelled Fumé Blanc. This is the principal grape used in making the dry white wines of the Graves region of Bordeaux and the white wines of Sancerre and Pouilly-Fumé in the Loire Valley of France. The grape is capable of producing as good a wine in California as it does in France. It is sometimes aged in small oak barrels.

Why is Sauvignon Blanc sometimes referred to as Fumé Blanc? Robert Mondavi found that no one was buying Sauvignon Blanc. So he changed its name to Fumé Blanc. Strictly a marketing maneuver—it was still the same wine. Result: Sales took off. The only mistake Mondavi made was not trademarking the name, so now anyone can use it (and many producers do).

1982

Napa Valley

FUMÉ BLANC

Dry Sauvignon Blanc

ALCOHOL 13% BY VOLUME

PRODUCED AND BOTTLED BY

ROBERT MONDAVI WINERY

OAKVILLE, CALIFORNIA

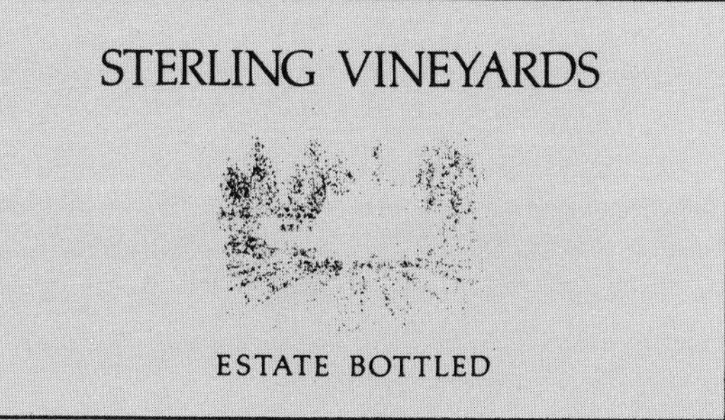

GROWN, PRODUCED AND BOTTLED BY

STERLING VINEYARDS

CALISTOGA, NAPA VALLEY, CALIF. ALCOHOL 13% BY VOLUME

Johannisberg Riesling—The true Riesling responsible for the best German wines of the Rhein and Mosel—and the Alsace wines of France—is called the White Riesling. This grape produces white wine of distinctive varietal character in every style from bone dry to very sweet dessert wines, which are often much better by themselves than with dessert. The nose of White Riesling at its finest is always lively, fragrant, and both fruity and flowery.

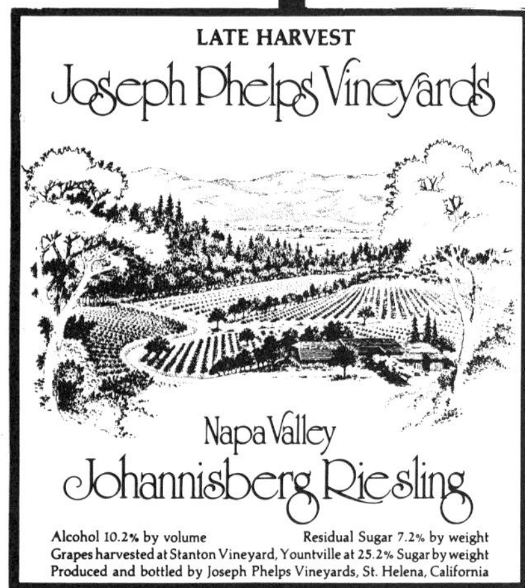

In 1981, BATF requested that the Wine Institute propose industry-wide standard definitions for the terms "Late Harvest" and other similar designations connecting wine style to picking time. The categories proposed with their associated grape sugar levels at harvest generally follow the terms established by the German Wine Law of 1971: (see page 71)

Early Harvest—Equivalent to a German Kabinett, this term refers to wine made from grapes picked at a *maximum* of 20° Brix.

Regular or Normal—No specific label designation will be used to connote wines made from fruit of traditional maturity levels, 20°–24° Brix.

Late Harvest—This term equates to a German Auslese and requires a *minimum* sugar level of 24° Brix at time of harvest.

Select Late Harvest—Equivalent to a German Beerenauslese, the sugar level *minimum* is 28° Brix.

Special Select Late Harvest—This, the highest maturity-level designation, requires that the grapes be picked at a minimum sugar content of 35° Brix, the same level necessary for a German Trockenbeerenauslese.

California Ingenuity

Several wineries in California started to market their Late Harvest Riesling with German names such as Trockenbeerenauslese. The German government complained and this practice was discontinued. One winemaker, though, began marketing his wine as T.B.A., the abbreviation for Trockenbeerenauslese. Again there was a complaint. This time the winemaker argued his case, saying that T.B.A. was not an abbreviation for Trockenbeerenauslese, but for *T*otally *B*otrytis *A*ffected. Stay tuned for more.

Chenin Blanc—This is one of the most widely planted grapes in the Loire Valley. In California, the grape yields a very attractive, soft, light-bodied wine. It is usually made very dry or semi-sweet; it is a perfect apéritif wine, simple and fruity.

Gewürztraminer—This grape is commonly grown both in Germany and in Alsace, France. The wine is usually finished in a slightly sweet to medium-sweet style to counter the grape's tendency towards bitterness, but dry versions have also shown quite well.

WINE AND food

Margrit Biever and Robert Mondavi (Robert Mondavi Winery)—With Chardonnay: oysters, lobster, a more complex fish with sauce *beurre blanc*, pheasant salad with truffles. With Sauvignon Blanc: traditional white meat or fish course, sautéed or grilled fish (as long as it isn't an oily fish).

Phil Baxter (Rutherford Hill)—With Chardonnay: pasta with a butter sauce, better yet with truffles. With Sauvignon Blanc: chilled shellfish, oysters on the half shell.

Francis Mahoney (Carneros Creek Winery)—With Chardonnay: fowl, ham, and seafood in sauces. With Sauvignon Blanc: fish, turkey, shellfish, and appetizers.

Katie Wetzel-Murphy (Alexander Valley Vineyards)—With Chardonnay: salmon with lemon or cream sauce, a light veal dish with mushrooms. With Riesling: chicken breasts poached with raspberry vinaigrette, cream of chanterelle soup.

Sam J. Sebastiani (Sebastiani Vineyards)—With Chardonnay: grilled baby salmon with shallots and fresh dill sauce. With Riesling: Brie tart with sliced green apples and Riesling glaze. With Sauvignon Blanc: rye toast triangles with fresh oysters and pesto.

David Stare (Dry Creek)—With Chardonnay: poached salmon with *beurre blanc*. With Sauvignon Blanc: simply prepared poultry and fish—except barbecued salmon.

Warren Winiarski (Stag's Leap Wine Cellars)—With Chardonnay: seviche, shellfish, salmon with a light Hollandaise sauce.

Angelo Papagni (Papagni Vineyards)—With Chardonnay: pesto linguini. With Sauvignon Blanc: salmon in a spicy mustard sauce with light cream.

Janet Trefethen (Trefethen Vineyards)—With Chardonnay: barbecued whole salmon in a sorrel sauce. With White Riesling: sautéed bay scallops with julienne vegetables.

California Trivia

Breeze through this potpourri of fascinating facts and figures. . . .

In 1875 California produced 4 million gallons of wine per year. By 1892 California almost quadrupled its production to 15 million gallons per year.

In 1920 there were 700 wineries in California. By the end of Prohibition there were 160.

André Tchelistcheff, dean of California winemakers, says, "It was simply unsociable in the United States to drink wine 50 years ago, contrary to the way we would socialize in Europe over a glass of wine."

I'm sure you'll recognize the names of some of the early European winemakers:

Czechoslovakia—Korbel Brothers—1882
Finland—Gustafe Niebaum (Inglenook)—1879
France—Paul Masson—1852
Etienne Thée and Charles LeFranc (Almaden)—1852
Pierre Mirassou—1854
Georges de Latour (Beaulieu)—1900
Germany—Beringer Brothers—1876
Carl Wente—1883
Ireland—James Concannon—1883
Italy—Giuseppe and Pietro Simi—1876
John Foppiano—1895
Samuele Sebastiani—1904
Louis Martini—1922
Adolph Parducci—1932

California's growth is absolutely phenomenal. The first major winery in the Napa Valley after Prohibition was established in 1966. At that time there were 15 wineries in Napa. Today there are 150 in the Napa Valley alone, and 540 in all of California.

"You can make the best wine in the world, but somebody's got to get it out there."—*Myron Nightingale (winemaker, Beringer Vineyards)*

The Advertising of Wine: "We will sell no wine before its time."—*Orson Welles for Paul Masson*
"All the best."—*Ernest & Julio Gallo*

Early California winemakers sent their sons to study oenology at Geisenheim (Germany) or Montpellier (France). Today many European winemakers send their sons to the University of California at Davis and Fresno State University.

"We knew that our message had reached *all* Americans—that California produces world-class wines—when the television show *Falcon Crest* entered the "Top Ten" in national ratings."—*Anonymous winemaker*

In California during Prohibition, vineyard owners started to plant heartier grapes, such as Alicante Bouschet, for shipment to the East Coast.

The University of California at Davis graduated only 5 students from their oenology department in 1966. Today—less than 20 years later—they have a waiting list of students from all over the world.

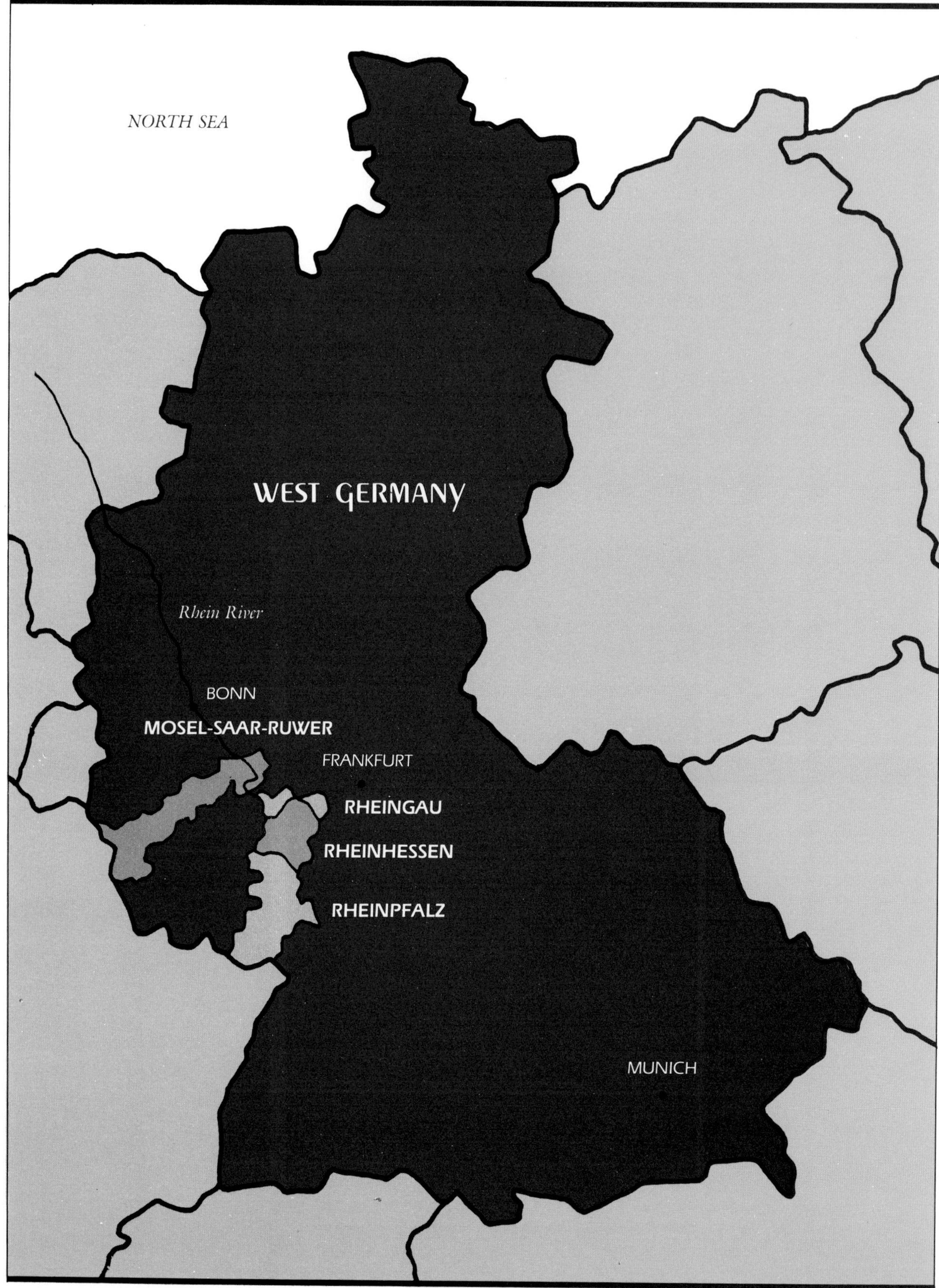
NORTH SEA
WEST GERMANY
Rhein River
BONN
MOSEL-SAAR-RUWER
FRANKFURT
RHEINGAU
RHEINHESSEN
RHEINPFALZ
MUNICH

The White Wines of Germany

Before we begin our study of the white wines of Germany, tell me this: Have you memorized the seven Grand Crus of Chablis, the 31 Grand Crus of the Côte d'Or, and the 150 different vineyards of the Napa Valley? I hope you have, so you can begin to memorize the 1,400 wine villages and the 2,600 vineyards of Germany. No problem, right? What's 4,000 simple little names?

Actually, if you were to have studied German wines before 1971, you would have had 30,000 different names to remember. There used to be very small parcels of land owned by many different people; that's why so many names were involved.

There has been a 10% increase in the vineyards planted over the last 10 years.

In an effort to make German wines less confusing, the government stepped in and passed a law in 1971. The new ruling stated that a vineyard must encompass at least 12.5 acres of land. This law cut the list of names considerably, though many of the vineyards today are divided among several owners.

In Germany, 100,000 grape-growers cultivate nearly 240,000 acres of vines.

The average holding per grower is 2.4 acres.

Germany produces only 2–3 percent of the world's wines. (Beer, remember, is the national beverage.) And what they *do* produce depends largely on the weather. Why is this? Well, look at where the wines are geographically. Germany is the northernmost country in which vines can grow. And 80 percent of the vineyards are located on hilly slopes. They can forget about mechanical harvesting.

France produces 10 times as much wine as Germany.

One mechanical harvester can do the work of 60 people.

As the German winemakers say, "100 days of sun will make a good wine, but 120 days of sun will make a *great* wine."

German wines tend to be 8–10% alcohol compared to an average 11–13% for French wine.

The chart below should help give you a better idea of the hilly conditions vintners must contend with in order to grow grapes and produce wines in Germany.

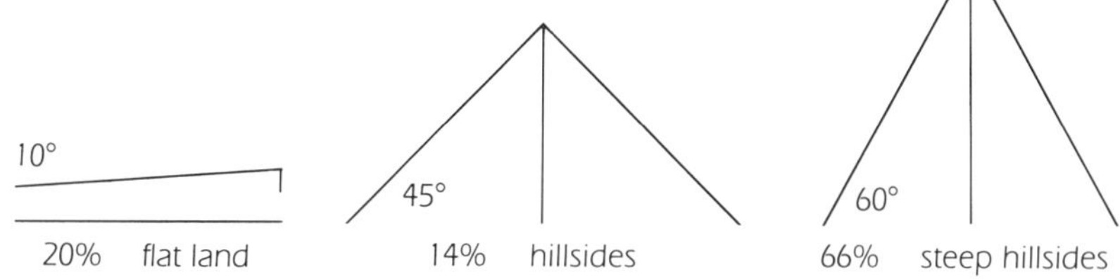

What are some of the problems of German wines in the American market?

For many people, the wines are not dry enough, especially to drink with most meals. Importers of German wines are trying to respond to this problem. They've been experimenting with drier wines; *trocken* (dry) and *halb-trocken* (semi-dry).

Have you ever noticed that one of the biggest drawbacks of German wines is the unpronounceable names? And wouldn't you know it, many wineries use Gothic script on the label to help you along! Peter Sichel, the largest exporter of German wines in the world, was one of the first exporters to make German names simpler for Americans. He realized we just weren't buying those wines with the hard-to-pronounce names, so he introduced Blue Nun. It is actually a Liebfraumilch wine, which translated means "milk of the blessed Mother." It has been popular in the United States for many years for many reasons: It's a nice, drinkable wine; it's consistent from year to year and it's very reasonably priced. The media ad campaign keeps people aware of the product, and besides, Blue Nun is a lot easier to ask for than Liebfraumilch!

Would You Believe?

Fifty years ago, most German wines were dry and very high in acidity. Even in the finest restaurants, you'd be offered a spoonful of sugar with a German wine to balance the acidity.

What is the style of German wines?

A balance of sweetness with acidity and low alcohol. Remember the equation:

Sugar + Yeast = Alcohol + Carbon Dioxide

Where does the sugar come from? The sun. If you have a good year and your wines are on a southerly slope, you'll get a lot of sun and therefore the right sugar content to produce a good wine. In many years, however, the winemakers are not so fortunate and they don't have enough sun to ripen the grapes. The result: higher acidity and lower alcohol. To compensate for this, the winemakers add sugar to the must before fermentation to increase the amount of alcohol. As mentioned before, this process is called chaptalization. (*Note*: Chaptalization is not permitted for higher-quality German wines.)

With German wines, 85 is the important number to remember.

- —85% of the wines Germany produces are white.
- —If a wine label gives the grape variety—Riesling, for example—85% of the wine must be made from the Riesling grape.
- —If a German wine shows a vintage on the label, 85% of the grapes used must be from that year.

A Note on Süss-Reserve

A common misconception about German wine is that fermentation stops and the remaining residual sugar gives the wine its sweetness naturally. On the contrary, the wines are fermented dry, and most German winemakers hold back a certain percentage of unfermented grape juice (called Süss-Reserve). This contains all the natural sugar and it is added back to the wine after fermentation. This adds sweetness to the wine and lowers the alcohol content.

What are the main winemaking regions of Germany?

There are eleven major winemaking regions. Do you have to commit them all to memory like the hundreds of other names I've mentioned in the book so far? Absolutely not. Why should you worry about all eleven when you only need to be familiar with four? Look at the eleven regions on the map for your own curiosity, but here are the four most important:

If you were to look at a map of the world, put your finger on Germany, and then follow that latitude across into North America, you'd be pointing to Nova Scotia.

Mosel-Saar-Ruwer
Rheingau
Rheinhessen
Rheinpfalz

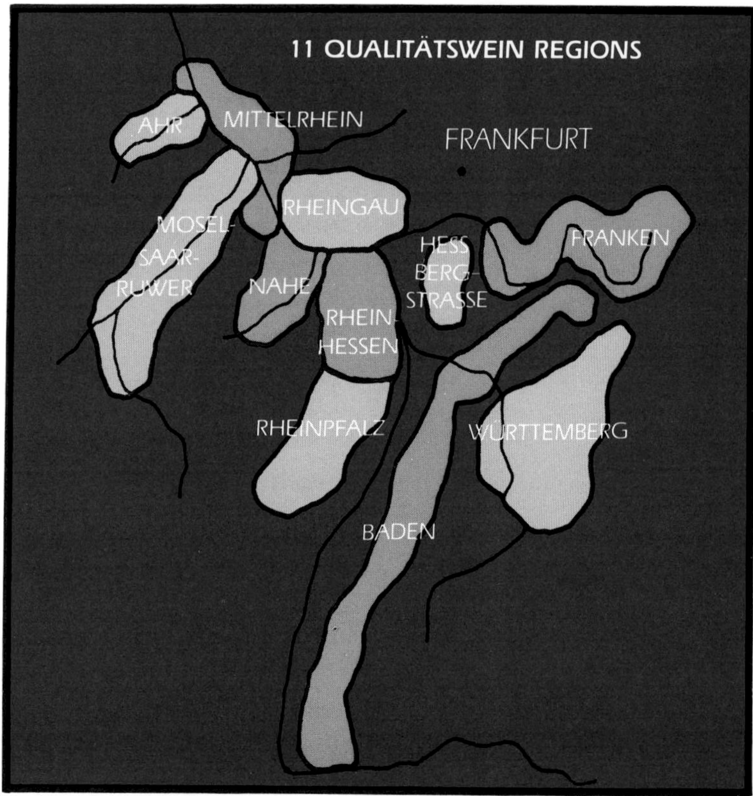

One of the reasons I emphasize these regions above the others is that you rarely see wine from the other German winegrowing regions in the United States. The other reason to look closely at these regions is because they produce the best German wines.

Germany produces red wines, too, but only 15%. Why? Red grapes simply do not grow well in the northerly climate.

One quick way to tell the difference between a Rhein and a Mosel wine on sight is to look at the bottle. Rhein wine comes in a brown bottle, Mosel in a green bottle.

"A Mosel is like a young girl—fresh, light, and fruity. A Rheingau is like a ripe woman of 30 years or more—mature." — *Walter Mueller* (*Bernkasteler Doktor*)

In 1921, the first Trockenbeerenauslese was made in the Mosel at the Bernkasteler Doktor estate.

58% of Mosel wines are made from the Riesling grape. 80% of Rheingau wines are made from Riesling.

Grapes in Germany:

Müller-Thurgau	31%
Riesling	23%
Silvaner	17%

What is the difference between Rhein and Mosel wines?

Rhein wines generally have more body than Mosels. In addition, Mosel wines often have a spritz—a natural effervescence. Mosels are also higher in acidity and lower in alcohol than Rhein wine.

MOSEL · SAAR · RUWER

What are the most important grape varieties?

Riesling—This is by far the best grape variety produced in Germany. If you don't see the name "Riesling" on the label, then there probably is very little, if any, Riesling grape in the wine. And remember, if the label gives the grape variety, then there must be at least 85 percent of that grape in the wine, according to German law. Of the grapes planted in Germany 23 percent are Riesling.

Silvaner—This is another variety that accounts for 17 percent of Germany's wines.

Müller-Thurgau—This is a combination of Riesling and Silvaner, the most widely planted grape in Germany.

There are many other grape varieties planted in Germany, and you may be familiar with some of them, such as Gewürztraminer, which is used to make the "spicy" Traminer wine, but for our purposes, we'll concentrate mostly on Riesling.

What are the quality levels of German wine?

As a result of the new German law of 1971, there are two main categories of quality. Either a wine is *Tafelwein*, which means "table wine," or *Qualitätswein*, "quality wine."

Tafelwein—The lowest designation given to a wine grown in Germany, it never carries the vineyard name. It is rarely seen in the United States.

Landwein—A new and higher category of table wine, which must have a higher concentration of grape sugar and can come only from certain areas. It will be either dry or semi-dry (*trocken* or *halb-trocken*).

Qualitätswein—literally, "quality wine."

1. *Qualitätswein bestimmter Anbaugebiete:* I'm giving you this one because you often see the abbreviation, QbA, on a label. QbA indicates a quality wine that comes from one of the eleven specified regions.

2. *Qualitätswein mit Prädikat:* This is quality wine with distinction—the good stuff. These wines may *not* be chaptalized: The winemaker is not permitted to add sugar. In ascending order of quality, price, and sweetness:

Kabinett:—Light, semi-dry wines made from normally ripened grapes. Cost: $4–$7.

Spätlese—Breaking up the word, *spät* means "late" and *lese* means "picking." Put them together and you have "late picking." That's exactly what the wine is made of—grapes that were picked after the normal harvest. The extra days of sun give the wine a more intense flavor. Cost: $6–$9.

Auslese—Translated as "out picked," this means that the grapes are selectively picked out from particularly ripe bunches. You probably do the same thing in your own garden if you grow tomatoes: You pick out the especially ripe ones, leaving the others on the vine. Cost: $8–$15.

Given good weather, the longer the grapes remain on the vine, the sweeter they become—but the winemaker takes a risk when he does this because all could be lost in the event of bad weather.

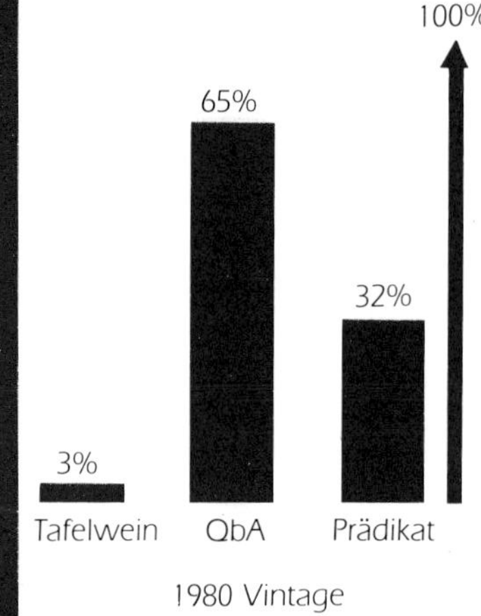

You could generalize with German wines—the longer the name, the higher the quality of the wine.

The Spätlese Rider: The First Late Harvest Wine

The story goes that at the vineyards of Schloss Johannisberg, the monks were not allowed to pick the grapes until the Abbot of Fulda gave his permission. During the harvest of 1775, the Abbot was away attending a synod meeting. That year the grapes were ripening early and some of them had started to rot on the vine. The monks, becoming concerned, dispatched a rider to ask the Abbot's permission to pick the grapes. By the time the rider returned, the monks believed all was lost, but they went ahead with the harvest anyway. To their amazement, the wine was one of the best they had ever tasted. That was the beginning of Spätlese-style wines.

Beerenauslese—Breaking the word down, you get *beeren* or "berries," *aus* or "out," and *lese* or "picking." Quite simply (and don't let the bigger names fool you), these are berries (grapes) that are picked out individually. These luscious grapes are used to create the rich dessert wines that Germany is known for. Beerenauslese is usually made only two or three times every ten years. It's not unheard of for a good Beerenauslese to cost up to $150.

Most German wines, including Beerenauslese and Trockenbeerenauslese, are bottled in spring and early summer. They no longer receive additional cask or tank maturation, because it has been discovered that this extra barrel maturation destroys the fruit.

Trockenbeerenauslese—A step above the Beerenauslese, but these grapes are dried (*trocken*), so they're more like raisins. These raisinated grapes produce the richest, sweetest, honey-like wine—and the most expensive, too.

Eiswein—A very rare, sweet, concentrated wine made from frozen grapes left on the vine. They are pressed while still frozen. According to Germany's new rules for winemaking, this wine must now be made from grapes that are at least ripe enough to make a Beerenauslese.

A Common Misnomer for German Wine

I know I just finished telling you about Spätlese wine and how you can remember the word by breaking it up to get "late picking." But, this is not always the case, even though it's a good general rule. The truth is that the winemaker can produce good Spätlese wine from grapes harvested earlier in the season—sometimes during the normal harvest—because the *time of picking* is not as important as the *ripeness* of the grapes. And the ripeness of the grapes, of course, depends on how much sun a vine receives, which brings us back to the location of the vine.

What is the difference between a $30 Beerenauslese and a $100 Beerenauslese (besides $70)?

The major difference is the grapes. The $30 bottle is probably made from Müller-Thurgau grapes or Silvaner, while the $100 bottle is from Riesling. In addition, the region the wine comes from will in part determine its quality. Traditionally, the best Beerenauslese and Trockenbeerenauslese come from the Rhein Valley. The most expensive come from the Rheingau.

What Is Botrytis Cinerea?

Botrytis cinerea, known as *Edelfäule* in German, is a mould that attacks grapes under special conditions, as we saw in the chapter on Sauternes. I say special because this "noble rot" is instrumental in the production of the better wines, namely Beerenauslese and Trockenbeerenauslese.

Noble rot occurs late in the season when the nights are cool and heavy with dew, the mornings have fog, and the days are warm.

When it attacks the grapes, they begin to shrivel and the water evaporates, leaving concentrated sugar. (Remember, 90 percent of wine is water.) Grapes affected by this mould may not look too appealing, but don't let looks deceive you: The proof is in the wine.

When I'm ordering a German wine in a restaurant or shopping at my local retailer, what should I look for?

The first thing I would make sure of is that it comes from either the Mosel-Saar-Ruwer or the Rheingau region, which in my opinion are the most important quality wine-producing regions in all of Germany. They are the German equivalent to wines from the Napa Valley, Bordeaux, Burgundy, and so forth.

Famous vineyards of the Rheingau are:
Schloss Johannisberg
Schloss Vollrads
Steinberg

Some important villages to look for:

Rheingau
Eltville
Erbach
Rüdesheim
Rauenthal
Hochheim
Johannisberg

Mosel-Saar-Ruwer
Piesport
Bernkastel
Graach
Wehlen
Ockfen
Serrig

VERBAND
DEUTSCHER
PRÄDIKATSWEIN-
VERSTEIGERER E. V.
Unsere Mitglieder besitzen
Lagen von Weltruf!
V
D P
750 ml
A. P. Nr. 2 576 510/14 82
MOSEL-SAAR-RUWER
QUALITÄTSWEIN MIT PRÄDIKAT
1981er
Graacher Himmelreich
Riesling - Spätlese
ERZEUGER-ABFÜLLUNG
S. A. Prüm Erben, S. A. Prüm, Wehlen/Mosel

Next, look to see if the wine is a Riesling. Anyone who studies and enjoys German wines finds that Riesling shows the best-tasting characteristics. It is a mark of quality.

Finally, be aware of the vintage. It's important, especially with German wines, to know if it was a good year.

Famous vineyards of the Mosel-Saar-Ruwer are:
Bernkasteler Doktor
Piesporter Goldtröpfchen
Scharzhofberg
Wehlener Sonnenuhr

Can you take the mystery out of reading German wine labels?

German wine labels give you plenty of information. For example, see the label below.

RUDOLF MÜLLER KG · WEINGUT - WEINKELLEREI · REIL/MOSEL
MOSEL - SAAR - RUWER
1976er
Reiler Sorentberg
Trockenbeerenauslese
Riesling - Qualitätswein mit Prädikat
A. P. Nr. 2 598 176/119/77
Erzeugerabfüllung
WEINGUT
Rudolf Müller

All Qualitätswein and Qualitätswein mit Prädikat must pass a test by an official laboratory and tasting panel to be given an official number prior to being released to the trade.

Impress your friends with this trivia:
A.P. Nr. 2 598 176/119/77

- 2 = the government referral office
- 598 = the registration of the shipper
- 176 = the application number
- 1/19 = the month and date the wine was tasted by the control authority
- 77 = the year the wine was tasted by the board

1. Mosel-Saar-Ruwer—This is the region of the wine's origin. Note that it's one of the big four we discussed earlier in the chapter.
2. 1976—The year the grapes were harvested.
3. Reil is the town and Sorentberg is the vineyard in which the grapes originate. The Germans add the suffix "er" to make Reiler, just as a person from New York is called a New Yorker.
4. Trockenbeerenauslese is the style of wine made from the grapes that were selectively picked from the vine.
5. Riesling is the grape variety. Therefore, this wine is at least 85 percent Riesling.
6. Qualitätswein mit Prädikat is the quality level of the wine.
7. A.P. Nr. 2 598 176/119/77 is the official testing number—proof that the wine was tasted by a panel of tasters and passed the strict quality standards required by the government.
8. Erzeugerabfüllung means estate-bottled.
9. Rudolf Müller is the producer of the wine.

Best Bets for Recent Vintages in Germany

1979 1981 1983

One of the greatest vintages of the century was 1976 (next to 1949 and 1921), but buy this vintage only at the Auslese levels or above; otherwise it will probably be past its peak.

The second-largest harvest after 1982 in quantity was 1983 and the best-quality vintage since 1976. As a result, you're going to see a lot of good-quality German wines in your retail store.

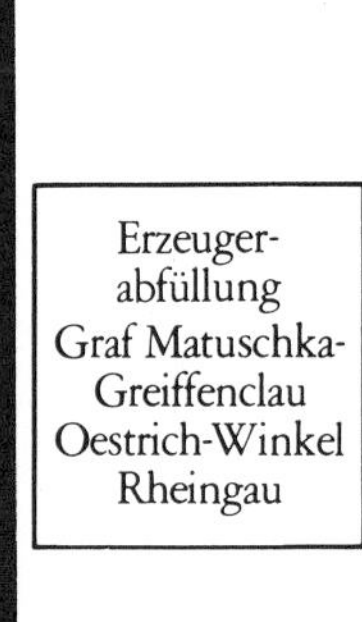

SCHLOSS VOLLRADS

Erzeuger-abfüllung Graf Matuschka-Greiffenclau Oestrich-Winkel Rheingau

Produce of Germany

A.P.Nr.

27074 013 84

Rheingau Riesling

1983er QUALITÄTSWEIN

grüngold

e 750 ml

wine and food

As we mentioned earlier, beer is the national beverage of Germany and the one served with meals by the German people. Most German wine is consumed between meals or after dinner. Recently this practice has been changing, and in an effort to show that German wines can complement meals many wine producers—such as Graf Matuschka, owner of Schloss Vollrads—have been serving German wine-and-food dinners throughout the United States. They tell me that Qualitätswein, Kabinett, and Spätlese wines go well with chicken, cold lobster, cold meats, and mild cheeses. The very sweet wines (Auslese, Beerenauslese, and Trockenbeerenauslese) are better consumed alone.

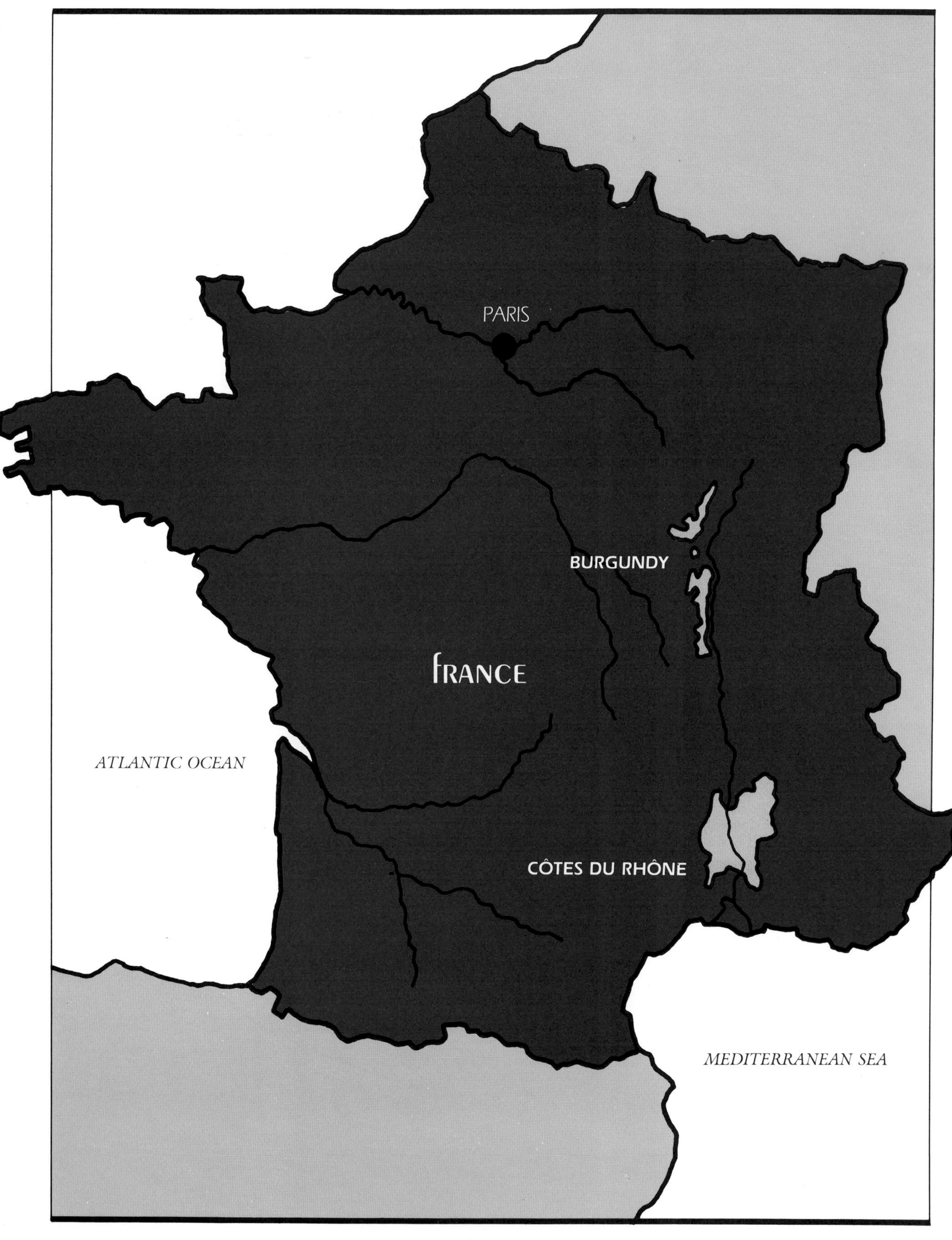
PARIS
BURGUNDY
FRANCE
ATLANTIC OCEAN
CÔTES DU RHÔNE
MEDITERRANEAN SEA

the red wines of burgundy and the rhône valley

Now we're getting into a whole new experience in wines—the reds. Generally, wine students get more intense and concentrate more when tasting red wines.

What's so different (beyond the obvious color)?

We're beginning to see more components in the wines—more complexities. In the white wines, we were looking mainly for the acid/fruit balance, but now in addition we're looking for other characteristics, such as tannin.

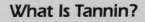

What Is Tannin?

Tannin is what gives wine its longevity and dryness. It comes from the skins, the pits, and the stems of the grapes. Another source of tannin is wood, especially the French oak barrels in which some wines are aged.

A word used to describe the taste sensation of tannin is "astringent." Let an aspirin dissolve in your mouth and you'll understand what I mean.

Tannin is also found in strong tea. And what can you add to the tea to make it less astringent? Milk—it softens the tannin. And so it is with a high tannic wine. If you take another milk by-product, such as cheese, and have it with the wine, it softens the tannin and makes the wine more appealing.

THE RED WINES OF BURGUNDY

Why is Burgundy so difficult to understand?

Before we go any further, I must tell you that there are no shortcuts. Burgundy is one of the most difficult subjects in the study of wines. People get uptight about Burgundy. They say, "There's so much to know," and "It looks so hard." Yes, there are a lot of vineyards and villages, and they are all important. But actually, there are only 25 to 50 names you need to familiarize yourself with, if you'd like to know and speak about Burgundy wines intelligently. Not to worry. I'm going to help you decode all the mysteries of Burgundy names, regions, and labels.

What are the main red-wine-producing areas of Burgundy?

Côte d'Or { **Côte de Nuits**, **Côte de Beaune** }

Beaujolais

Côte Châlonnaise

What major grape varieties are used in red Burgundy wines?

The two major grape varieties are Pinot Noir and Gamay. Under Appellation Contrôlée laws, all red Burgundies, excluding Beaujolais, must be made from the Pinot Noir grape. Beaujolais is produced from the Gamay grape variety.

Let's take a closer look at the red-wine-producing regions of Burgundy.

BEAUJOLAIS

Made from 100 percent Gamay grapes, this wine's style is typically light and fruity. It is meant to be consumed young. Beaujolais is the largest-selling Burgundy in the United States by far, probably because it's so easy to drink. It can be chilled and it's very affordable. Most bottles cost between $5 and $7, although the price varies with the quality and the grade.

What are the quality levels of Beaujolais?

Beaujolais—the basic Beaujolais. The only difference between this wine and Beaujolais Supérieur is that Supérieur has more alcohol, but the quality is the same. The basic Beaujolais accounts for the majority of all Beaujolais produced (Cost: $).

Beaujolais-Villages—comes from certain villages in Beaujolais. There are 35 villages that consistently produce better wines. Most Beaujolais-Villages is a blend of wines from these villages, and usually no particular village name is included on the label (Cost: $$).

"Cru"—a total of nine in Beaujolais. A "cru" is actually the name of a village that produces the highest quality of Beaujolais (Cost: $$$$).

Here are the nine "crus" (villages):

Brouilly
Morgon
Moulin-à-Vent
Fleurie

These four are the most popular of the "crus" and account for 75 percent of Beaujolais production.

Côte de Brouilly
Chiroubles
Chénas
Juliénas
Saint-Amour

What is Beaujolais Nouveau?

Beaujolais Nouveau is a fruity, light-style wine that is best to drink young. Isn't that what I've been saying about *all* Beaujolais wines? Yes, but Nouveau is different. This "new" Beaujolais is picked, fermented, bottled, and available at your local retailer in a matter of weeks. (I don't know what you call that in your business, but I call it good cash flow in mine. It gives the winemaker practically an instant return.)

There is another purpose behind Beaujolais Nouveau: It gives the public a sample of the quality and style that the winemaker produces in his regular Beaujolais.

Over 40% of the Beaujolais crop is used to make Beaujolais Nouveau.

Beaujolais Nouveau is meant to be consumed within six months of bottling. So if you're holding a 1976 Beaujolais Nouveau, now is the time to give it to your "friends."

Beaujolais Nouveau Madness

The exact date of release is November 15, and Beaujolais Nouveau is introduced to the consumer amidst great hoopla. The restaurants and retailers all vie to be the first to offer Beaujolais to their customers. Some of these wine buyers go so far as to fly the wine into the country on the Concorde; others stretch the rules a little so they have it earlier.

How long should I keep a Beaujolais?

It depends on the level of quality and the vintage. Beaujolais is meant to last between one and two years, except for the "cru" Beaujolais. "Crus" can last longer because they are more complex. I've tasted Beaujolais "crus" that were more than ten years old and still in excellent condition. This is the exception, though, not the rule.

At the restaurant, people often ask me for white Beaujolais. Yes, white Beaujolais exists, but only one percent of total Beaujolais production is white. If this is the style that appeals to you, I think you'd be much better off with a Mâcon Blanc. It's a similar pleasing style and easier to find.

Wines from the nine "crus" of Beaujolais usually do not bear the name "Beaujolais" on the label—just the name of the village. This is because the producers of "cru" Beaujolais don't want to have their wines confused with basic Beaujolais.

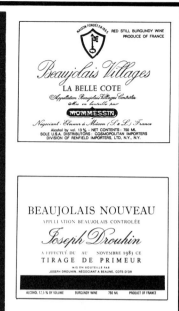

"Beaujolais is one of the very few red wines that can be drunk as a white. Beaujolais is my daily drink. And sometimes I blend one-half water to the wine. It is the most refreshing drink in the world."—*Didier Mommessin*

What shippers/producers should I look for when buying Beaujolais?

Bouchard
Drouhin
Duboeuf
Jadot
Mommessin
Piat

Best Bets for Recent Vintages of Beaujolais

1981—"cru" Beaujolais only
1982—all Beaujolais
1983—probably the best vintage in Beaujolais since 1976

WINE AND FOOD

Beaujolais goes well with almost anything—especially light, simple meals and cheeses—nothing overpowering. Generally, try to match your Beaujolais with light food, such as veal, fish, or fowl. Here's what some of the experts say:

Jean-François Bouchard—"A perfect picnic wine; good for the first course, charcuterie, cold meats, and salads."

André Gagey (Louis Jadot)—"Beaujolais with simple meals, light cheeses, grilled meat—everything except sweets."

Robert Drouhin—"Should be served slightly cool . . . a wine to drink more than sip, instead of talking about it."

Didier Mommessin—"Serve with an extremely strong cheese, such as Roquefort, especially when the wine is young and strong enough for it. Also with white meat and veal."

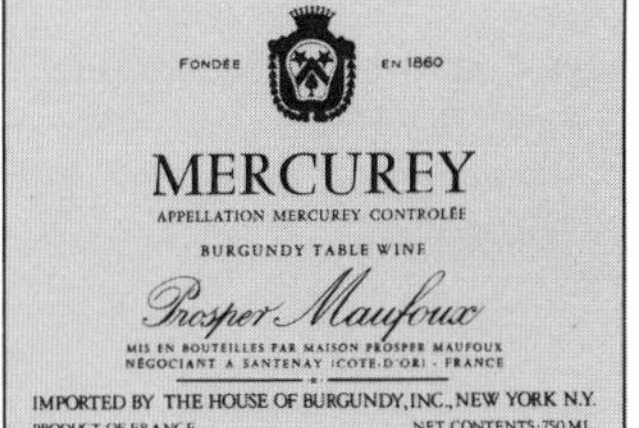

CÔTE CHÂLONNAISE

You should know three villages from this area:
Mercurey
Givry
Rully

Mercurey is the most important, producing wines of high quality. Because they are not well known in the United States, Mercurey wines are often a very good buy.

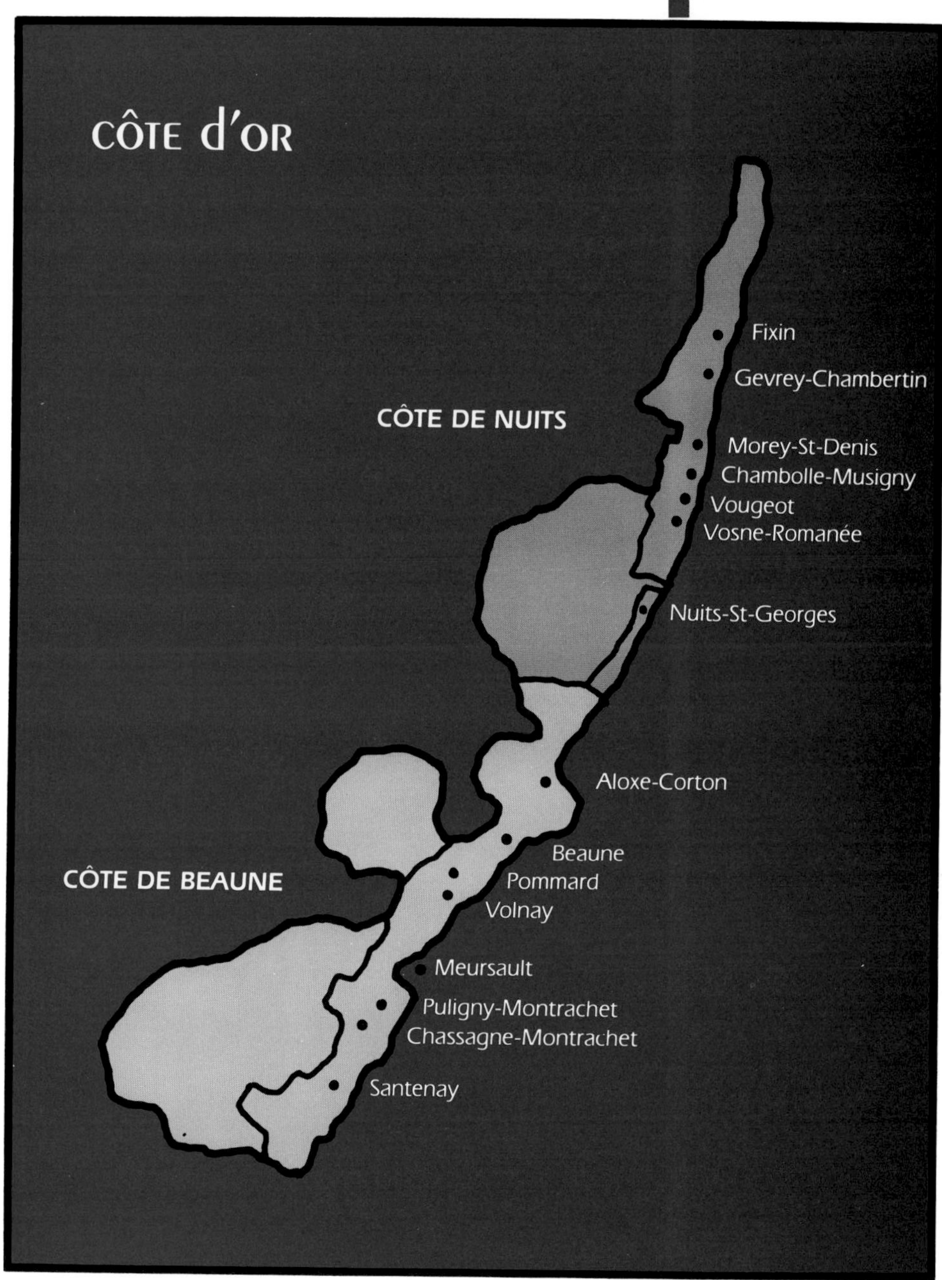

CÔTE d'OR

Now we're getting to the heart of Burgundy—the Côte d'Or (pronounced "door") and meaning "golden slope." One reason this name is appropriate is because of the color of the foliage on the mountainside in autumn. Another reason this region is golden is because of the income it brings the winemakers—and the wines are not exactly the $2.99 specials of the day. The Côte d'Or is divided into two regions:

Côte de Beaune—red and white wines
Côte de Nuits—where quality red Burgundy wines come from

The Côte d'Or is only 30 miles long and a half-mile wide.

A good trivia question for your friends:
How many red Grand Crus are there in the Côte de Beaune?
Answer: only one—Corton, from the village of Aloxe-Corton.

What's the best way to understand the wines of the Côte d'Or?

First you need to know that these wines are distinguished by quality levels—Generic, Village, Premier Cru and Grand Cru. Let's look at the quality levels with the "Double Pyramid" shown below. As you can see, not a lot of Grand Cru wine is produced, but that small amount is top quality. Generic, on the other hand, is available in abundance. Although much is produced, very few generic wines can be classified as "outstanding."

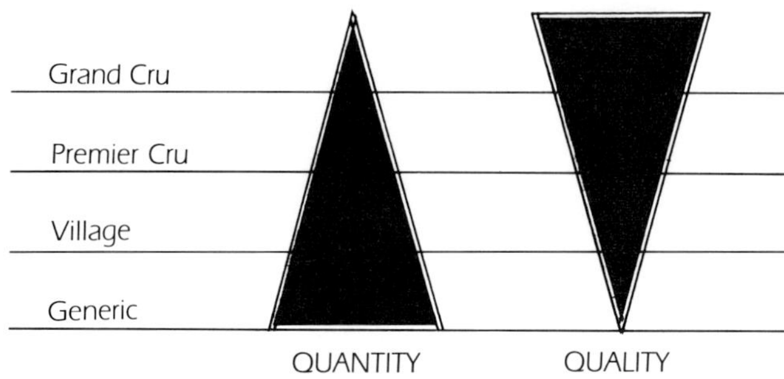

Another way to understand the wines of the Côte d'Or is to become familiar with the most important villages and vineyards.

CÔTE DE BEAUNE

Villages	Premier Cru Vineyards	Grand Cru Vineyards
Aloxe-Corton	Corton Clos du Roi Corton Bressandes Corton Maréchaudes Corton Renardes	Corton
Beaune	Grèves Fèves Marconnets Bressandes Clos des Mouches	None
Pommard	Epenots Rugiens	None
Volnay	Caillerets Santenots Clos de Chênes	None

ALOXE CORTON LATOUR
APPELLATION ALOXE-CORTON CONTROLEE
MIS EN BOUTEILLE PAR
LOUIS LATOUR.NÉGOCIANT A BEAUNE (CÔTE D'OR)

CÔTE DE NUITS

Finally, we reach the Côte de Nuits. If you're going to spend any time studying your geography, do it now. Most of the big, full-bodied reds come from this area. The most important names (also the most expensive) for you to remember when you go to your local retailer or dine out are:

Village	Premier Crus Vineyards	Grand Crus Vineyards
Gevrey-Chambertin	Clos St-Jacques	Chambertin
		Chambertin Clos de Bèze
		Latricières-Chambertin
		Mazis-Chambertin
		Mazoyères-Chambertin
		Ruchottes-Chambertin
		Chapelle-Chambertin
		Charmes-Chambertin
		Griotte-Chambertin
Morey-St-Denis	Clos des Lambrays	Clos de Tart
		Clos St-Denis
		Clos de la Roche
		Bonnes Mares (part)
Chambolle-Musigny	Amoureuses	Musigny
	Charmes	Bonnes Mares (part)
Vougeot		Clos de Vougeot
Vosne-Romanée	Grande-Rue	Romanée-Conti
	Beaux-Monts	La Romanée
	Malconsorts	La Tâche
		Richebourg
		Romanée-St-Vivant
Nuits-St-Georges	Les St-Georges	None
	Vaucrains	
	Porets	

Joseph Drouhin

CHAMBERTIN-CLOS DE BÈZE

APPELLATION CONTROLÉE

MIS EN BOUTEILLE PAR

JOSEPH DROUHIN

Maison fondée en 1880

NÉGOCIANT A BEAUNE, COTE-D'OR

AUX CELLIERS DES ROIS DE FRANCE ET DES DUCS DE BOURGOGNE

Chambertin Clos de Bèze was the favorite wine of Napoleon, who is reported to have said: "Nothing makes the future look so rosy as to contemplate it through a glass of Chambertin." Obviously, he ran out of Chambertin at Waterloo.

MIS EN BOUTEILLE AU DOMAINE
PRODUCE OF FRANCE
APPELLATION CONTROLÉE
NUITS S^T GEORGES
Les St-Georges
750 ml
Domaine Henri Gouges à Nuits St Georges
FRANCE
Bourgogne

If you look at a map, you'll notice there are many more names. I'm only listing the ones you need to know—to make life easier.

The Importance of Soil to Burgundy Wines

If you talk to any producers of Burgundy wines, they'll tell you the most important element in making their quality wines is the soil in which the grapes are grown. This, together with the slope of the land (and the sunshine), determines whether the wine is a Village wine, a Premier Cru, or a Grand Cru.

When I was in Burgundy recently, it rained for five straight days. On the sixth day, the workers were at the bottom of the slopes with their pails and shovels, collecting the soil that had run down the mountain and returning it to the vineyard.

Why are we bothering with all this geography? Must we learn the names of all the villages and vineyards?

I thought you'd never ask. First of all, the geography is important because it helps make you a smart buyer. If you are familiar with the most important villages and vineyards, you're more likely to make an educated purchase.

No, you really don't have to memorize verbatim *all* the villages and vineyards. I'll let you in on a little secret of how to choose a Burgundy wine and tell at a glance if it's a Premier Cru, a Village wine or a Grand Cru. You will, however, have to remember when you look at a label that:

Village (only) = Village wine

Vineyard (only) = Grand Cru

Village + Vineyard = Premier Cru

It's that simple.

This is the method I use to teach Burgundy wine. Ask yourself the following:

Where is the wine from?
France.

What type of wine is it?
Burgundy.

What region is it from?
Côte d'Or.

Which area?
Côte de Nuits.

What village is the wine from?
Vosne-Romanée.

SOCIÉTÉ CIVILE DU DOMAINE DE LA ROMANÉE-CONTI
PROPRIETAIRE A VOSNE-ROMANÉE (COTE-D'OR)

LA TACHE
APPELLATION LA TACHE CONTROLÉE
32.280 Bouteilles Récoltées
N° 11022
ANNÉE 1972
LES ASSOCIÉS-GÉRANTS
Mise en bouteille au domaine

Does the label give more details?
Yes, it tells you the wine is from a vineyard called La Tâche, which is designated as a Grand Cru vineyard.

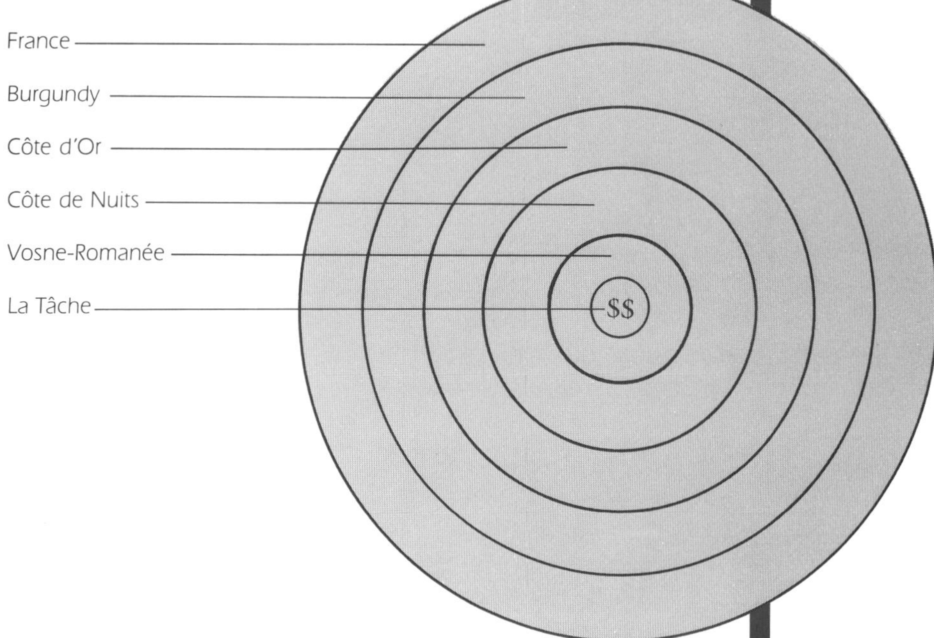

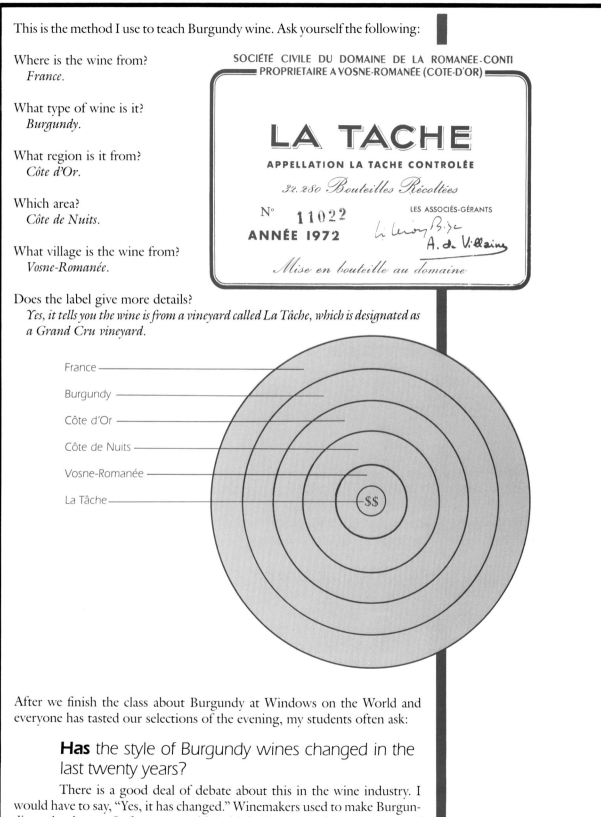

After we finish the class about Burgundy at Windows on the World and everyone has tasted our selections of the evening, my students often ask:

Has the style of Burgundy wines changed in the last twenty years?

There is a good deal of debate about this in the wine industry. I would have to say, "Yes, it has changed." Winemakers used to make Burgundies to last longer. In fact, you couldn't drink a Burgundy for several years, if you wanted to get the fullest flavor. It simply wasn't ready. Today the

If you don't want to be disappointed by the Burgundy wine you select, make sure you know your vintages.

Years ago, only the best Burgundy vintages were shipped to the United States. Today, *all* vintages are exported to the United States.

"To Decant, or not to Decant?" It has been my experience that in Burgundy, wine is rarely decanted, whereas in Bordeaux, it is almost always decanted. (more about decanting on page 171).

In Burgundy in the 1960s, wines were fermented and vatted for up to three weeks. Today's Burgundy wines are usually fermented for six to twelve days.

Because of erratic weather conditions in Burgundy, only one year in three is considered a good vintage.

winemakers of Burgundy are complying with consumer demand for Burgundy they can drink earlier. In America, it seems no one has the patience to wait. A compromise had to be made, however, and that is in the body. Many wines are lighter in style and they can be consumed just a few years after the vintage.

The other question I'm always asked in wine class:

Why are the well-known great Burgundies so expensive?

The answer is simple—supply and demand. The Burgundy growers and shippers of the Côte d'Or have a problem all business people would envy—not enough supply to meet the demand. It has been this way for years and will continue, because Burgundy is a small region that produces a limited amount of wine.

Take a look at the following wine harvest chart. It gives you a better idea of the limited supply of Burgundy wine. The region's wine production is broken down into cases. For instance, if you look under "Grand Crus of the Côte de Nuits" and find La Tâche, you'll see that they produced under 1,500 cases of wine. That's not very much for world consumption—of course, it's an expensive wine.

Burgundy Wine Harvest

(average number of cases over a five-year period)

	RED	WHITE
REGIONAL APPELLATIONS	1,851,120	625,264
Chablis		
Petit Chablis		42,757
Chablis		419,491
Premier Cru		243,878
Grand Cru		49,062
		755,188
CÔTE D'OR		
Côte de Nuits		
Chambolle-Musigny	43,700	
Gevrey-Chambertin	145,787	
Morey-St-Denis	22,899	233
Nuits-St-Georges	82,695	166
Vougeot	4,040	477
Vosne-Romanée	51,426	
Other	69,086	
	419,633	876
Côte de Beaune		
Aloxe-Corton	45,865	178
Auxey-Duresses	35,698	11,699
Beaune	121,545	5,528
Chassagne-Montrachet	79,132	58,375
Fixin	13,364	
Meursault	9,368	167,654

Pommard	104,772	
Puligny-Montrachet	3,374	99,212
Santenay	116,317	1,754
Volnay	79,609	
Other	365,233	30,414
	974,277	376,757
Côte Châlonnaise	285,436	72,103
Mâconnais		
Pouilly-Fuissé		358,908
Other	597,003	1,180,763
	597,003	1,539,671
Beaujolais	8,255,070	56,399
Beaujolais Villages and Crus	3,192,148	
Grand Crus of the Côte de Nuits		
Bonne Mares	3,740	
Chambertin	5,483	
Chambertin Clos de Bèze	4,717	
Chapelle-Chambertin	2,086	
Charmes-Chambertin	10,254	
Clos de la Roche	4,872	
Clos St-Denis	1,731	
Clos de Tart	1,875	
Clos de Vougeot	13,908	
Échézeaux	10,922	
Grands Échézeaux	2,609	
Griotte-Chambertin	666	
La Tâche	1,487	
Latricières-Chambertin	2,541	
Mazis-Chambertin	2,297	
Musigny	2,397	66
Richebourg	2,353	
La Romanée	210	
Romanée-Conti	499	
Romanée-St-Vivant	2,231	
Ruchottes-Chambertin	777	
	77,655	66
Grand Crus of the Côte de Beaune		
Bâtard-Montrachet		5,128
Bienvenue-Bâtard-Montrachet		1,431
Chevalier-Montrachet		2,020
Corton	28,216	477
Corton-Charlemagne		13,197
Criots-Bâtard-Montrachet		521
Montrachet		2,508
	28,216	25,282
	15,680,558	3,451,606
Total Burgundy Wine	19,132,164	

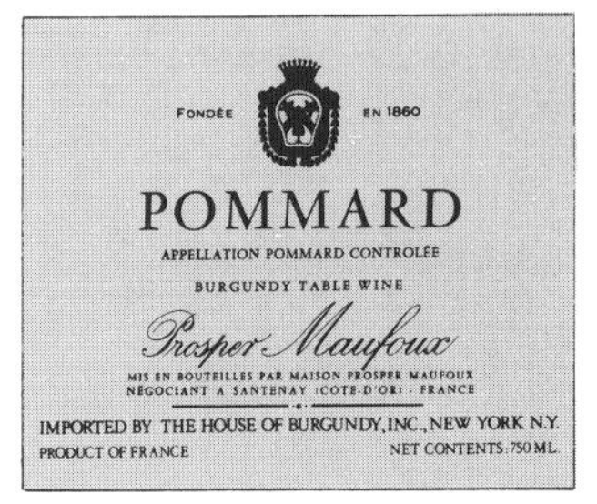

Best Bets for Recent Vintages of Côte d'Or

1978 1979 1981 1983

Who are the most important shippers to look for when buying red Burgundy wine?

Bouchard Père & Fils	Louis Jadot
Joseph Drouhin	Louis Latour
Faiveley	Prosper Maufoux

Although 80 percent of Burgundy wines are sold through shippers, some fine estate-bottled wines are available in limited quantities in the United States. Look for the following:

Domaine Henri Gouges (Nuits-St-Georges)
Domaine Prince de Merode (Aloxe-Corton)
Domaine Dujac (Morey-St-Denis)
Domaine Louis Trapet, Domaine Pierre Damoy (Gevrey-Chambertin)
Domaine de La Romanée-Conti, Domaine Henri Lamarche (Vosne-Romanée)
Domaine J. Prieur, Domaine Comte de Voguë (Chambolle-Musigny)
Domaine Clerget, Domaine Parent (Pommard)

Wine and food

To get the most flavor from both the wine and the food, some of Burgundy's famous winemakers offer these suggestions:

Jean-François Bouchard—"Lamb cooked in its own sauce—not too spicy . . . or veal with mushroom sauce."

Robert Drouhin—"For light red Burgundies, white meat—not too many spices; partridge, pheasant, and rabbit. For heavier-style wines, lamb and steak are good choices." Personally, Mr. Drouhin does not enjoy red Burgundies with cheese—especially goat cheese.

André Gagey (Louis Jadot)—"For lighter-style wines such as Volnay—roast chicken, roast duck, and veal. For big wines such as Corton, Gevrey-Chambertin, Chambolle-Musigny—venison or steak cooked with red wine. For older Burgundian wines—goat cheese, such as Gruyère and Brie."

Louis Latour—"Red wines need strong foods, such as venison, duck, or chicken in a red wine sauce."

THE RED WINES OF THE RHÔNE VALLEY

Fondée
En 1860
COTES DU RHONE
APPELLATION COTES DU RHONE CONTROLÉE
RHONE TABLE WINE
Prosper Maufoux
MIS EN BOUTEILLES PAR MAISON PROSPER MAUFOUX
NÉGOCIANT A SANTENAY (COTE-D'OR) - FRANCE
IMPORTED BY THE HOUSE OF BURGUNDY, INC., NEW YORK N.Y.
PRODUCT OF FRANCE
NET CONTENTS 750 ML.

Many times at Windows on the World, customers may ask me to recommend a big robust red Burgundy wine to complement their Chateaubriand or filet mignon. To their surprise, I don't recommend a Burgundy at all. Their best bet is a Rhône wine.

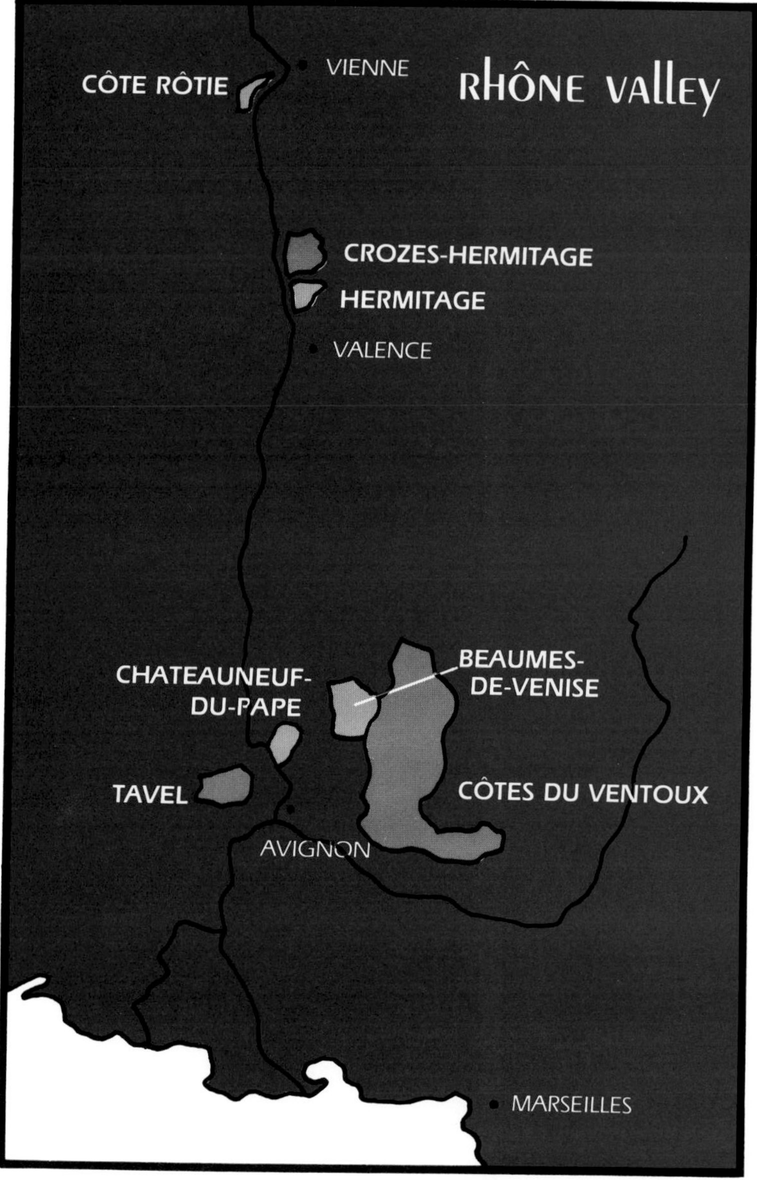

What is a Rhône wine?

95% of all the wines made in the Rhône Valley are red.

A Rhône wine is typically a bigger, fuller wine than those of Burgundy, and it has a higher alcoholic content. The reason for this is quite simple. It all goes back to location—geography.

Where is the Rhône Valley?

A simple Côtes du Rhône is similar to a Beaujolais wine except it has more body and alcohol. A Beaujolais, by A.O.C. standards, must contain a minimum 9% alcohol—a Côtes du Rhône, 10.5%.

The Rhône Valley is in southeastern France, below the Burgundy region. Here the climate is hot and the conditions are sunny. The extra sun gives the wines that added boost of alcohol because as you know, the sun gives the grapes the sugar that turns into alcohol. The soil is full of rocks that retain the intense summer heat during both day and night.

Some of the oldest vineyards in France are in the Rhône Valley. Hermitage, for example, has been in existence for over 2,000 years.

I just told you that Rhône wines are known to have more alcohol than other French wines. That's a fact. It's also a fact that the winemakers of the Rhône Valley are required by law to make sure their wines have a specified amount of alcohol. For example, the minimum alcoholic content required by the A.O.C. is 10.5 percent for Côtes du Rhône and 13 percent for Chateauneuf-du-Pape.

What are the winemaking regions in the Rhône Valley?

The region is divided into two distinct areas: northern and southern Rhône. Wines that come from the northern region are:

Côte Rôtie
Crozes-Hermitage
Hermitage

Hermitage is the best and the longest-lived of the Rhône wines. In a great vintage, Hermitage wines can last for 50 years.

There is a white Chateauneuf-du-Pape and a white Hermitage, but only a few thousand cases are produced each year.

You may be more familiar with the wines from the southern region:

Chateauneuf-du-Pape
Tavel

Two distinct microclimates separate the north from the south. It is important for you to understand that these areas make distinctly different wines because of:

1. soil
2. location
3. different grape varieties used in making the wines of each area.

What are the main grape varieties used in the Rhône Valley?

Now we're going to consider some new grapes:

Grenache
Syrah
Cinsault

For those who prefer sweet wines, try Beaumes-de-Venise. It's a fortified wine made from the Muscat grape.

What wines do they make from these grapes?

The Côte Rôtie, Hermitage, and Crozes-Hermitage from the north are made solely from the Syrah grape. These are the biggest, fullest wines from that region.

Chateauneuf-du-Pape and Tavel acquire their style primarily from the Grenache grape. Chateauneuf-du-Pape is usually a blend of 65 percent Grenache and 35 percent Syrah, although as many as thirteen separate grape varieties may be included in the blend.

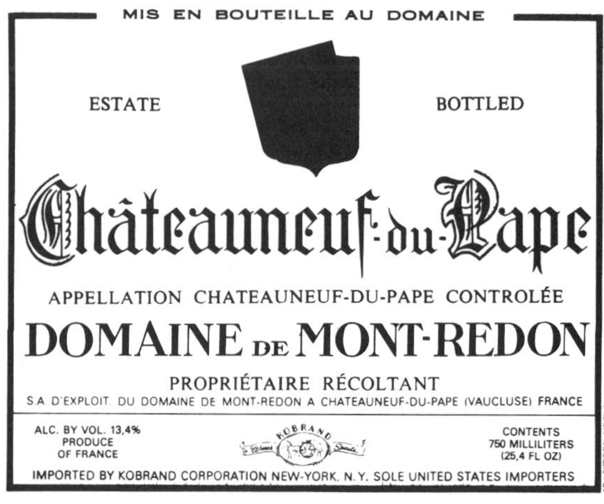

What is Tavel?

We have already established that it's made from the Grenache grape. However, it's a rosé—an unusually dry rosé, which separates it from most others. When you come right down to it, Tavel is just like a red wine with all of the components but less color. How do they make a rosé wine with red wine characteristics but less color? It's all in the vatting process.

Tavel is considered the best rosé of France.

The Rhône Valley has had six good vintages in a row due to great weather conditions: 1978–1983.

There is no official classification for Rhône Valley wines.

What is the difference between short-vatted wines and long-vatted wines?

When a wine is "short-vatted," the skins are allowed to ferment with the must (grape juice) for a short period of time—only long enough to take on that rosé color. It's just the opposite when a winemaker is producing other red Rhône wines like Chateauneuf-du-Pape or Hermitage. The grape skins are allowed to ferment with the must for a longer time, and that is evident from the rich, ruby color of the wine.

Chateauneuf-du-Pape is the most popular wine from the Rhône Valley sold in the United States.

Chateauneuf-du-Pape means "new castle of the Pope," for the palace in which Pope Clement V resided in the fourteenth century.

The old Papal coat of arms appears on some Chateauneuf-du-Pape bottles. Only owners of vineyards are permitted to use this coat of arms on the label.

Two wines from the largest and best domains in Chateauneuf-du-Pape, which are available in the United States: Mont-Redon and Beaucastel.

What is the difference between a $5 bottle of Chateauneuf-du-Pape and a $20 Chateauneuf-du-Pape?

Besides longer vatting time, a winemaker is permitted to use thirteen different grapes for his Chateauneuf-du-Pape recipe, as I mentioned earlier. It's only logical then, that the winemaker who uses a lot of the best grapes (which is equivalent to cooking with the finest ingredients) will produce the best-tasting wine and the most expensive.

For example, a $5 bottle of Chateauneuf-du-Pape may contain only 20 percent of top-quality grapes (Grenache, Syrah, and Cinsault) and 80 percent of lesser-quality grapes; a $20 bottle may contain 90 percent of the top-quality grapes and 10 percent of others.

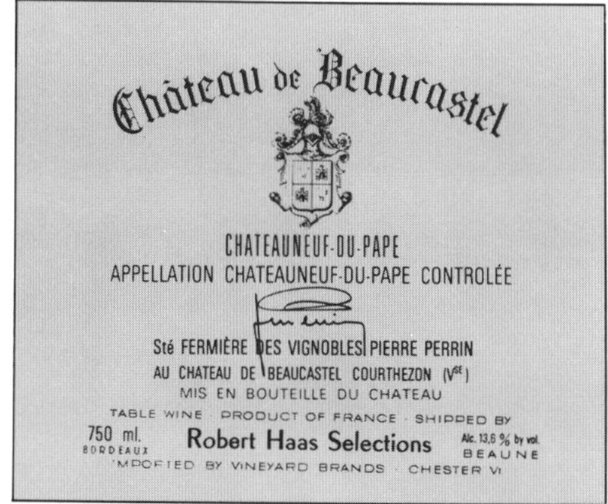

Best Bets for Red Rhône Valley Wines

As I've already stated, the last six vintages have all been good, but three of them are outstanding. They are:

1976 1978 1983

"1983 in the North is considered to be the best vintage since 1929."—*Paul Jaboulet*

How do I buy a red Rhône wine?

As with all the wines discussed in this book, you should first decide if you prefer a light Côtes du Rhône wine or a bigger, more flavorful one. Since the last few years have been good vintages, that shouldn't be a worry. Also, it's important to buy from a reliable producer. Two of the oldest and best-known firms are M. Chapoutier and Paul Jaboulet Ainé. Their wines are widely available in the United States.

The Rhône wines, to me, represent some of the best values in French wines. Too many people concentrate on the wines of Burgundy and Bordeaux and neglect these fine wines.

When should I drink my Rhône wine?

Tavel—two years
Côtes du Rhône—within three years
Crozes-Hermitage—five years
Chateauneuf-du-Pape—five years, but higher-quality Chateauneuf-du-Pape is better at ten years
Hermitage—seven to eight years, but best at fifteen years

The Rhône Valley Roundup

Northern wines
Côte Rôtie
Hermitage
Crozes-Hermitage

Grapes
Syrah

Southern wines
Chateauneuf-du-Pape
Tavel

Grapes
Grenache
Syrah
Cinsault

(Côtes du Rhône is a regional wine, that can be produced from grapes grown in either or both the northern and the southern Rhône regions.)

The Differences
Microclimates
Grapes
Vintages (A good year in the north may be a bad year in the south and vice versa.)

WINE AND food

Paul Jaboulet—"A simple Côtes du Rhône is good to have with poultry, such as chicken, in a light sauce.

"To have Chateauneuf-du-Pape with food," says Mr. Jaboulet, "the wine must be at least three to four years old." He likes a good simple steak with his Chateauneuf-du-Pape, and says the wine overpowers lamb.

"An aged Hermitage should be reserved for that special evening.

"Tavel should be slightly chilled and is a good picnic wine; it goes especially well with cold chicken." Mr. Jaboulet notes: "As the temperature goes up, so do the Tavel sales."

Marc Chapoutier—With a Côtes du Rhône wine he recommends poultry, light meats, and cheese.

Côte Rôtie goes well with white meats and small game.

Chateauneuf-du-Pape complements the ripest of cheese, the richest venison, and the most lavish civet of wild boar.

A Hermitage is suitable with beef, game, and any full-flavored cheese.

Tavel rosé is excellent with white meat and poultry.

A good value is: Côtes du Ventoux.
This relatively new appellation was started in 1973. The wines that come into the American market are generally a good value because not too many consumers know about them. One of the most widely available wines to look for in this category is La Vieille Ferme: It is inexpensive and a good value.

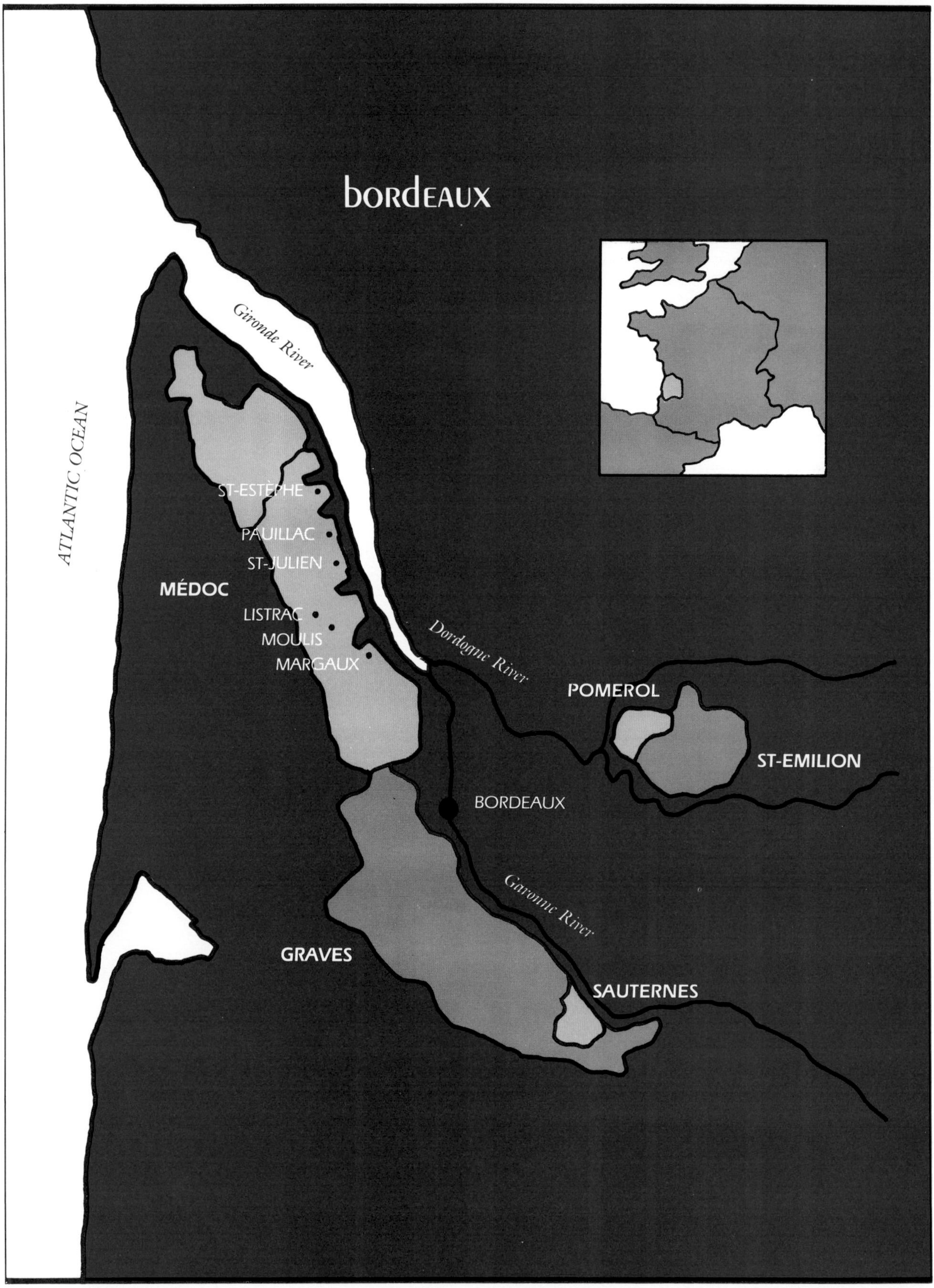

bordeaux

Gironde River

ATLANTIC OCEAN

ST-ESTÈPHE

PAUILLAC

ST-JULIEN

MÉDOC

LISTRAC

MOULIS

MARGAUX

Dordogne River

POMEROL

ST-EMILION

BORDEAUX

Garonne River

GRAVES

SAUTERNES

THE RED WINES OF BORDEAUX

This province of France is rich with excitement and history, and the best part is that the wines speak for themselves. You'll find this region much easier to learn about than Burgundy. For one thing, the plots of land are bigger, and they're owned by fewer landholders. And, as Samuel Johnson once said, "He who aspires to be a serious wine drinker must drink claret."

The English word "claret" refers to dry red wines from Bordeaux.

Some 40 wine regions in Bordeaux produce high-quality wine that enables them to carry the A.O.C. designation on the label. Of these 40 places, five stand out in my mind:

Of all the A.O.C. wines of France, 25% come from the Bordeaux region.

Médoc—26,683 acres (produces only red wines)
Pomerol—1,800 acres (the smallest red-wine-producing region in Bordeaux)
Graves—4,702 acres (produces both red and dry white wines)
St-Emilion—12,401 acres (produces only red wines)
Sauternes—4,890 acres (produces only sweet white wines)

In the Médoc, there are four important *inner* appellations you should be familiar with. From north to south they are:

St-Estèphe
Pauillac
St-Julien
Margaux

While these are very popular, most people are already familiar with them, so I suggest you also look for two others:

Bordeaux is much larger in acreage than Burgundy.

Moulis
Listrac

In dollar value the United States is the largest importer of Bordeaux wines: 25% white, 75% red.

Since we've already covered the white wines of France earlier in the book, here we'll concentrate mainly on the four red regions of Bordeaux.

What grape varieties are grown in Bordeaux?

The three major grapes are:

Cabernet Sauvignon
Merlot
Cabernet Franc

Unlike Burgundy, where the winemaker must use 100 percent Pinot Noir to make most red wines (100 percent Gamay for Beaujolais), the red wines in Bordeaux are almost always made from a blend of grapes.

In all of Bordeaux, there are some 42,000 acres of Cabernet Sauvignon, 79,000 acres of Merlot, and 24,000 acres of Cabernet Franc.

Some of the major shippers of regional wines from Bordeaux are:
Barton & Guestier (B & G)
Calvet
Cordier
Ginestet
Dourthe Frères
Eschenauer
Sichel

What are the different quality levels of Bordeaux wine?

Look to see if a Bordeaux is labelled by a "regional," "proprietary," or "château" name. These are the grades of quality.

Regional—Regional wines come from a defined area. Only grapes and wines made in that area can be called by its regional name. For example, Médoc and St-Emilion.

Proprietary—Proprietary wines are table wines that have been given specific names and are marked as such. For instance, when most people buy a wine like Mouton-Cadet or Lacour Pavillon, they buy it because it's a nice, inexpensive, and consistent drinking wine.

Château—Château wines are the products of individual vineyards: The grapes are harvested, the wine is made *and* bottled at a particular château. Château wines are usually considered the best quality wines from Bordeaux.

The "bread and butter" wines of Bordeaux are the regional and proprietary wines. These wines are meant to be consumed within two to three years from the harvest.

Examples of proprietary wines you may be familiar with:
Grand Marque
Maitre d'Estournel
Lacour Pavillon
Mouton-Cadet

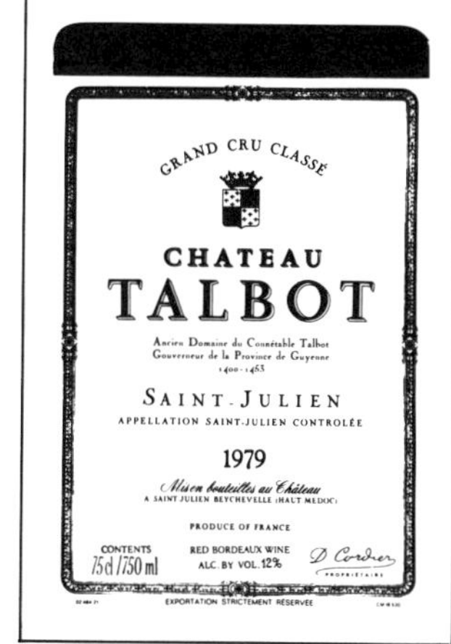

What is a château?

When most people think of a château, they picture a grandiose home filled with Persian rugs and valuable antiques and surrounded by rolling hills of vineyards. Well, I'm sorry to shatter your dreams, but most châteaus are not like this at all. Yes, a château could be a mansion on a large estate, but it could also be a split-level home with a two-car garage.

According to French law, a château is a house attached to a vineyard having a specific number of acres, as well as winemaking and storage facilities on the property. A wine may not be called a château wine unless it meets these criteria.

How do I know if the wine I buy was really bottled at the château?

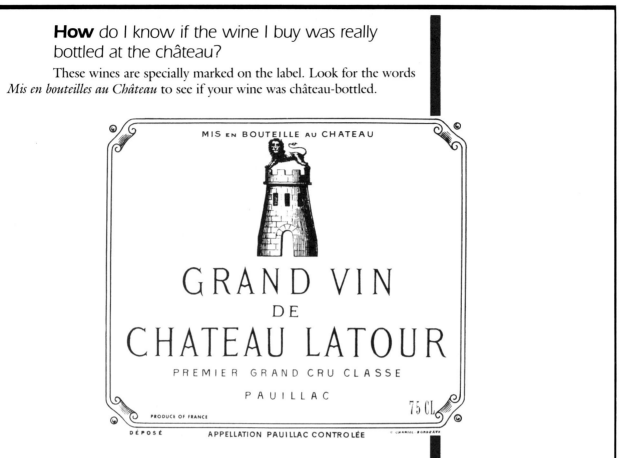

These wines are specially marked on the label. Look for the words *Mis en bouteilles au Château* to see if your wine was château-bottled.

MIS EN BOUTEILLE AU CHATEAU
GRAND VIN
DE
CHATEAU LATOUR
PREMIER GRAND CRU CLASSE
PAUILLAC
75 CL
PRODUCE OF FRANCE
DÉPOSÉ
APPELLATION PAUILLAC CONTROLÉE

Let's take a closer look at the château. One fact I've learned from my years of teaching wine is that no one wants to memorize the names of thousands of châteaus, so I'll shorten the list by starting with the most important classification in Bordeaux.

Now is the time to start memorizing. In Bordeaux there are over 3,000 individual châteaus!

GRAND CRU CLASSÉ
CHATEAU LA LAGUNE
HAUT·MÉDOC
APPELLATION HAUT-MÉDOC CONTROLÉE
1978
SOCIÉTÉ CIVILE AGRICOLE DU CHATEAU LA LAGUNE
PROPRIÉTAIRE A LUDON (GIRONDE) FRANCE
MIS EN BOUTEILLE AU CHATEAU

Médoc

When and how were the château wines classified?

Over 100 years ago in the Médoc region of Bordeaux, a wine classification was established. Brokers from the wine industry were asked at a Paris exhibition in 1855 to rate the top Médoc wines according to price, which at that time was directly related to quality. (After all, don't we class everything, from cars to restaurants?) The brokers agreed, provided the classification would never become official. Behold, the Official Classification of 1855!

The Classification of 1855 was broken down into three parts:
Grand Crus Classés
Grand Crus Exceptionnels
Crus Bourgeois

The next classification is for the Grand Crus Classés—the top 61 châteaus in Médoc.

THE OFFICIAL (1855) CLASSIFICATION OF THE GREAT RED WINES OF BORDEAUX

Out of the top five châteaus rated in the 1855 classification, two are not owned by Frenchmen:

Château Haut-Brion is owned by an American family (Dillon).

Château Latour is owned by an English concern.

THE MÉDOC

FIRST GROWTHS—PREMIERS CRUS

Vineyard	Commune
Château Lafite-Rothschild	Pauillac
Château Latour	Pauillac
Château Margaux	Margaux
Château Mouton-Rothschild	Pauillac
Château Haut-Brion	Pessac (Graves)

SECOND GROWTHS—DEUXIÈMES CRUS

Vineyard	Commune
Château Rausan-Ségla	Margaux
Château Rauzan Gassies	Margaux
Château Léoville-Las Cases	St-Julien
Château Léoville-Poyferré	St-Julien
Château Léoville-Barton	St-Julien
Château Durfort-Vivens	Margaux
Château Gruaud-Larose	St-Julien
Château Lascombes	Margaux
Château Brane-Cantenac	Cantenac-Margaux
Château Pichon-Longueville (Baron)	Pauillac
Château Pichon-Longueville-Lalande	Pauillac
Château Ducru-Beaucaillou	St-Julien
Château Cos d'Estournel	St-Estèphe
Château Montrose	St-Estèphe

THIRD GROWTHS—TROISIÈMES CRUS

Vineyard	Commune
Château Kirwan	Cantenac-Margaux
Château d'Issan	Cantenac-Margaux
Château Lagrange	St-Julien
Château Langoa-Barton	St-Julien
Château Giscours	Labarde
Château Malescot-St-Exupéry	Margaux
Château Cantenac-Brown	Cantenac-Margaux
Château Boyd-Cantenac	Margaux
Château Palmer	Cantenac-Margaux
Château La Lagune	Ludon
Château Calon-Ségur	St-Estèphe
Château Ferrière	Margaux
Château Marquis d'Alesme-Becker	Margaux

FOURTH GROWTHS—QUATRIÈMES CRUS

Vineyard	Commune
Château St-Pierre-Sevaistre	St-Julien
Château St-Pierre-Bontemps	St-Julien
Château Talbot	St-Julien
Château Branaire-Ducru	St-Julien
Château Duhart-Milon-Rothschild	Pauillac
Château Pouget	Cantenac-Margaux
Château La Tour-Carnet	St-Laurent
Château Lafon-Rochet	St-Estèphe
Château Beychevelle	St-Julien
Château Prieuré-Lichine	Cantenac-Margaux
Château Marquis de Terme	Margaux

FIFTH GROWTHS—CINQUIÈMES CRUS

Vineyard	Commune
Château Pontet-Canet	Pauillac
Château Batailley	Pauillac
Château Haut-Batailley	Pauillac
Château Grand-Puy-Lacoste	Pauillac
Château Grand-Puy-Ducasse	Pauillac
Château Lynch-Bages	Pauillac
Château Lynch-Moussas	Pauillac
Château Dauzac	Labarde
Château Mouton-Baronne-Philippe (called Château Mouton d'Armailhacq until 1956)	Pauillac
Château du Tertre	Arsac
Château Haut-Bages-Libéral	Pauillac
Château Pédesclaux	Pauillac
Château Belgrave	St-Laurent
Château Camensac	St-Laurent
Château Cos Labory	St-Estèphe
Château Clerc-Milon	Pauillac
Château Croizet Bages	Pauillac
Château Cantemerle	Macau

Don't be misled by the term "growth." It might make it easier to understand if you substitute the word "classification." Instead of saying a wine is "first growth," you could say, "first classification."

"The classified growths are divided in five classes and the price difference from one class to another is about 12%."—*Traité Sur Les Vins du Médoc, William Frank, 1855*

Why weren't the wines of St-Emilion and Pomerol classed with the wines of the Médoc area in 1855?

I compare this to the hotel classification that was done in the mid-70s in New York City. They never listed the best hotels located on the West Side, which was certainly not chic enough to merit listing, even though it had some excellent hotels. It's the same with wine classifications. St-Emilion and Pomerol were simply not chic enough; these two areas were considered out of touch with the rest of the Bordeaux wine world.

The only château included in the 1855 classification that was not a part of the Médoc was Château Haut-Brion of Graves. This château was so famous at the time that the wine brokers had no choice but to include it.

CHATEAU HAUT BRION
1978
GRAVES
Premier Grand Cru Classé
Appellation Graves Contrôlée
75 cl
PRODUCE OF FRANCE
MARQUE ET BOUTEILLE DEPOSEES

Is the 1855 classification still in use today?

Every wine person knows about the 1855 classification, but much has changed since then. Some châteaus no longer exist. Other vineyards have doubled or tripled their production by buying up their neighbor's land, which is permitted by law. In some well-known "first growth" vineyards, such as Château Margaux, the quality of the wine degenerated for a while when the family that owned the château weren't putting enough money and time into the vineyard. In 1977, Château Margaux was sold to a Greek family by the name of Mentzenopoulos for $16 million, and since then the quality of the wine has come back up to its "first growth" standards.

CHÂTEAU MARGAUX
GRAND VIN
1981
PREMIER GRAND CRU CLASSÉ 1855
MIS EN BOUTEILLE AU CHÂTEAU
FRANCE
APPELLATION MARGAUX CONTROLÉE
75 cl
SOCIÉTÉ CIVILE AGRICOLE CHATEAU MARGAUX

Château Gloria, in the commune of St-Julien, is an example of a vineyard that did not exist at the time of the 1855 classification. The mayor of St-Julien, Henri Martin, bought many parcels of "second growth" vineyards. As a result, he produces top-quality wine that is not included in the 1855 classification. It's also important to consider the techniques used to make wine today. They're a lot different from those of 1855. Once again, the outcome is better wine. As you can see, some of the châteaus listed in the 1855 classification deserve a lesser ranking, while others deserve a better one.

On the 1945 Mouton-Rothschild bottle, there is a big "V" that stands for "Victory" and the end of World War II. Every year since, Philippe de Rothschild has asked a different artist to design his labels. Some of the most famous artists in the world have agreed to have their work grace the Mouton label, among them:
Jean Cocteau—1947
Salvador Dali—1958
Henry Moore—1964
Joàn Miró—1969
Marc Chagall—1970
Pablo Picasso—1973
Robert Motherwell—1974
Andy Warhol—1975

Have there ever been any changes in the 1855 classification?

Yes, but only once. It was in 1973. Château Mouton-Rothschild was elevated from a "second growth" to a "first growth" vineyard. There's a little story behind that, which is related in the box.

Exception to the Rule . . .

In 1920 when the Baron Philippe de Rothschild took over the family vineyard, he couldn't accept the fact that back in 1855 his château was rated a "second growth." He thought it should have been classed a "first growth" from the beginning—and he fought to get to the top for some fifty years. While the Baron's wine was classified as a "second growth," his motto was:

First, I cannot be.
Second, I do not deign to be.
Mouton, I am.

When his wine was elevated to a "first growth" in 1973, Rothschild had to stop using his old motto. He replaced it with a new one:

First, I am.
Second, I was.
But Mouton does not change.

"For a given vintage there is quite a consistent ratio between the prices of the different classes, which is of considerable help to the trade. So a fifth growth would always sell at about half the price of a second. The thirds and fourths would get prices halfway between the seconds and the fifths. The first growths are getting about 25% over the second growths."—*Bordeaux et Ses Vins, Ch. Cocks, 1868*

I've always found the 1855 classification to be a little cumbersome, so one day I sat down and drew up my own chart. I separated the classification into "growths" (first, second, third, etc.) and then I listed the communes (Pauillac, Margaux, St-Julien, and so on) and set down the number of distinctive vineyards in each one. My chart shows which communes of Bordeaux have the most "first growths"—all the way down to "fifth growths." It also shows which commune corners the market on *all* "growths." Since I was inspired to figure this out during the World Series, my chart is actually a box score of the 1855 classification.

A quick glance at my box score gives you some instant facts that may guide you when you want to buy a Bordeaux wine from Médoc.

Kevin Zraly's Box Score of the 1855 Classification

Commune	1st	2nd	3rd	4th	5th	Total
Margaux	1	5	10	3	2	21
Pauillac	3	2	0	1	12	18
St-Julien	0	5	2	4	0	11
St-Estèphe	0	2	1	1	1	5
St-Laurent	0	0	0	1	2	3
Haut-Médoc	0	0	1	0	1	2
Graves	1	0	0	0	0	1
	5	14	14	10	18	61

Total = 61 Châteaus

Tallying the score, Pauillac has three of the five "first growths." Margaux practically clean-sweeps the "third growths." In fact, Margaux is the overall winner, because it has the biggest total of classed vineyards in all of Médoc. Margaux is also the only area to have a château rated in every category. St-Julien has no "first" or "fifth growths," but is very strong in the "second" and "fourth."

What does "Cru Bourgeois" mean?

Cru Bourgeois is actually one section of the complete Médoc classification of 1855. The vineyards that fell under this category, although very good, did not meet the price/quality image of the 61 Grand Crus Classés.

POMEROL

This is the smallest of the top wine districts in Bordeaux that produces red wines. Pomerol produces only 15 percent as much wine as St-Emilion; as a result, Pomerol wines are relatively scarce. And if you do find them, they'll be expensive. Although no official classification exists, here is a list of some of the finest Pomerol wines on the market:

The major grape used to produce wine in the Pomerol region is Merlot. Very little Cabernet Sauvignon is used in these wines.

Château Pétrus, the most expensive wine of Bordeaux, is made with 95% Merlot.

The red wines of Pomerol tend to be softer, fruitier, and ready to be drunk sooner than the Médoc wines.

Château Pétrus
Château La Conseillante
Château Petit-Village
Château Trotanoy
Château L'Évangile
Vieux Château-Certan
Château Lapointe
Château Lafleur
Château La Fleur-Pétrus
Château Gazin
Château Beauregard
Château Nénin
Château Latour à Pomerol

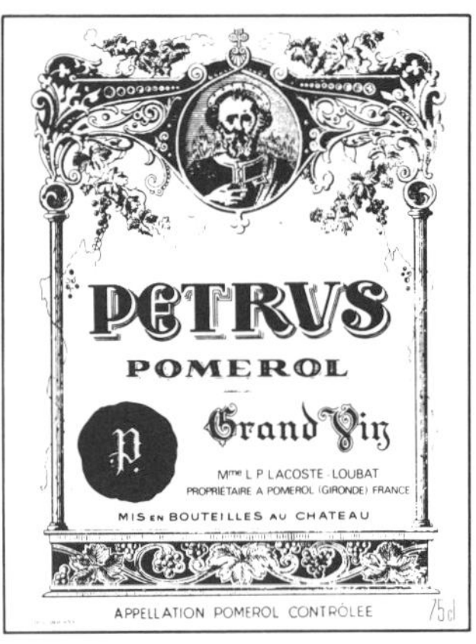

ST-EMILION

This area produces about two-thirds as much wine as the entire Médoc, and it is one of the most beautiful villages in France (my own bias). The wines of St-Emilion were finally classified officially in 1955, one century after the Médoc classification. There are 12 "first growths" comparable to those "Cru Classé" wines of the Médoc, and some 70 Grand Crus Classés.

The Twelve First Growths of St-Emilion
Château Ausone
Château Cheval Blanc
Château Beauséjour-Duffau
Château Beauséjour-Fagout
Château Bel-Air
Château Canon
Château Figeac
Château La Gaffelière
Château La Magdelaine
Château Pavie
Château Trottevieille
Château Clos Fourtet

Important "Grand Crus Classés" and Other St-Emilion Wine Available in the U.S.
Château L'Angélus
Château Canon-La Gaffelière
Château La Tour-Figeac
Château Trimoulet
Château Dassault
Château Simard
Château Monbousquet
Clos des Jacobins

The Graves region is equally divided between red and white wine.

About vintages, noted wine expert Alexis Lichine says: "Great vintages take time to mature. Lesser wines mature faster than the greater ones. . . . Patience is needed for great vintages, hence the usefulness and enjoyment of lesser vintages." He sums it up: "Often vintages which have a poorer rating—if young—will give a greater enjoyment than a better-rated vintage—if young."

GRAVES

The most famous château—we have already seen it in the 1855 classification—is Château Haut-Brion. Other good red Graves classified in 1959 are:

Château Bouscaut
Château Haut-Bailly
Château Carbonnieux
Domaine de Chevalier
Château de Fieuzal
Château Olivier
Château Malartic-Lagravière
Château La Tour-Martillac
Château Smith-Haut-Lafitte
Château Pape-Clément
Château La Mission-Haut-Brion
Château La Tour-Haut-Brion

Now that you know all the greatest red wines of Bordeaux, let me take you a step further and show you some of the best vintages.

Best Bets . . . for Millionaires

If your love of wine is such that money is no object, these are the vintages for you. They shouldn't be too difficult to remember:

1900—turn of the century
1929—for those of you on Wall Street
1945—the end of World War II
1961—the year we were all born

Best Bets for Red Bordeaux

For us commonfolk who don't have the money or the patience to seek out these older vintages, let's take a look at some more recent excellent vintages:

1978
1979—represents the best price/value relationship
1981
1982
1983 '81–'83 represent the first time in many years that there were three consecutive good vintages.

How do I buy a red Bordeaux?

The first question you need to ask yourself is how much you want to spend. Then look at the vintage. I don't expect that you'll go out and buy one of the four famous vintages I told you about, but you should find out how the weather was before you buy a questionable vintage. You don't even have to be familiar with all of the châteaus of Bordeaux, as long as you know something about the years.

Bordeaux's largest harvest ever took place in 1979. This means that the 1979s are easier to find at your retailer, and they won't be as expensive as other vintages.

On Drinking the Wines of Bordeaux

The French drink their Bordeaux wines young, being afraid that the Socialist government will take it away from them.

The English drink their Bordeaux wines very old, because they like to take their friends down to their wine cellars with the cobwebs and the dust to show off their old bottles.

And the Americans drink their Bordeaux exactly when they are ready to be drunk, because they don't know any better.

—Author Unknown

What separates a $5 red Bordeaux from a $25 red Bordeaux?

- The place where the grapes are grown.
- The age of the vines themselves (usually the older the vine, the better the wine).
- The yield of the vine (lower yield means higher quality).
- Winemaking technique (for example, how long the wine is aged in wood).
- The vintage.

La Rose-Trintaudon is the largest vineyard in the Médoc area, making close to 70,000 cases of wine per year.

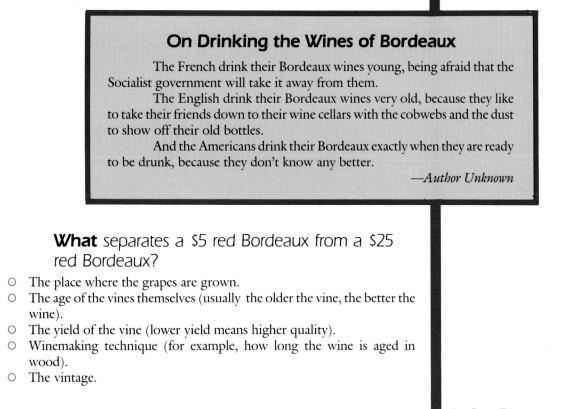

Is it necessary to pay a tremendous sum of money to get a great-tasting red Bordeaux wine?

It's nice if you have it to spend, but sometimes you don't. The best way to get the most for your money is to use what I call the "Petit Château" method. For example: Let's say you like Château Lafite-Rothschild, but you don't have the money to pay for it. Look at the region. It's from Pauillac. You have a choice here: Either you can buy a regional wine called "Pauillac," which isn't going to be the best, or you can find another château which is rated less than Lafite. Go to the 1855 classification, to the "fifth growths" and look for other Pauillacs. They may not be one-fifth of the price, but they will be considerably less than the Lafite.

Since I didn't memorize the 3,000 châteaus myself, when I go to my neighborhood retailer, I look at the shelf and find a château I've never heard of. If it's from Pauillac, from a good vintage, and it's $7.50, I buy it. My chances are good. Everything in wine is hedging your bets.

While Napoleon Bonaparte preferred the Burgundy Chambertin, former President Richard Nixon's favorite wine is Château Margaux. Nixon always has a bottle of his favorite vintage waiting at his table from the cellar of the "21" Club.

Here is a list of my favorite red Bordeaux wines:

Château Lafite-Rothschild
Château Margaux
Château Latour
Château Haut-Brion
Château Mouton-Rothschild
Château Léoville-Las Cases
Château Léoville-Poyferré
Château Léoville-Barton
Château Gruaud-Larose
Château Pichon-Longueville-Lalande
Château Ducru-Beaucaillou
Château Cos d'Estournel
Château Giscours
Château Palmer
Château La Lagune
Château Calon-Ségur
Château Branaire-Ducru
Château Talbot
Château Duhart-Milon-Rothschild
Château Beychevelle
Château Prieuré-Lichine
Château Haut-Batailley
Château Grand-Puy-Lacoste
Château Lynch-Bages
Château Mouton-Baronne-Phillippe
Château Kirwan
Château Lascombes
Château Pétrus
Château Trotanoy
Château Ausone
Château Cheval Blanc
Château Figeac
Château Pavie
Château Clos Fourtet
Château La Mission-Haut-Brion
Château Carbonnieux
Château Pichon-Longueville
Château Canon
Château Haut-Bailly

Still more recommended wines to look for that are not classified:

Château Gloria
Château Lanessan
Château Angludet
Château de Pez
Château Phélan-Ségur
Château Chasse-Spleen
Château Fourcas-Hosten
Château La Rose-Trintaudon
Château Greysac
Château Simard
Château Monbousquet
Château Puy-Blanquet

A Bordeaux for Valentine's Day: Château Calon-Ségur

At one time the Marquis de Ségur owned Château Lafite, Château Latour, and Château Calon-Ségur. He said: "I make my wines at Lafite and Latour, but my heart is at Calon." Hence the label.

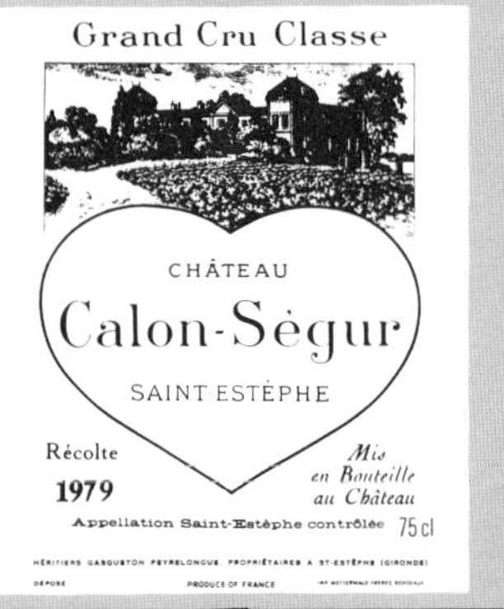

wine and food

Alain Querre (Château Monbousquet)—With St-Emilion or Pomerol wine, he recommends roast beef or grilled beef without sauce, seasoned with shallots, or in its own sauce. (A St-Emilion sauce is one of his favorites.) St-Estèphe goes well with lamb or lamprey eel, and red Graves is most enjoyable with fresh salmon.

Denise Lurton Moulle (Château La Louviere, Château Clos Fourtet)—She recommends plain grilled lamb chops served with a plate of herbed pasta; roast duck served either with a plain sauce or juniper berries.

Jean Kressman (Château La Tour-Martillac)—With white meats, serve the lightest Bordeaux or some light Médocs of the 1971 or 1980 vintages. With red meats, roasted or not, all sorts of cheeses (if not fermented), and nuts, serve a strong Bordeaux.

Alexis Lichine (Château Prieuré-Lichine)—Since fish are so good in the Atlantic region, he admits having a definite preference for them. In the relaxed atmosphere of his dining room, he would have bass or any other Atlantic fish in a red wine sauce.

Bruno Prats (Château Cos d'Estournel)—He recommends simple food that is not too rich or served with too much sauce: leg of lamb in its own juice with a touch of garlic, veal with butter sauce, and roast duck with eggplant.

Jean-Jacques de Bethmann (Château Olivier)—*Confit de canard, magret de canard* (duck) over wild mushrooms from the estate. *Entrecôte de Bordelaise.*

Had you dined at the Four Seasons restaurant in New York when it first opened in 1959, you could have had a 1918 Château Lafite-Rothschild for $18 or a 1934 Château Latour for $16. Or if those wines were a bit beyond your budget, you could have had a 1945 Château Cos d'Estournel for $9.50.

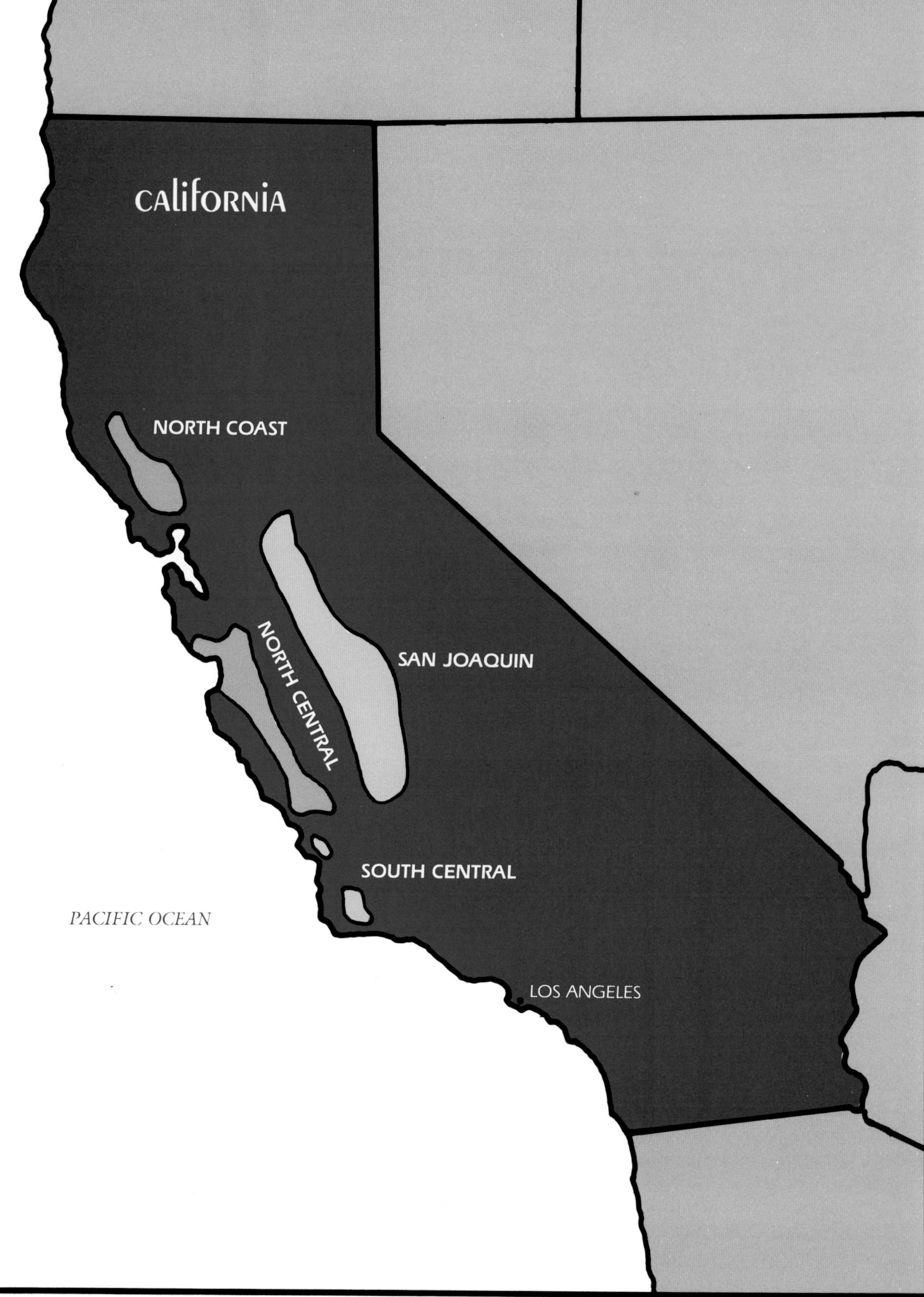
California
NORTH COAST
NORTH CENTRAL
SAN JOAQUIN
SOUTH CENTRAL
PACIFIC OCEAN
LOS ANGELES

THE RED WINES of CALIFORNIA

If I were to ask you what type of wine Americans prefer—red or white—what would you say? If you answered white, you are absolutely correct. But why am I bringing this up in the chapter on California red wine? Because, until recently, there were more red grapes grown in California than white grapes.

That doesn't sound right, does it? Perhaps not, but there was a good reason for planting more red grapes than white ones, and it stemmed from American drinking habits. In 1960, Americans were consuming 83 percent red wines (including rosé); in 1970 only 76 percent of the wines they consumed were red. If you were a vineyard owner in 1970, you would probably have planted red grapes.

Acreage in California: Currently there are 174,000 in red grapes, 190,000 in white grapes.

Then in the late'70s a new trend began to develop. Americans began drinking more white wines than red wines. Ideally, you'd think the vineyard owner could rip out the red vines and replace them with white grapes to give the consumer what he wanted, but it's not that simple. As you already know, it takes three to five years from planting of the vines to the day the winemaker can produce wine from the grapes. That's the maturing process and its slow turnaround time.

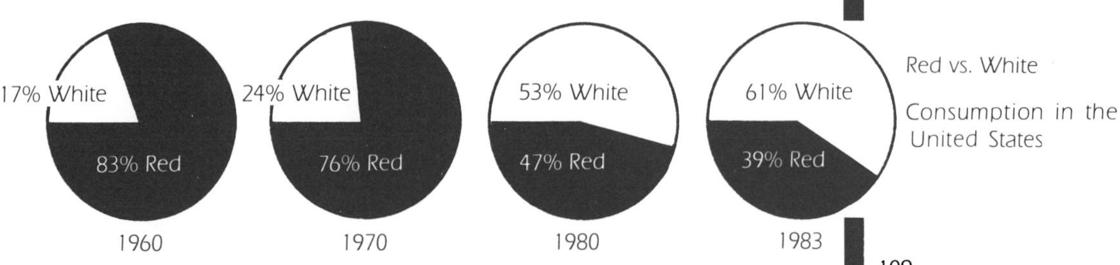

Red vs. White

Consumption in the United States

To keep up with the trend, California winemakers created a new style of wine. They began making white wine from red grapes. This explains the white Zinfandels, Pinot Noir Blanc, and so on. To produce these types of wine, they minimize the contact of the grape skins with the juice.

At Windows on the World, we sell 75% white wine to 25% red wine.

On the average, one ounce of table wine = 18 calories.

Alcohol comparison: 5 oz. white wine = 12 oz. beer = 1¼ oz. liquor.

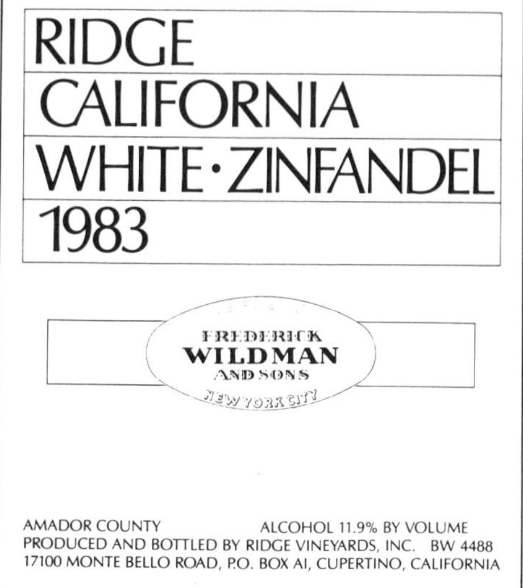

RIDGE
CALIFORNIA
WHITE·ZINFANDEL
1983
FREDERICK
WILDMAN
AND SONS
NEW YORK CITY
AMADOR COUNTY
ALCOHOL 11.9% BY VOLUME
PRODUCED AND BOTTLED BY RIDGE VINEYARDS, INC. BW 4488
17100 MONTE BELLO ROAD, P.O. BOX AI, CUPERTINO, CALIFORNIA

The Switch Is On

Here are some of the reasons Americans switched from drinking red wines to white:

1. White wine became synonymous with health. It is *perceived* to have fewer calories than any other alcoholic beverage (but it's not true).
2. Businessmen replaced their martini habits with white wine, at least in part because of America's new health consciousness, and the feeling that wine is better for you than gin, Scotch, and rye. White wine was the natural substitute because it can be mixed as a drink (spritzer); it's the same color as a martini; and the bartender may even add a twist of lemon.
3. The "refrigerator consciousness of Americans" was at work. Americans like to drink everything cold and often prefer their drinks with ice.
4. Women became the primary purchasers of wine, and studies show they tend to prefer the lighter style of the whites.
5. Americans changed their eating habits. They started to switch their regimen from the standard meat and potatoes to fish and vegetables. The lighter wine lends itself well to the lighter meal.
6. Wine became the chic drink (thanks to all of the above). Instead of cocktail parties, people went to wine and cheese parties. Bars that never used to stock wine—or at least nothing decent—now serve an assortment of fine wines.
7. And, once again, for beginning wine drinkers, it's natural to drink white wines before progressing to red.

Red Grape Plantings

Look at the chart below to see how many acres of red grapes were planted in California by 1969 and how it increased in ten years. In that time the total acreage of wine grapes planted in California tripled. That rapid expansion is characteristic of California's wine industry.

Total Acreage of Wine Grapes Planted

1969—110,000 acres
1979—340,000 acres

Grape-by-Grape Comparison

Grape	**1969**	**1979**
Cabernet Sauvignon	5,098	23,592
Pinot Noir	2,715	9,769
Gamay Beaujolais	969	4,339
Zinfandel	21,704	29,884
Gamay	1,640	5,347
Petite Sirah	4,332	13,168
Merlot	(two acres in 1960)	2,778

"You see? I've always told you California wines weren't so bad."

Today winemakers are planting more white grapes, such as Chardonnay and Sauvignon Blanc. But don't underestimate California reds. The winemakers are still developing their own style, but even today California produces some world-class red wines.

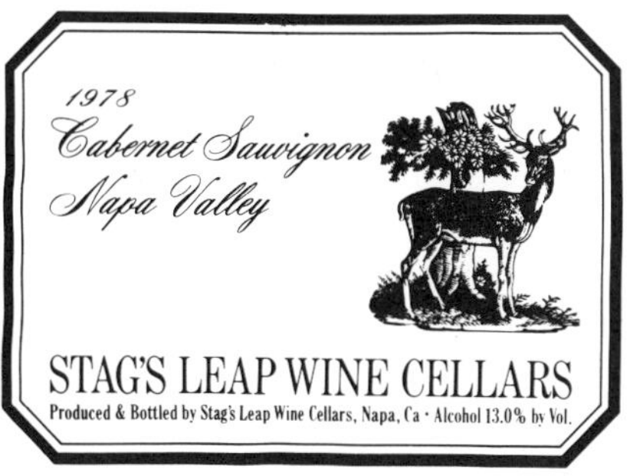

1980

OPUS ONE

ROBERT MONDAVI

BARON PHILIPPE DE ROTHSCHILD

What are the major red grapes winemakers use to make California reds?

Cabernet Sauvignon—Considered the most successful red *vinifera* grape in California, this grape yields some of the greatest red wines in the world. It is the predominant variety used in the finest red Bordeaux wines, such as Château Lafite-Rothschild and Château Latour. Almost all California Cabernets are dry and, depending on the producer, range in style from light to extremely full-bodied. Excellent vintages come into their own only after five to ten years of bottle aging.

Opus One

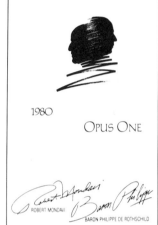

Amidst grand hoopla in the wine world, Robert Mondavi and Philippe de Rothschild released their newest wine creation—Opus One. Opus One is made primarily from Cabernet Sauvignon grapes and is produced at the Robert Mondavi Winery in the Napa Valley.

Opus One in its first vintages sells for $35–$50 at your local retailer (if you can find it) and a lot more if you order it at a restaurant. Only a small amount is being produced. "It isn't Mouton and it isn't Mondavi," says Robert Mondavi.

"Pinot Noir represents one of the biggest challenges to winemakers in California."—*John Parducci*

Pinot Noir—Known as the "headache" grape, because of its fragile quality, it is difficult to grow and work with. The great grape of the Burgundy region of France—responsible for such famous wines as Pommard, Nuits-St-Georges, and Gevrey-Chambertin—it is also one of the principal grapes in French Champagne. In California, a tremendous amount of experimentation is being done with this grape in location of plantings and fermentation techniques. Recent samples have proven these experiments fruitful in achieving the richness and complexity of French Burgundies. Pinot Noir is usually less tannic than Cabernet and matures more quickly, generally in four to six years. Because of all the extra expense involved in growing this grape, the best examples of Pinot Noirs from California may cost more than other varietals.

The Carneros district is one of the better places to grow Pinot Noir because of its cooler climate.

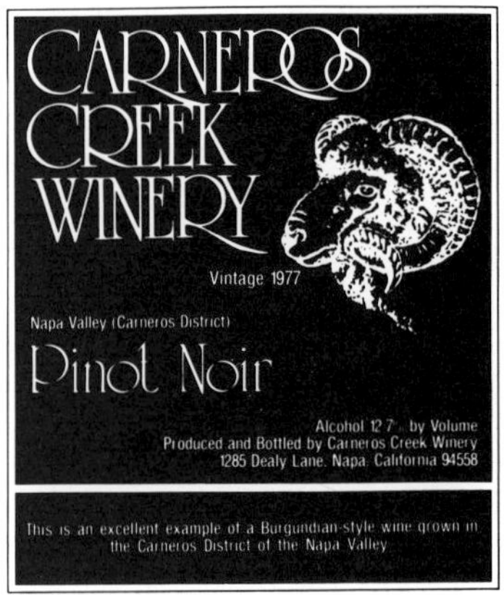

Zinfandel—The surprise grape of California, it was used to make "generic" or "jug" wines in the early years of California winemaking. Over the past ten years, however, it has developed into one of the best red varietal grapes. It is unique among grapes grown in the United States in that its European origin is unknown. The only problem in choosing a Zinfandel wine is that so many different styles are made. Depending on the producer, the wines can range from big, rich, intensely flavored types with substantial tannin, to very light, fruity wines.

Merlot—For many years Merlot was thought of as a grape to be blended with the Cabernet Sauvignon, because its tannins are softer and its texture more supple. It is now achieving its own identity as a premium varietal. Over 50 wineries in the United States now market this varietal as compared to five less than ten years ago. It produces a soft, round wine, and generally it does not need the same aging as the Cabernet Sauvignon.

There were only two acres of Merlot planted in all of California in 1960.

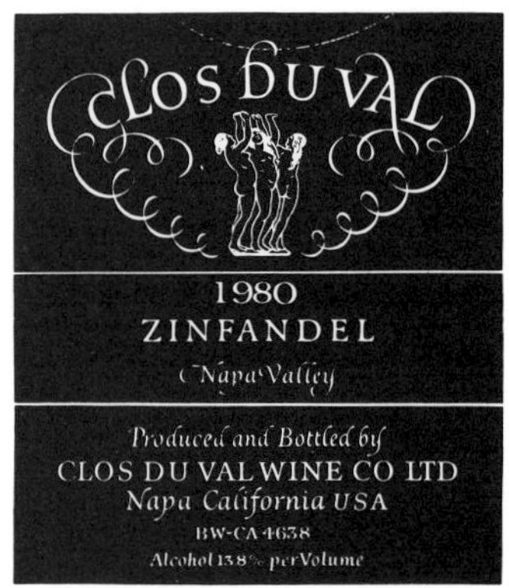

Gamay—In California, two different types of grapes are associated with Gamay wine: Gamay Beaujolais and Napa Gamay. Gamay Beaujolais, until recently, was thought by California viticulturists to be the true grape of the Beaujolais district of France. Now it is identified as one of many clones of the Pinot Noir grape. Depending on the producer, the wine may be light or medium in body. Now viticulturists think that it was Napa Gamay which was always the real grape of Beaujolais. Gamay is used to produce a style very similar to that of the French Beaujolais. Gamay is a light, fruity wine that should be consumed young, the same as its French counterpart, but it lacks the fruitiness associated with the French Beaujolais.

Petite Sirah—Like the Zinfandel grape, the Petite Sirah was long used for the blending of generic Burgundies. The grape yields inky-colored wines that are high in tannin, full-bodied with a spiciness in the aroma, and taste that can stand up to hearty foods.

Jordan

1977
Cabernet Sauvignon
Alexander Valley

Produced & Bottled by Jordan Vineyards & Winery
Alexander Valley, Healdsburg, Calif. Alcohol 12.8% by Volume

When I buy a Cabernet, Zinfandel, Merlot, Pinot Noir, or any other red varietal, how do I know what style I'm getting? Do they indicate the style of the wine on the label?

Unless you just happen to be familiar with a particular vineyard's wine, you're stuck with trial-and-error tastings, because the winemaker does not usually indicate on the label whether a wine is ready to drink, or if it should be aged, or any other basic information. You're one step ahead, though, just by knowing that you'll find drastically different styles of the same wine.

To avoid any unpleasant surprises, I can't stress emphatically enough the importance of an educated wine retailer. One of the strongest recommendations I give—to a new winedrinker, especially—is to find the right retailer, one who understands wine and your taste.

1977
NAPA VALLEY
CABERNET SAUVIGNON
ALCOHOL 13½% BY VOLUME
PRODUCED AND BOTTLED IN OUR CELLAR BY
HEITZ WINE CELLARS
ST. HELENA, CALIFORNIA

Do California wines age?

I've already come across a problem with this question, because California hasn't been producing fine varietals long enough for us to judge them as we judge the European wines. Even those wineries that have been in business for about twenty years have little, if any, of their first vintages left, because they needed the cash and couldn't afford to let their wines go unsold.

From my personal experience, I think California wines have the potential to age as well as any Burgundy or Bordeaux, but we won't get a chance to find out for another few years, since the California wineries are only just beginning to hold back a certain amount of wine for posterity.

What's the future for California wines?

We are nowhere near tapping the potential of California wines yet. Everything is still in a nebulous stage and experimentation is constant. Consider these two points: (1) Vineyard owners in California are still learning about their land in terms of what grapes will grow where. (2) Many California winemakers are young themselves, and are gradually finding their own winemaking style.

RESERVE
1979
Napa Valley
CABERNET SAUVIGNON
ALCOHOL 13% BY VOLUME
PRODUCED AND BOTTLED BY
ROBERT MONDAVI WINERY
OAKVILLE, CALIFORNIA

WINE AND FOOD

Margrit Biever and Robert Mondavi—With Cabernet Sauvignon: lamb, wild game such as grouse and caribou. With Pinot Noir: pork loin, milder game such as domestic pheasant, coq au vin.

Angelo Papagni (Papagni Vineyards)—With Zinfandel: rack of lamb in a mustard paste with rosemary and olive oil.

Katie Wetzel-Murphy (Alexander Valley Vineyards)—With Cabernet Sauvignon: salad, cheese (especially chèvre), steak with pepper. With Pinot Noir: veal with red wine or tomato sauces. With Zinfandel: New Zealand lamb stuffed with spinach.

Louis Martini—With Cabernet Sauvignon: ripe Camembert cheese. With Pinot Noir: roast beef and good beef stew.

Sam J. Sebastiani—With Cabernet Sauvignon: sliced tongue with blueberry sauce. With Pinot Noir: barbecued lamb with basting sauce of chopped chiles, olive oil, Pinot Noir, and honey. With Zinfandel: breast of veal stuffed with a combination of hot and mild Italian sausage, beef heart, toasted pine nuts, and chard.

David Stare (Dry Creek)—With Cabernet Sauvignon: beef, charcoal broiled steak; "Sometimes I smear blue cheese over the beef before broiling." With Zinfandel: butterflied leg of lamb marinated in garlic, onion, rosemary, and Zinfandel.

Warren Winiarski (Stag's Leap Wine Cellars)—With Cabernet Sauvignon: lamb or veal with light sauces.

Justin Meyer (Silver Oak Cellars)—With Cabernet Sauvignon: Caesar salad, leg of lamb with rosemary, pasta in a pesto sauce. "I couldn't cook without garlic!"

Janet Trefethen (Trefethen Vineyards)—With Cabernet Sauvignon: prime cut of well-aged grilled beef, also—believe it or not—with chocolate and chocolate chip cookies. With Pinot Noir: roasted quail stuffed with peeled kiwi fruit in a Madeira sauce. Also with pork tenderloin in a fruity sauce.

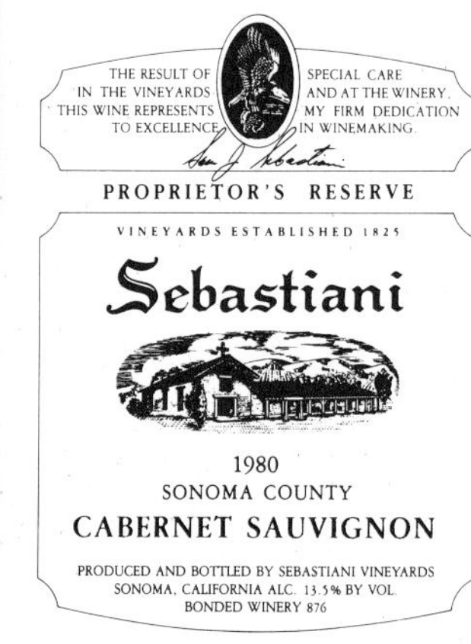

THE RESULT OF IN THE VINEYARDS THIS WINE REPRESENTS TO EXCELLENCE
SPECIAL CARE AND AT THE WINERY. MY FIRM DEDICATION IN WINEMAKING.
PROPRIETOR'S RESERVE
VINEYARDS ESTABLISHED 1825
Sebastiani
1980
SONOMA COUNTY
CABERNET SAUVIGNON
PRODUCED AND BOTTLED BY SEBASTIANI VINEYARDS
SONOMA, CALIFORNIA ALC. 13.5% BY VOL.
BONDED WINERY 876

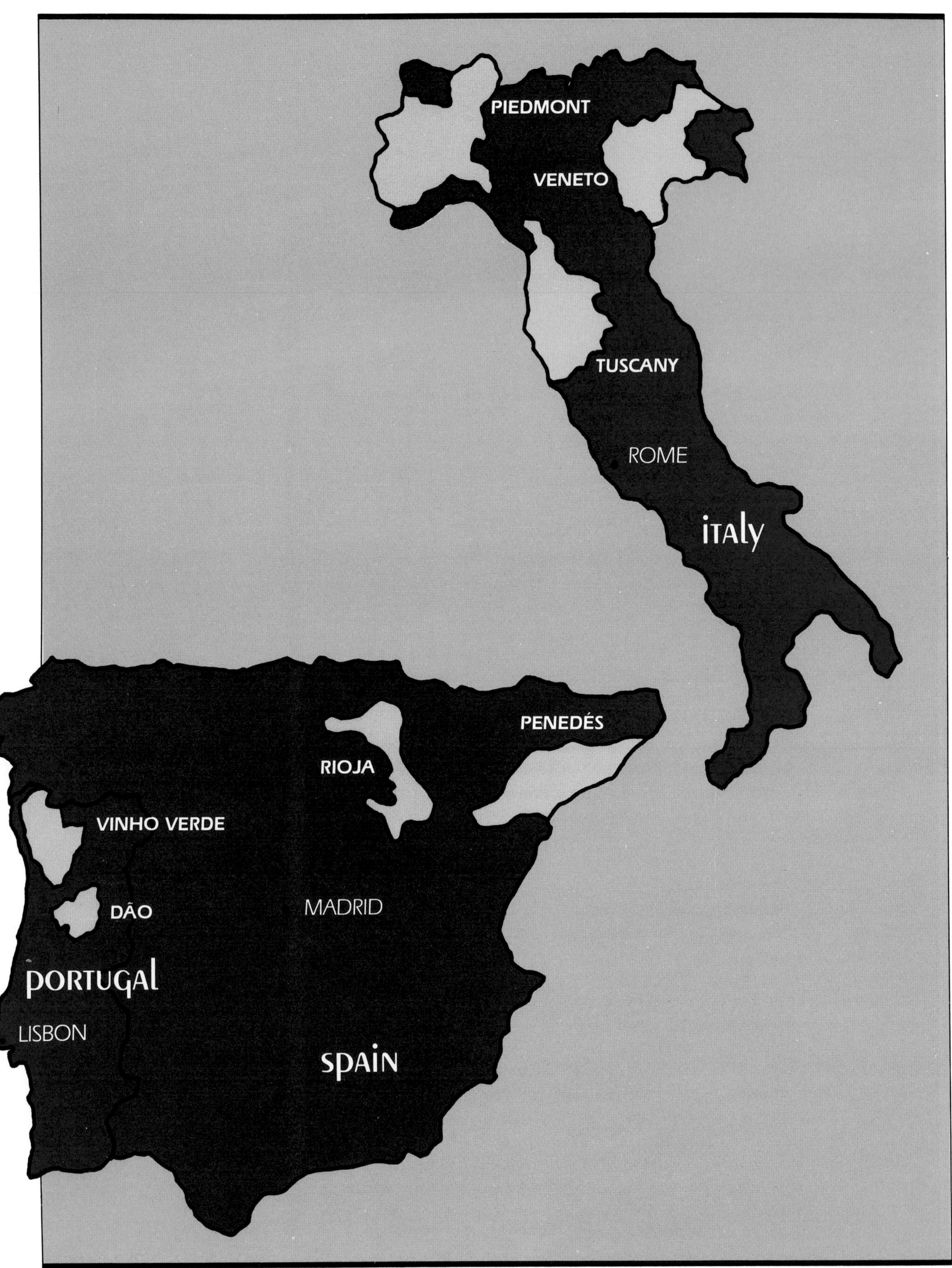

PIEDMONT
VENETO
TUSCANY
ROME
ITALY
PENEDÉS
RIOJA
VINHO VERDE
DÃO
MADRID
PORTUGAL
LISBON
SPAIN

THE RED WINES OF ITALY, SPAIN, AND PORTUGAL

Why group Italy, Spain, and Portugal together?

These countries share a common casual attitude towards wine. Wine is a drink to be enjoyed at practically any time of the day without fanfare. All three experience the warm climate of southern Europe, which is one of the reasons they produce wines of a similar style. In fact, all these areas produce more red wines than whites, and that's what their reputation is based upon.

Another reason I group these three winemaking countries together is that they are relative newcomers in books about wine. People will read about the wines of France, the wines of Germany, and those California—but not about the wines of Italy, Spain, or Portugal. At least not as much.

And that's a cause of good news. Since many people don't concentrate on these areas in any great detail, good values are waiting out there for those who do!

Just to show you how important these countries are in the wine world, here are a few interesting statistics:

Worldwide Consumption Rank
#1 Italy
#3 Portugal
#5 Spain

Worldwide Production Rank
#1 Italy
#3 Spain
#6 Portugal (but Portugal's production is equal to all U.S. wine production)

ITALY

Italy is the world's biggest producer, as well as the top consumer, of wine. It has been producing wine for almost 3,000 years, and the vines grow *everywhere*. As one retailer of fine Italian wines says: "There is no country. Italy is one vast vineyard from north to south."

Italian wines are good for any occasion—from quaffing to tasting. Some of my favorite wines are Italian. In fact, 25 percent of my personal wine cellar is stocked with them.

In Italy, Spain, and Portugal, vineyards are not classified as they are in Bordeaux. There are no Grand Crus or Premier Crus.

There are 23,000 different wine labels, if you care to memorize them, 20 regions and 93 provinces. But don't worry. If you want to know the basics of Italian wines, concentrate on the three regions listed below, and you'll be well on your way to having Italy in the palm of your hand.

Piedmont
Tuscany
Veneto

What are the major red grape varieties in Italy?

Most of the best Italian red wines use Sangiovese or Nebbiolo grapes. There are several others, but these are the best.

How are Italian wines controlled?

There are more than 200 D.O.C. wines. They account for 12% of Italy's wine production.

As mentioned before, the Denominazione di Origine Controllata, abbreviated D.O.C., is the Italian equivalent of the French A.O.C., which controls the quality of the wine. Italy's D.O.C. laws went into effect in 1963.

D.O.C. Laws

The D.O.C. governs:

1. The geographical limits of each region.
2. The grape varieties that can be used.
3. The percentage of each grape used.
4. The maximum amount of wine that can be produced per acre.
5. The minimum alcohol content of the wine.
6. The aging requirements, such as how long a wine should spend in wood or bottle, for certain wines.

The biggest difference between the A.O.C. of France and the D.O.C. of Italy: the D.O.C. has aging requirements.

Recently, the Italian wine board took quality control one step beyond the regular D.O.C. They have added the higher-ranking D.O.C.G. The "G" stands for *Garantita*, meaning they absolutely guarantee the superior quality of a wine through tasting-control boards.

Only five wines qualify for the D.O.C.G. label at present:

Barbaresco—from Piedmont
Barolo—from Piedmont
Brunello di Montalcino—from Tuscany
Chianti—from Tuscany
Vino Nobile di Montepulciano—from Tuscany

As you can see, two wines are from Piedmont and the other three are from Tuscany. Now you understand why these are two of the regions you should study.

Before the D.O.C. laws were set up, some producers of Chianti established their own minimum standards that were quite strict. Their symbol was the black rooster, sometimes found on Chianti bottles.

TUSCANY—THE HOME OF CHIANTI

Why did Chianti have such a bad image until recently?

One reason was the little straw-covered flasks (*fiaschi*) that the wine was bottled in—nice until restaurants hung the bottles from the ceiling next to the bar along with the sausage and the provolone. So Chianti developed a bad image as a cheap little wine to be bought for $3 a jug.

My own feeling is that one of the best values in Italian wine today is unquestionably the wine of Chianti.

How many of you, during your college days, bought a bottle of Chianti to use as a candleholder?

Today you'll find the best Chiantis in Bordeaux-style bottles.

Chianti was recently elevated to D.O.C.G. status, effective with the 1984 harvest.

What are the different quality levels of Chianti?

Chianti—the first quality level (Cost: $)
Chianti Classico—from the inner district of Chianti (Cost: $$)
Chianti Classico Riserva:—from a Classico area, aged for three years (Cost: $$$$)

How should I buy Chianti?

First of all, find the style of Chianti you like the best. There is a considerable variation in Chianti styles. Second, always buy from a shipper or producer that you know—one with a good, reliable reputation. Some quality Chianti producers are: Antinori, Badia à Coltibuono, Brolio, Frescobaldi, Melini, Nozzole, Ricasoli, Ruffino, and Villa Banfi.

If you were to ask someone to name a red Italian wine, chances are the person would answer "Chianti." Yes, Chianti *is* red, but did you know it is really a blend of both red *and* white grapes?

What Is Chianti?

Red Grapes Minimum—Maximum
Sangiovese: 50%—80% (for body and character)
Canaiolo: 10%—30% (adds fruitiness)

White Grapes Minimum—Maximum
Trebbiano and Malvasia: 10%—30%: (both soften the wine)

What follows are two typical, but different blends of Chiantis:

Number 1
Sangiovese: 80%
Canaiolo: 10%
Trebbiano: 10%

Number 2
Sangiovese: 50%
Canaiolo: 20%
Trebbiano: 30%

As you can see, the blends are very different. Can you tell which one will be fuller and which one will be lighter?

Number 1 is the fuller, more robust Chianti, because it is made primarily of the Sangiovese, which is a red grape and, as shown above, the one that gives the wine body and character. There is only 10% Trebbiano, the white grape.

Number 2 is the lighter-style Chianti, with only 50% of the red Sangiovese and a lot more Trebbiano. As a general rule, the more white grapes the wine has, the lighter the style.

Since the recent D.O.C.G. passed its new requirements, winemakers are required to use at least 80% Sangiovese to produce Chianti. Besides decreasing the amount of white grapes that may be used, the D.O.C.G. is also encouraging the use of "non-traditional" grapes, such as Cabernet Sauvignon, by allowing an unprecedented 10% "optional grape."

What other high-quality wines come from Tuscany?

Two of the greatest Italian red wines are Brunello di Montalcino and Vino Nobile di Montepulciano. If you purchase the Brunello, keep in mind that it probably needs more aging before it will be ready to drink. The best-known producers of Brunello are: Biondi-Santi (one of the most expensive wines in Italy), Barbi, Il Poggione, and Col D'Orcia. Those of Vino Nobile are: Fassati and Poggio alla Sala.

When is the best time to drink a Brunello?

You can drink a Brunello wine after it ages from five to ten years. If the wine is from a good vintage and you want it to be at its best, lay it down in your cellar for ten or even closer to twenty years from the vintage date on the bottle.

Piedmont—The Big Reds

Two D.O.C.G. wines come from this region in northwest Italy: Barolo and Barbaresco. The greatest variety of fine red wines are produced here.

The Grapes of Piedmont
Barbera—Côtes du Rhône style (Cost: $)
Dolcetto—Beaujolais style (Cost: $$)
Nebbiolo—The best! (Cost: $$$$)

It is said that when you begin drinking Italian wines, you start with the lighter style Barbera and Dolcetto, move on to the fuller-bodied Barbaresco, until finally you can fully appreciate a Barolo. For this, Renato Ratti says, "Barolo is the wine of arrival."

There are 300 different labels of Barolo.

Barolo and Barbaresco, the heavyweight wines from Piedmont, are made from the Nebbiolo variety. These wines have the fullest style and a high alcoholic content. Be careful when you try to match young vintages of these wines with dinner as they may overpower the food.

Piedmont's production:
90% red
9% spumante (sparkling white)
1% white

Barolo vs. Barbaresco

BAROLO	BARBARESCO
Nebbiolo grape	Nebbiolo grape
Minimum 13% alcohol	12½% alcohol
More complex flavor; more body	Lighter; less body
Must be aged at least three years (two in wood)	Requires two years of aging (one in wood)
"Riserva" = five years of aging	"Riserva" = four years of aging

Getting to know Dolcetto

Dolcetto is a Piedmontese wine that is not well known in the United States. It is a light, drinkable, Beaujolais-style red—just the kind of simple wine I love to consume at home. Because it is not well known, it is very inexpensive and therefore an excellent value—a real find!

Two-thirds of all Italian wines are red.

60% of all Italian D.O.C. wines are red.

The best producers of Piedmont wines are: Antoniolo, Antonio Vallana, Bersano, Borgogno, Fontanafredda, Gaja, Pio Cesare, Prunotto, and Renato Ratti.

VENETO—THE HOME OF SOAVE

This is one of Italy's largest wine-producing regions. Even if you don't recognize the area immediately, I'm sure you've had a Veronese wine at one time or another. They are Valpolicella, Bardolino, and Soave. All three are very consistent, easy to drink, and ready to be consumed whenever you buy them. They do not fit into the category of a Brunello di Montalcino or a Barolo, but they are very good table wines and within everyone's budget.

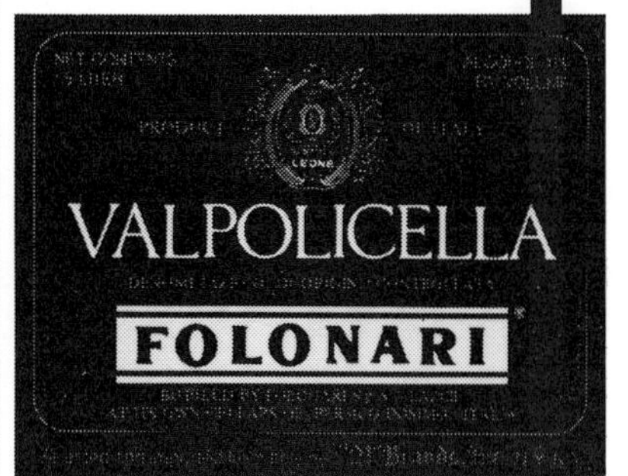

What is Amarone?

Amarone is a type of wine made by a special process in the region of Veneto. Only the ripest grapes from the top of each bunch are used. After picking, they are left to raisinate (dry and shrivel) on straw mats. Does this sound familiar to you? It should, because this is similar to the process used to make German Trockenbeerenauslese and French Sauternes. One difference is that with Amarone, the winemaker ferments most of the sugar, bringing the alcohol content to 14–16 percent.

ITALIAN WHITES

I am often asked why I don't teach a class on Italian white wines. The answer is quite simple. Take a look at the most popular white wines: Soave, Frascati, Pinot Grigio, Orvieto, Corvo, and Verdicchio, among others. Every one of them retails for about $5. The Italians just don't put the same effort into most of their white wines as they put into their reds—in terms of style or complexity—and they are the first to admit it. All the same, Italian white wines are easy to drink and represent good value.

Overview

When you buy Italian wines, how do you know what you're getting?

It depends. Wines are usually known by the grape they're made from or their village or district of origin. (A few others are just given a marketable proprietary name.)

How Italian Wines Are Named

Grape	Village or District	Proprietary
Barbera	Chianti	Principato
Nebbiolo	Barolo	Bell'agio
Trebbiano	Barbaresco	
	Soave	

62% of the Italian wines imported into the U.S. are Lambruscos.

For a new experience with Italian whites, try Gavi, and wines from the region of Friuli.

Have Piedmont wines changed over the last ten years? Many have. The wines of the past were more tannic and difficult to appreciate, while the present-day wines are easier to drink.

The top five wines imported to the U.S. from Italy are:
1. Riunite
2. Cella
3. Canei
4. Folonari
5. Bolla

The above wines equal 40% of all imported table wine in the U.S.

An interesting note: Riunite Lambrusco marketed in the United States is not sold in Italy. It is a wine that was developed specifically for the American market.

What are the best vintages for Italian wines?

Of course, the best vintages will depend on the location of the vines, the weather conditions, and several other variables. You can be sure that these "Best Bets" come from a reliable source; they're the direct suggestions of some Italian wine producers.

Best Bets for Chianti

Dr. Ambrogio Folonari, Ruffino

1974 1975* 1977 1979

Best Bets for Barbaresco

Angelo Gaja

1970 1978* 1979 1982

Best Bets for Piedmont

Renato Ratti	Pio Cesare
1964 1971* 1978	1971 1978 1982

Mr. Ratti suggests allowing 20 years for a good Barolo or Barbaresco to show its full flavor.

Best Bets for Barbaresco and Barolo

Giuseppe Colla, of Prunotto

Mr. Colla offers his "Best Bets" in the form of advice. His general rule: In a good vintage, set a Barbaresco aside for a minimum of four years before drinking. In the same situation, put away a Barolo for six years. However, in a great vintage year, lay down a Barbaresco for six years and a Barolo for eight years. As they say, "Patience is a virtue"—especially with wine.

*Indicates an exceptionally good year.

What's in the winemaking future of Italy?

It's very lucrative. The Italian wine producers are just beginning to build up their businesses for export. Until the 1960s, wine consumption was a fact of life for the Italians. As one wine producer commented, "They didn't drink the wine; they *ate* the wine." To the Italians, wine was wine. They didn't scrutinize a label, but only looked to see if the wine was red, white, or rosé.

Then they discovered wine as a business. Their philosophy changed considerably from casually drinking wine to making it more marketable, and improving and enhancing the quality. As technology cleared the way for experimentation, the Italians entered the business with enthusiasm. Their success in the United States is indicated by Americans' obvious zest for Italian wines.

In Italy at present, they're planting a lot more Chardonnay and Cabernet Sauvignon. In fact, Tuscany could be just the right spot for Cabernet Sauvignon and Chardonnay—in particular, in Montalcino.

Some of these new Italian wines are in the marketplace now, and there will be more in the future.

An interesting trend in Italy: Beer consumption is going up, while wine consumption is going down.

In the last five or six years, Italians have become more weight and health conscious, so they're changing their eating habits. As a result, the long lunch hour is a thing of the past. Yes, all good things must come to an end.

WINE AND FOOD

In Italy, the wine is made to go with the food. No meal is served without wine. Take it from the experts:

"When you're having Italian wines, you must not taste the wine alone. *You must have them with food.*"—*Giuseppe Colla of Prunotto*

"Piedmontese wines show better with food than in a tasting."—*Angelo Gaja*

The following food and wine suggestions are based on what some of the Italian wine producers enjoy eating with their wine. You don't have to take their word for it. Get yourself a bottle of wine, a tasty dish, and *mangia!*

Ambrogio Folonari (Ruffino)—He enjoys Chianti with prosciutto, chicken, pasta, and of course, pizza. When it comes to a Chianti Classico Riserva, Dr. Folonari prefers a hearty prime rib dinner or a steak.

Ezio Rivella (Villa Banfi)—He says that Chianti is good with all meat dishes, but he saves the Brunello for "stronger" dishes, such as steak, wild boar, pheasant, and other game.

Angelo Gaja—He has Barbaresco with meat and veal, and also with mature cheeses that are "not too strong," such as Emmentaler and fontina. Mr. Gaja advises against Parmesan and goat cheese when you have a Barbaresco.

Giuseppe Colla (Prunotto)—Mr. Colla says light-style Dolcetto goes well with all first courses and all white meat—chicken and veal especially. He prefers not to have Dolcetto with fish. The wine doesn't stand up well to spicy sauce, but it's great with tomato sauce and pasta.

Renato Ratti—Both Barbera and Dolcetto are good with chicken and lighter foods. However, Barolo and Barbaresco need to be served with heavier dishes to match their own body. Mr. Ratti suggests:

- a roast in its natural sauce or better yet, try Brasato al Barolo—cooked with Barolo
- meat cooked with wine
- pheasant, duck, wild rabbit
- cheeses
- for a special dish, try *risotto al Barolo* (rice cooked with Barolo wine)

Mr. Ratti says that Italians even serve wine with dessert—his favorite: strawberries or peaches with Dolcetto wine. The dryness in the wine contrasted with the natural sweetness of the fruit makes for a taste sensation!

Lorenza de'Medici and Stucchi-Prinetti (Badia)—Since Tuscan cooking is very simple, these two winery owners recommend an assortment of simple foods. They prefer herbs to heavy sauces. With young Chianti, they suggest roast chicken, pigeons, or pasta with meat sauce. To complement an older Chianti, they recommend a wide pasta with:

- braised meat in Chianti
- pheasant or other game
- wild boar
- roast beef

Piero Antinori (Antinori)—Mr. Antinori enjoys Chianti with the grilled foods for which Tuscany is famous, especially its *bistecca alla Fiorentina* (beefsteak). He suggests poultry and even hamburgers as other tasty possibilities.

For Chianti Classico Riserva, Mr. Antinori enjoys having the best of the vintages with wild boar and fine aged Parmesan cheese. He says the wine is a perfect match for roast beef, roast turkey, lamb, or veal.

For further reading on Italian wine: *Vino* by Burton Anderson; *The Pocket Guide to Italian Wines* by Burton Anderson; *Italian Wine* by Victor Hazan.

SPAIN

Marqués de Cáceres is owned by a Bordeaux producer. He also owns La Rose-Trintaudon and Château Camensac in Bordeaux.

The three main winemaking regions in Spain are:

Rioja
Penedés
Sherry

We'll put aside the region of Sherry for now, since you'll become a Sherry expert in the next chapter. That leaves us with Rioja and Penedés, both located in northern Spain, very near the French border.

In fact, it's only a five-hour drive to Bordeaux from Rioja, so it's no coincidence that the Rioja wines often have a Bordeaux style. Back in the 1800s, many Bordeaux wine producers brought their expertise to this region.

Why would a Frenchman leave his château in Bordeaux to go to a Spanish bodega in Rioja, Spain?

I'm glad you asked. It so happens that Frenchmen did travel from Bordeaux to Rioja at one point in history. Do you remember Phylloxera (see page 20)? It was a plant louse that killed all the vines and almost wiped out the Bordeaux wine industry.

Phylloxera started in the north and moved south. I'm not kidding when I say this (everyone thinks it's a joke), but the Phylloxera had trouble getting over the Pyrenees because it had to go over the mountains. Phylloxera destroyed all of the vines of Bordeaux first. Some of the Bordeaux vineyard owners decided to establish vineyards and wineries in the Rioja district. It was a logical place for them to go because of the similar climate and growing conditions. The influence of the Bordelaise is sometimes apparent even in today's Rioja wines.

What grapes are used in Rioja wines?

The two major grapes used in Spanish wine are:

Garnacha (related to the Grenache of the Rhône Valley)
Tempranillo

These grapes are blended to give Rioja wines their distinct taste: After the shippers buy the grapes, they blend wines from several vintages to keep the style consistent. If you do see a vintage on a Rioja label, you'll find it next to the word *consecha*, which means harvest.

Although Spanish wine laws have changed recently, years ago it was not uncommon to find Rioja wine labelled with a very old date, selling at a very inexpensive price.

From Innocence to Experience . . .

I remember going to Rioja and visiting a winemaker's cellar while he pulled out all of these old wines—from 1918, 1925, 1938—great vintages from his private cellar, and I hadn't even made a formal appointment with him! So I was really astounded. I was 22 years old and looked the part back in those days, and I couldn't believe he was taking all of these wines out for me.

I was drinking the wines and getting happier and happier, when I told the Spanish winemaker, "It's so nice of you to show me these wines." I remarked at how amazing the wine's color was, especially considering some of them were 1918s and 1925s. "Look at the way the color is lasting in this 1925," I told him. "It doesn't look 50 years old."

"It's not 50 years old," he replied.

"But look at the label," I countered. "It says '1925'."

"1925 was a very good year," the man said.

"What do you mean?"

"It was the year my son was born," he announced proudly. "It was a very good year for me. Since then, I name my best wine after the year of my son's birth."

Have Rioja wines changed in style over the last ten years?

Yes, without a doubt. One of the problems with Rioja wines has been, until recently, prolonged storage in wooden casks. They used to keep the wine in wood until they were ready to sell it—as long as ten years!

In fact, it used to be that you were better off drinking a red Rioja than a white one for just that reason. The Spaniards used almost identical techniques to make their white wine as they did for their red. As a result, the white wines were overly wooded; their crispness and fruitiness were lost. It was like eating a two-by-four.

Don't get me wrong—the Spaniards liked this style. They only started to change the style of the wine when they became interested in exporting Spanish wines. Today, many bodegas don't use wood at all in their winemaking. They use stainless-steel tanks instead, which makes for a lighter, more agreeable wine. The stainless-steel tanks have also helped the Rioja winemakers refine their reds, so you can taste the fruit of the grape.

Look for the word "Reserva" on a Spanish wine label. It means that the shipper especially selected this wine and gave it further aging in cask and bottle.

Why are Rioja wines so easy to understand?

All you need to know when buying a Rioja wine is the style and the reputation of the Rioja winemaker/shipper. The grape varieties are not found on the wine labels, and there is no classification system to be memorized.

"Gran Reserva" means that the wine had to undergo at least seven years of aging.

How would I know which Rioja wine to buy in the store?

You mean besides going with a name producer and the reputation of the winemaker/shipper? You may also be familiar with a Rioja wine by its proprietary name. The following are some shippers to look for, along with some of their better-known proprietary names:

Federico Paternina—Banda Azul
C.U.N.E.—Imperial, Viña Real
Bodegas Bilbaines—Brillante, Viña Pomal
Marqués de Cáceres
Marqués de Riscal
Domecq Domain
Marqués de Murrieta
Bodega Santiago—Gran Condal
Bodegas Muerza
Lopez de Heredia—Viña Tondonia, Viña Bosconia
Ollara

The other famous winegrowing region in Spain is Penedés. That name may not sound too familiar until you hear the name "Torres." The Torres family is the best-known producer of wine from the Penedés area—the wines of Jean Leon are also prevalent.

Stacking the Cellar

Now that you have all of your wine certificates (I'm assuming that you have already sent away to correspondence courses for your certificates in French, German, and Spanish wines) and a place to put them (presumably in your wine cellar), you have to fill that cellar. So what do you do?

You buy really inexpensive wines, at $3–$4 a bottle. But when you show someone your wine cellar, don't take your guests over to those inexpensive bottles. Keep them at a distance with the explanation, "Oh, those. You can't touch *those* wines. They must rest."

Then you take your guests over to the expensive stuff. You ever so carefully pull out the 1945 bottle. (You always have one really old bottle in your cellar just for show.) Then you slowly put back the 1945 and say, "Oh, these are all of my '45s and '61s."

Get the idea?

If you're purchasing Spanish wines, what you should really start looking for—especially now, and I've been saying this for the last couple of years—are the wines of Rioja. That is, if you want to fill up your wine cellar with wines you can drink now and also put away. Buy something like a Marqués de Cáceres or a C.U.N.E. wine. Try a bottle, and if you like it, buy the case—it will be remarkably inexpensive. And it's good drinking wine. Every wine cellar should have some Riojas.

Best Bets for Rioja Reds

1974 1978 1981 1982

Wine and Food

The lighter-style Rioja reds go well with chicken and veal. The more full-bodied "Reservas" complement pork, lamb, and steak. The new-style Rioja whites (only the most recent vintages) should be served alone as an apéritif, with light fish dishes, or with langoustines or shrimp.

PORTUGAL

Are you ready for a 30-second lesson on Portuguese wines? That's all I'm going to give you here, because Portugal is more famous for its Ports than its table wines. Don't worry—you'll learn all about Port in the next chapter.

In Portugal, they don't think about wine—they drink it.

There's not much to say about Portuguese table wines, because the best ones usually remain in Portugal. Of six designated winegrowing regions, only two produce wine that is available in the United States. They are *Vinho Verde* for the white wines, and *Dão* (pronounced "down") for the reds.

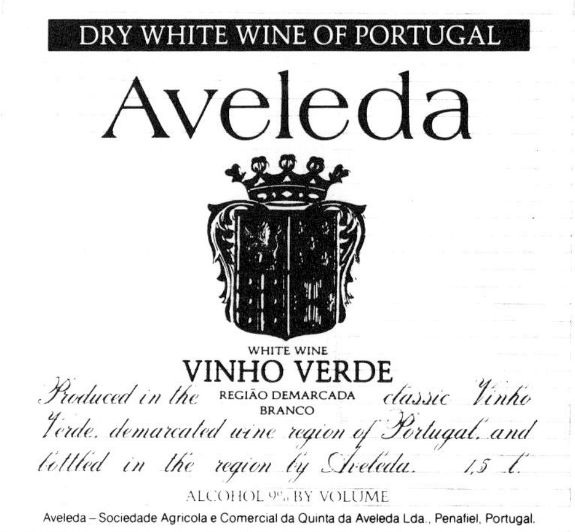

Vinho Verde—They can be either red or white, though the white is more commonly found in the United States. A light wine—sometimes having a slight spritz—it is a good summertime wine and goes well with shellfish and light fish dishes.

Dão—The best-known red table wine in Portugal, it is big, rich, and sometimes compared to Bordeaux in style.

Rosé—Without question, the best-known Portuguese wines are rosés. I'm sure you're familiar with Mateus and Lancers. Although they've lost some of their popularity, both wines remain on the list of the "Top 10 Imported Wines" in the United States.

The following are three important definitions you should be familiar with when you're looking for a good Portuguese wine: *Colheita*, which means vintage, and *Reserva* and *Garrafeira*, which usually signify higher quality and longer aging.

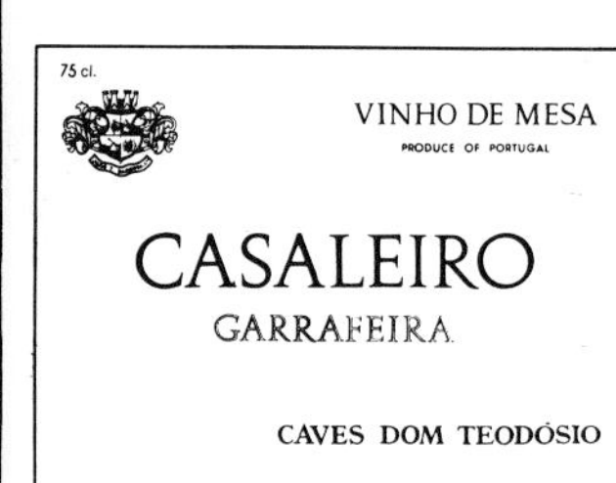

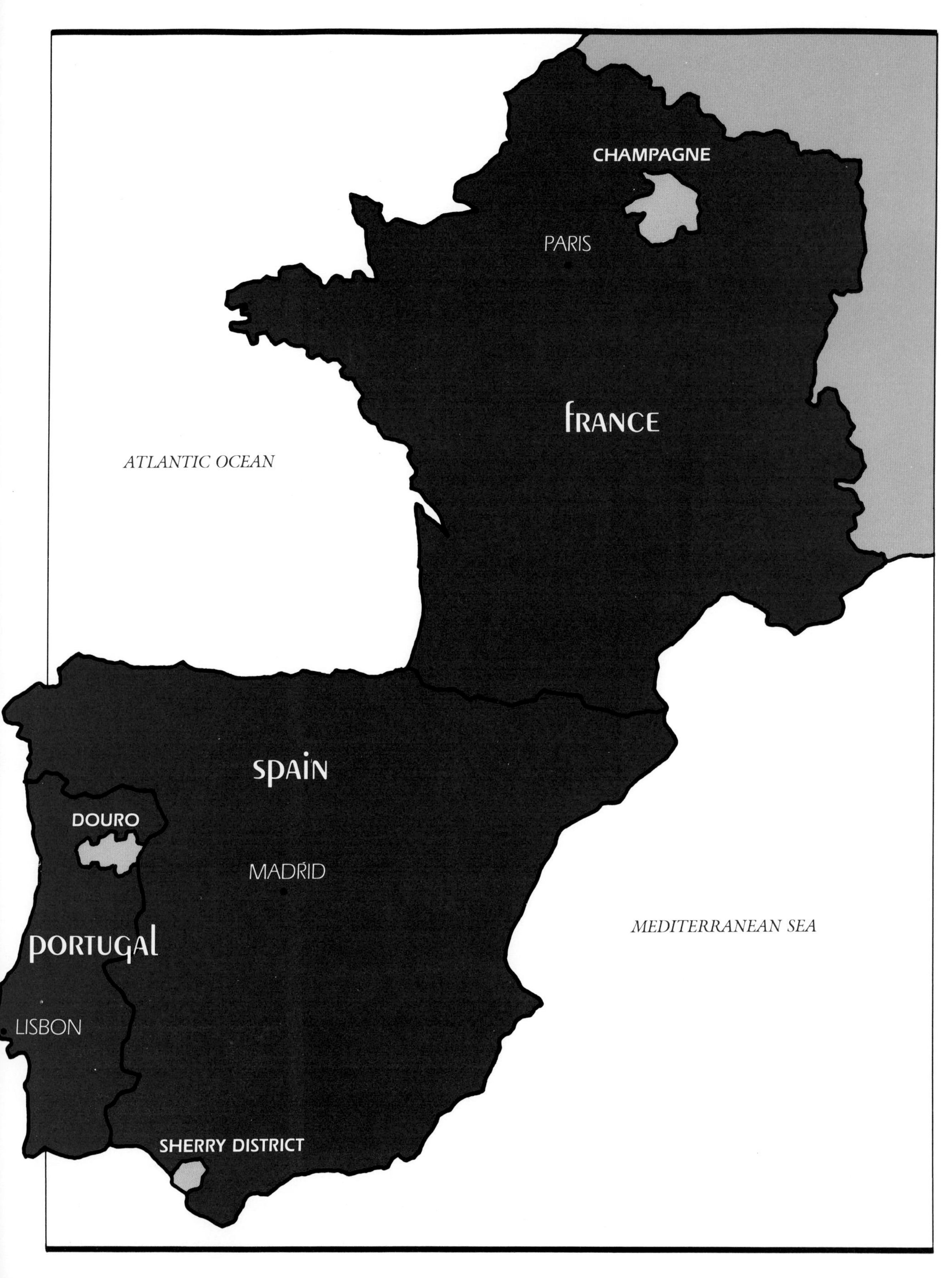
CHAMPAGNE
PARIS
FRANCE
ATLANTIC OCEAN
SPAIN
DOURO
MADRID
MEDITERRANEAN SEA
PORTUGAL
LISBON
SHERRY DISTRICT

CHAMPAGNE, SHERRY, AND PORT

Now we're beginning our last class—the last chapter on the wine itself. This is where the class ends—on a happy note, I might add. What better way to celebrate than with Champagne?

Why do I group Champagne, Sherry, and Port together? Because as diverse as these wines are, the way the consumer will buy them is through the reputation and reliability of the shipper. Since these are all blended wines, the shipper is responsible for all phases of the production. In Champagne, for example, Moët & Chandon is a well-known house; in Port, the house of Sandeman; and in Sherry, the house of Pedro Domecq.

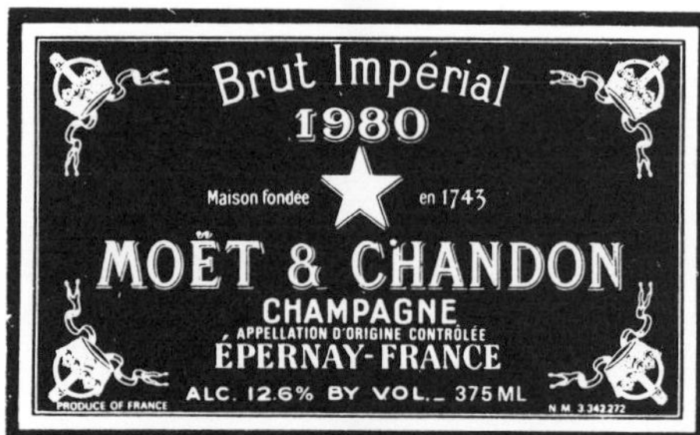

CHAMPAGNE

What is Champagne?

We all know that Champagne is a sparkling bubbly that everyone drinks on New Year's Eve. It's more than that. Champagne is a region in France—the northernmost winemaking region, to be exact—and it's an hour and a half northeast of Paris.

Why do I stress its northern location? Because this is going to affect the taste of the wine. Champagne is a high-acid, sparkling wine. In the region of Champagne, the growing season is shorter; thus, the grapes are picked with higher acidity than in most other regions. The Champagne region is divided into three main areas:

Valley of the Marne
Mountain of Reims
Côte des Blancs

To evaluate Champagne, look at the bubbles. The better wines have smaller bubbles and more of them. Also, with a good Champagne, the bubbles last longer.

Acidity in Champagne not only gives freshness to the wine, but is also important to its longevity.

The acidity, together with the bubbles (CO_2), is what makes good Champagne.

Ten million bottles of Champagne were sold in the United States in 1983.

"In victory you deserve it; in defeat you need it."—*Christian Pol Roger*

Blanc de Blancs is white wine made from 100% white grapes—Chardonnay.

All Appellation Contrôlée sparkling wines made in France, including Champagne, must be made by the *Méthode Champenoise* process.

Less than 10% of the sparkling wines made in the United States are made by the *Méthode Champenoise* process.

Most Champagnes are fermented in stainless steel.

"Fermentation in barrels is absolutely out of date."—*Bertrand Mure, Ruinart*

Wine presses are placed in the vineyards during the harvest to allow the winemaker to press the red grapes immediately without extracting any of their color.

Over 75% of the Champagne produced is non-vintage. This means it's a blend of several years' harvests.

Three grapes can be used to produce Champagne:

Pinot Noir (red)—accounts for 37 percent of all grapes planted
Pinot Meunier (red)—accounts for 32 percent of all grapes planted
Chardonnay (white)—accounts for 31 percent of all grapes planted

In France, only sparkling wines that come from the region of Champagne may be called "Champagne." Some American producers have borrowed the name "Champagne" to put on the label of their sparkling wines. These cannot and should not be compared with French Champagne.

How is Champagne made?

All French Champagne is made by a process called *Méthode Champenoise*, which is described below, step by step.

MÉTHODE CHAMPENOISE

Harvest—The normal harvest usually takes place in late September or early October.

Pressing the Grapes—Only three pressings of the grapes are permitted. The first pressing produces high-quality Champagne, while the second and third pressings are either made into inexpensive Champagne or sold to other firms.

Fermentation—All Champagnes undergo a first fermentation when the grape juice is converted into wine. Remember the formula: Sugar + Yeast = Alcohol + CO_2. The carbon dioxide dissipates. The first fermentation takes two to three weeks.

Blending—The blending is the most important step in Champagne production. The winemaker has to make a lot of decisions here. Three of the more important ones are: (1) What grapes to blend—how much Chardonnay, Pinot Noir, and Pinot Meunier? (2) From which vineyards should the grapes come? (3) What years or vintages should be blended?

Liqueur de Tirage—After the blending process, the wine is placed in its permanent bottle. At this point, the winemaker adds *Liqueur de Tirage*—a blend of sugar and yeast—which will begin the wine's second fermentation.

Second Fermentation—During this fermentation, the carbon dioxide stays in the bottle. This is where the bubbles come from. The second fermentation also leaves a natural sediment in the bottle. Now the problems begin. How do you get rid of the sediment without losing the carbon dioxide? Go on to the next step.

Riddling—The wine bottles are now placed in A-frame racks, neck down. The remueur, or riddler, goes through the racks of Champagne bottles and gives each bottle a slight turn while gradually tipping the bottle further downwards. After six to eight weeks, the bottle stands almost completely upside down with the sediment resting in the neck of the bottle.

Aging—The amount of time the wine spends aging on its sediment is one of the most important factors in determining the quality of the wine.

Dégorgement—The top of the bottle is dipped into a brine solution to freeze it, and then the temporary bottle cap (the kind that's used for soft drinks) is removed and out flies the iced sediment, due to the carbon dioxide.

Dosage—This combination of wine and cane sugar is added to the bottle after dégorgement. At this point, the winemaker can determine whether he wants a sweeter or a drier Champagne.

Recorking—The wine is recorked with real cork instead of a bottle cap.

Non-vintage Champagne must be kept in the bottle for at least one year. (In practice, most of the fine houses age non-vintage Champagne for three years, and vintage for five years.) Vintage Champagne cannot be sold until three years after the harvest.

Bollinger R.D. (Recently Disgorged), 1970, was left on its sediment for 13 years.

Champagne is put into heavy bottles to hold the pressurized wine. This is another reason that Champagne is more expensive than ordinary wine.

Two methods of making rosé Champagne: (1) add red wine from the vineyards of Bouzy; (2) leave the red grape skins in contact with the must for a short period of time.

Dosage

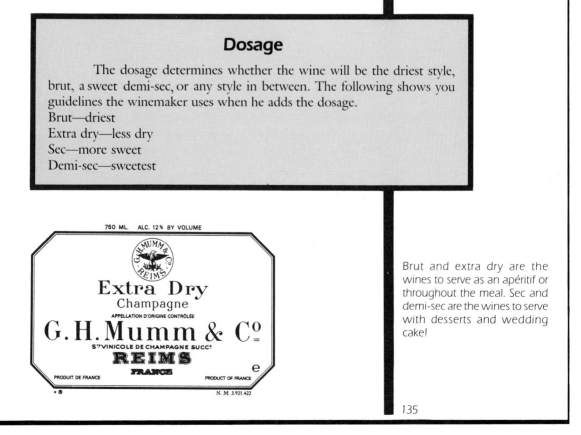

The dosage determines whether the wine will be the driest style, brut, a sweet demi-sec, or any style in between. The following shows you guidelines the winemaker uses when he adds the dosage.

Brut—driest
Extra dry—less dry
Sec—more sweet
Demi-sec—sweetest

Brut and extra dry are the wines to serve as an apéritif or throughout the meal. Sec and demi-sec are the wines to serve with desserts and wedding cake!

The top five Champagne houses that export to the United States are: Moët & Chandon, Mumm, Piper Heidsieck,, Perrier-Jouët, and Taittinger.

How do I buy a good Champagne?

First, determine the style you prefer, whether full-bodied or light-bodied, a dry brut or a sweet demi-sec. Then make sure you buy your Champagne from a reliable shipper/producer. The following are some brands in national distribution to look for:

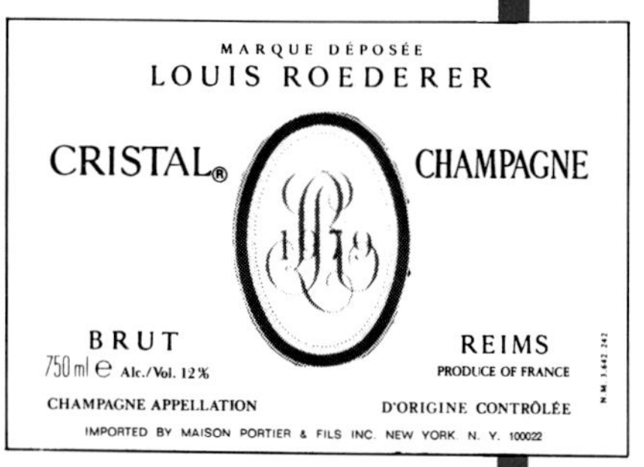

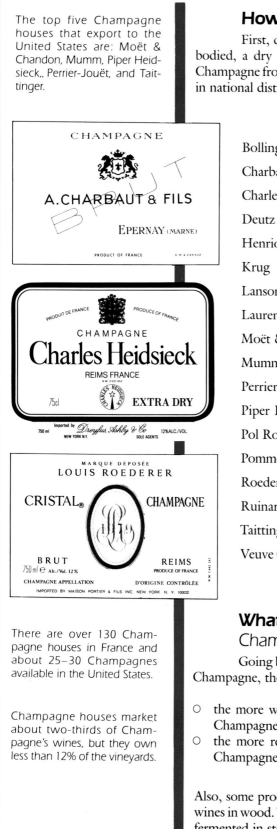

- Bollinger
- Charbaut
- Charles Heidsieck
- Deutz
- Henriot
- Krug
- Lanson
- Laurent-Perrier
- Moët & Chandon
- Mumm
- Perrier-Jouët
- Piper Heidsieck
- Pol Roger
- Pommery
- Roederer
- Ruinart Père & Fils
- Taittinger
- Veuve Cliquot

There are over 130 Champagne houses in France and about 25–30 Champagnes available in the United States.

Champagne houses market about two-thirds of Champagne's wines, but they own less than 12% of the vineyards.

What accounts for the different styles of Champagne?

Going back to the three grapes we talked about that are used to make Champagne, the general rule is:

- the more white grapes used in the blend, the lighter the style of the Champagne.
- the more red grapes used in the blend, the heavier the style of the Champagne.

Also, some producers such as Bollinger, Krug, and Roederer ferment their wines in wood. This gives the Champagne stronger characteristics than those fermented in stainless steel.

Is every year a vintage year?

No, but the vintages of the 1970s were: 1971, 1973, 1975, 1976, and 1979. *Note:* These were vintage years for most Champagne houses. "Vintage" in Champagne is different from other wine regions, because each house makes its own determination on whether or not to declare a vintage year.

Shippers don't always agree on the quality of the wines produced in any given vintage, so the years for vintage Champagnes vary from shipper to shipper. Each house usually declares a vintage three years out of each decade.

Looking Over the Body

Full-Bodied	**Medium-Bodied**	**Light-Bodied**
Bollinger	Veuve Cliquot	Perrier-Jouët
Krug	Ruinart	Pol Roger
Roederer	Pommery	Taittinger
	Mumm	Charbaut
	Moët & Chandon	Laurent-Perrier
	Deutz	

Why is there such a tremendous price difference between non-vintage and "luxury" Champagne?

Luxury Champagne must meet the following requirements to be designated as such:

- made from the best grapes at the highest-rated vineyards
- usually made from the first pressing of the grapes
- spends more time aging in the bottle than non-vintage Champagne
- made only in vintage years
- made in small quantity, and the demand is high. Price is dictated largely by supply and demand.

Vintage Champagne must contain 100% of that vintage year's harvest.

Dom Perignon, for example, is aged five to six years before it is put on the market.

Now that we've gone through the different levels of Champagne, I'll let you in on a little secret. When I buy Champagne, I prefer non-vintage over both vintage and luxury Champagnes. That's what tastes best for me, and it's definitely the best value for the money.

Non-vintage Champagne is more typical of the house style than vintage Champagne.

"It's not a Burgundy; it's not a Bordeaux; it's a white wine; it's a sparkling wine that should be kept no longer than two to three years. It should be consumed young."—*Claude Taittinger*

Rule: You can save vintage Champagne for up to ten years from the vintage on the bottle.

The pressure in a bottle of Champagne is about 90 pounds per square inch (or roughly three times the pressure in your automobile tire).

When is your Champagne ready to drink?

As soon as you buy it. You can keep the bottle for three to four years after you purchase it, but the wine will not improve. Champagne is something you shouldn't put away. So if you're still saving that Dom Perignon that you received for your tenth wedding anniversary fifteen years ago, it is long past its prime.

What is the correct way to open Champagne?

Before we sip Champagne in class, I always take a few moments to show everyone how to properly open a bottle of Champagne. I do this for good reason. Opening a bottle of Champagne is extremely dangerous, and I'm not kidding. I stress this to all the waiters, waitresses, and captains at Windows on the World. If you know the pounds per square inch that are under pressure in the bottle, you know what I'm talking about.

Opening Champagne Correctly

1. Remove the foil from the top of the bottle.

2. Place your hand on top of the cork, never removing your hand until the cork is pulled out completely. (I know this may seem a bit awkward, but it's very important.)

3. Take the wire off.

4. Wrap a towel around the bottle for safety and spillage, "just in case."

5. Remove the cork gently, slowly turning the bottle in one direction, and the cork in another. The idea behind opening a bottle is to ease the cork out gently rather than cracking the bottle open with a festive pop and letting it foam. That may be a lot of fun, but it does nothing for the Champagne. When you pop the cork off, you allow the carbon dioxide to escape. That carbon dioxide is what Champagne is all about.

What do you do if you forget?

How many times have you realized you forgot to put the Champagne on ice and company is due any minute? What do you do?

Usually, you put it in the freezer. Bad idea: *Don't* put Champagne in the freezer unless you tie a string to your finger to remind you it's in there! It can freeze and explode in a matter of fifteen minutes. Always chill Champagne in the warmest part of your refrigerator—the vegetable bin, for example. But if you're in a bind, and company is ringing the doorbell, and you realize the Champagne is not yet chilled, you have two options: (1) offer them a martini; (2) put the Champagne into an ice-filled bucket with water. It should be ready in twenty minutes.

For even quicker results, try chilling the Champagne in a brine solution made of water, ice, and salt.

Champagne Pet Peeves

After so many years in this business, I still can't figure out why so many people ruin perfectly good Champagne.

For instance, the Champagne Royale. You know what that is? It's a Kir Royale, when the bartender adds crème de cassis (black currant brandy) to Champagne. It takes out the acidity and adds sweetness to the wine, which is a shame after the winemaker took so many years to get the wine just right.

The worst offender is the Mimosa, the Sunday brunch drink—Champagne and orange juice. I love the people who will only drink Dom Perignon Mimosas. They're not going to taste anything. They may as well drink orange juice with club soda.

The other real offender is the Champagne Cocktail. The bartender adds bitters, orange peel, and sugar. Put it all together and then you add a great Champagne. What are you doing? Destroying the taste of Champagne.

Should I go on?

Some people order Champagne in a restaurant, and then swirl the wine real fast, mixing up the Champagne in their glass until they lose all of the carbon dioxide, which, of course, is the bubbles. All they're left with is a nice kind of dry wine with no sparkle to it.

There is a time and place for everything. And the above examples are the best times to buy an inexpensive sparkling wine at $4.99–$6.99 a bottle. If you use French Champagne for mixed drinks, you're actually wasting your money—unless, of course, you want to impress someone.

What glasses should Champagne be served in?

No matter what you decide to serve, you should serve it in the proper glass. There's a little story behind the Champagne glass, dating back to Greek mythology. The first "coupe" was said to be moulded from the breast of Helen of Troy. The Greeks believed that wine-drinking was a sensual experience, and it was only fitting that the most beautiful woman take part in shaping the chalice.

Centuries later, Marie Antoinette, Queen of France, decided it was time to create a new Champagne glass. She had coupes moulded to her own breasts, which changed the shape of the glass entirely, since Marie Antoinette was—shall we say—a bit more endowed than Helen of Troy.

The glasses shown below are the ones commonly used today—the flute and the tulip-shaped glass. Champagne does not lose its bubbles as fast in these glasses as it did in the old-fashioned model.

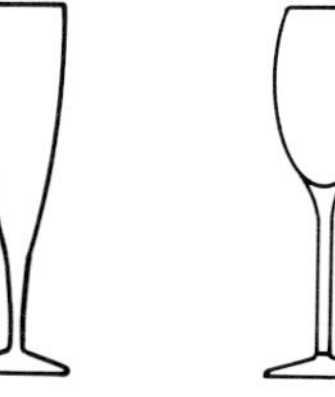

The cost of French Champagne soared in recent years because 1978, 1980, and 1981 were very low-quantity years.

Rejoice! 1982 and 1983 are the largest harvests ever in Champagne. The result will be price stabilization.

As beautiful as Helen was, the resulting glass was admittedly wide and shallow.

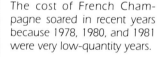

"I like it because it always tastes as though my foot's asleep."—*Art Buchwald*

Women, particularly those attached to the royal courts, deserve much of the credit for Champagne's international fame. Madame de Pompadour said that Champagne was the only drink that left a woman still beautiful after drinking it. Madame de Parabère once expressed that Champagne was the only wine to give brilliance to the eyes without flushing the face.

WINE AND FOOD

Champagne is one of the most versatile wines that you can drink with a number of foods from apéritif to dessert. Here are some Champagne and food combinations that some of the experts suggest:

Christian Bizot (Bollinger)—Mr. Bizot's favorite accompaniments to Champagne are a cheese soufflé made with a mild cheese like Gruyère, or grilled fish with a light cream sauce, but not too spicy. He explains: "The heavier the food, the heavier the style of Champagne."

Another favorite of Mr. Bizot is Bollinger R.D. with game meats.

Some dishes that Mr. Bizot finds do *not* do justice to the wine: melon, because the sugary taste offsets the taste of the Champagne; vinegar, as in a salad dressing, or vinaigrette; any dessert with Brut Champagne.

When the late Madame Lilly Bollinger was asked when she drank Champagne by a London reporter, she replied: "I drink it when I'm happy and when I'm sad. Sometimes I drink it when I'm alone. When I have company I consider it obligatory. I trifle with it if I'm not hungry and drink it when I am. Otherwise I never touch it—unless I'm thirsty."

Claude Taittinger (Taittinger)—First of all, Mr. Taittinger's general rule is: "Never with sweets." He prefers to serve Champagne with warm, cooked oysters, or as an apéritif with small hors d'oeuvres. He doesn't serve Champagne with cheese, because, he says, "The bubbles do not go well." He prefers red wine with cheese.

Christian Pol Roger—With Brut non-vintage: light hors d'oeuvres, mousse of pike. With vintage: pheasant, lobster, other seafood. With rosé: a strawberry dessert.

What is the difference between Champagne and sparkling wine?

As I've already mentioned, Champagne is the wine that comes from the Champagne region. It is the best sparkling wine in the world, because the region has the ideal combination of elements conducive to excellent sparkling

In France, all sparkling wines not produced in Champagne are called *Mousseux.*

winemaking. The soil is fine chalk, the grapes are the best grown anywhere for sparkling wine, and the location is perfect. This combination of soil and climate is reflected in the wine.

Sparkling wine, on the other hand, is produced in many areas and the quality varies from wine to wine. The Spanish produce the popular Codorniu and Freixenet—both excellent values and good sparkling wines. The German version is called Sekt; you probably have seen Henkell-Trocken at your retailer. This is the most popular brand of Sekt in the United States. Italy has spumante, which means "sparkling." The most popular Italian sparkling wine in the United States is Asti Spumante.

New York State and California are the two main producers of sparkling wine in this country. New York is known for Great Western, Taylor, and Gold Seal. California produces many fine sparkling wines, such as Domaine Chandon, Korbel, Piper-Sonoma, and Schramsberg.

Most of the larger California wineries also market their own sparkling wine.

Is there a difference in the way Champagne and sparkling wines are made?

Sometimes. All French Champagne and many fine sparkling wines are produced by the *Méthode Champenoise* process, which is laborious, intensive, and very expensive (see page 134). If you see a bottle of sparkling wine for $1.99, you can bet that the wine was not made by this process. The inexpensive sparkling wines are made by other methods. For example, in one of them, the secondary fermentation takes place in large tanks. Sometimes these tanks are big enough to produce 100,000 bottles of sparkling wine.

Domaine Chandon is owned by the Moët-Hennessy Group, which is responsible for the production of Dom Perignon in France. In fact, the same winemaker is flown into California to make the blend for the Domaine Chandon.

Piper-Sonoma is a joint venture of Sonoma Vineyards and the French Champagne house of Piper Heidsieck.

Schramsberg
BLANC DE NOIRS
NAPA VALLEY
CHAMPAGNE
VINTAGE 1979
PRODUCED AND BOTTLED BY
SCHRAMSBERG VINEYARDS
CALISTOGA, CALIFORNIA
ALCOHOL 12.5% BY VOLUME
CONTENTS 750 MLS

Is Schramsberg only for Republicans? I'm not sure, but former President Richard Nixon took some Schramsberg with him on his first visit to China. Also, President Ronald Reagan brought Schramsberg along with him on his 1984 visit to China.

Making Sparkling Wine

There are ways to make a sparkling wine that are quicker and cheaper than the Champagne method.

The Charmat process is widely used, whereby the second fermentation takes place in a large container instead of the individual bottle. Other producers simply add the spritz to their wines—a simple shot of carbon dioxide like a soft drink manufacturer would use.

Another method is called the transfer process. After the second fermentation takes place and the wine has aged for a few months, the wine is transferred to tanks. Dosage is added and the wines are refiltered and rebottled. By using this technique, the winemaker doesn't have to disgorge each bottle separately, which saves a lot of time and expense.

That's why you have to read the label carefully. A California wine made in the true French Champagne method will say on the label either: "Individually fermented in *this* bottle," or "Individually fermented in *the* bottle."

SHERRY

The two greatest fortified wines in the world are Port and Sherry. These wines have much in common, although the end result is two very different styles.

What exactly is fortified wine?

Fortified wine is made when a neutral grape brandy is added to wine to raise the alcoholic content. What sets Port apart from Sherry is *when* the winemaker adds the neutral brandy. It is added to the Port *during* fermentation. The extra alcohol kills the yeast and stops the fermentation, which is why Port is a relatively sweet wine. For Sherry, on the other hand, the brandy is added *after* fermentation.

What are the unique processes that characterize Sherry?

Controlled oxidation and fractional blending. Normally a winemaker guards against letting any air into the wine during the winemaking process. But that's exactly what *makes* Sherry—the air that oxidizes the wine. The winemaker places the wine in barrels and stores it in a bodega.

What is a bodega?

No, I don't mean a grocery store at 125th Street and Lexington Avenue in New York City. It's an above-ground structure used to store wine. Why do you think winemakers would want to store the wine above ground? For the air. Sherry is an oxidized wine. They fill the barrels approximately two-thirds full instead of all the way, and they leave the bung (cork) loosely in the barrel to let the air in.

Another fortified wine is Madeira. Although not as popular as it once was, Madeira wine was probably the first wine imported into America. It was favored by the colonists, including George Washington, and was served to toast the Declaration of Independence.

The neutral grape brandy, when added to the wine, raises the alcohol content to 16%–20%.

Two other famous fortified wines are Marsala (from Italy) and Vermouth (from Italy and France).

Sherry accounts for less than 3% of Spanish wine production.

"Styles of Sherry suit a variety of tastes, which range from the very dry and pale to the very dark and sweet."—*Muricio Gonzalez*

The Angel's Share

When Sherry is made, not only do winemakers let air into the barrels, but some wine evaporates as well. Each year they lose a minimum of 3% of their Sherry to the angels, which translates into 7,000 bottles per *day* lost through evaporation!

Why do you think the people of Sherry are so happy all the time? Besides the excellent sunshine they have, the people breathe in oxygen *and* Sherry.

So much for the controlled oxidation. Now for the fractional blending. Fractional blending is carried out through the *Solera System*.

There are 295 days of sunshine in Sherry.

What is the Solera System?

The Solera System is an aging and maturing process that takes place through the dynamic and continuous blending of several vintages of Sherry that are stored in rows of barrels and never moved. Wine is drawn out of these barrels—never more than one third the content of the barrel. The purpose of this type of blending is to maintain the "house" style of the Sherry by using the "mother" wine as a base and refreshing it with a portion of the younger wines.

Here's how it works: The barrels are stacked in such a way that the oldest wines are in the barrels at the bottom and the younger wines are stacked on top. Each year, the bodega foreman draws some wine from the oldest barrels, and transfers it to the barrels containing younger wine (from the following vintage). It is a continuous process, since the winemaker must keep all the barrels two-thirds full.

Some Soleras can be a blend of 10–20 different harvests.

In today's Sherry, only American oak is used to age the wine.

If you buy a bottle of Sherry with a year such as 1908 on the label, that's not the vintage, but rather the year the Solera was established. There is no such thing as vintage Sherry.

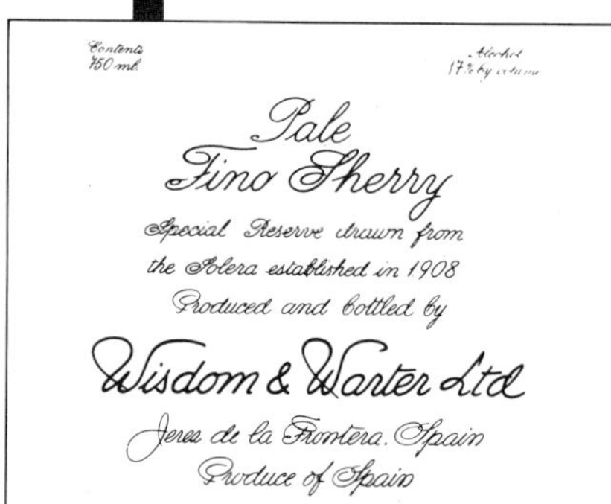

Where do they make Sherry?

Sherry is produced in sunny southwestern Spain in Andalusia. An area within three towns makes up the Sherry triangle. They are:

Jerez de la Frontera
Puerto de Santa Maria
Sanlúcar de Barrameda

What grapes are used to make Sherry?

There are two main varieties:

Palomino (this shouldn't be too difficult for horse lovers to remember)
Pedro Ximénez (named after Peter Siemons who brought the grape to Sherry from Germany)

There are five basic types of Sherry:

Manzanilla
Fino
Amontillado
Oloroso
Cream

The oldest Sherry is in the bottom row. That row is called the Solera. The next oldest row (or scale) is called the first Criadera; the third-oldest wines are called the second Criadera, and so on.

For you historians, Puerto de Santa Maria is where Christopher Columbus's ships were built and where all the arrangements were made with Queen Isabella for his journey.

The Palomino grape accounts for 90% of the planted vineyards in Sherry.

Here's another abbreviation for you—PX. Do you remember B.A.T.F., T.B.A., QbA, A.O.C., and D.O.C.? If you want to know Sherry you may have to say "PX." PX is the abbreviation for Pedro Ximénez.

How is Sherry made?

All Sherry begins as wine, the same as Champagne. The process changes when the winemaker adds neutral grape brandy. After the harvest, the winemaker decides which grapes will be made into what style Sherry—a Fino or an Oloroso. These are the only *styles* from which the five main *types* evolve.

To clarify the Sherry and rid it of all sediment, beaten egg whites are added to the wine. The question always comes up: "What do they do with the yolks?" Did you ever hear of flan? That's the puddinglike dessert made from all the yolks. In Sherry country, this dessert is called *toscina del cielo*, which translated means "the fat of the angels."

fino

After fermentation is completed, the winemaker adds neutral grape brandy to increase the alcohol content to 15½% percent. The next and most important step is dictated by nature. With the proper alcohol content and temperature, a "flor" develops on the Sherry. *Flor* is a layer of living yeast that forms on the wine. It continues to grow every spring and fall. This flor is responsible for the unique taste of a Fino-style Sherry. Sometimes this flor does not continue or maintain itself. Then it gradually dies off, the wine takes on a deeper, fuller taste and is reclassified as an Amontillado.

The Magic 15s: The flor develops when the alcohol content is 15–15½% and the temperature is 15°C. (59°F.).

There is another type of Fino called Manzanilla. This wine is made by the exact same process as a Fino, except for the fact that the grapes are grown and the wine is made in Sanlúcar, which is located on the coast. Between the salt air and the humidity in Sanlúcar—actually the microclimate—the flor layer is much denser, giving the wine a slightly briny taste.

It has been said that if you take a Fino to Sanlúcar de Barrameda, it will develop Manzanilla characteristics. Conversely, if you take a Manzanilla to Jerez or Puerto de Santa Maria, it will develop Fino characteristics.

Of the Sherry consumed in Spain, 90% is Fino. As one winemaker said, "We ship the sweet and drink the dry."

oloroso

The Palomino grapes used to make Sherry are left in the sun to dry. After fermentation, the winemaker once again adds neutral grape brandy to bring the alcohol content to 15½ percent. Eighteen to 24 months later, if no flor has developed, alcohol is added again, raising the alcohol content to 18 percent, and the wine becomes an Oloroso.

What is the difference between Fino and Oloroso Sherry?

The grapes used to produce Fino Sherry are immediately fermented. The grapes for Oloroso are sun-dried for 12–24 hours: the sun evaporates some of the water in the grapes and adds to their sweetness.

What is another difference between Fino and Oloroso? The flor does not form on an Oloroso Sherry.

pedro ximénez—PX

To make Pedro Ximénez Sherry, the winemaker sun-dries the PX grapes for 10–14 days. As a result, the grapes become raisins with a very high residual sugar content. What do you think the wine will look and taste like? The Sherry will be very dark, thick, syrupy, viscous, *and* sweet.

PX is used to make Cream Sherry, such as Harvey's Bristol Cream, among others. Cream Sherry is a blend of PX and Oloroso.

Pale Cream Sherry is a mixture of PX and Fino Sherry.

The Making of Sherry Step by Step

1—Harvest (September/October)

2—Fermentation

3—Winemaker decides to make a Fino–style or Oloroso–style Sherry.

4—Addition of alcohol (neutral grape brandy)

Fino			Oloroso
15½%			18%

5—The flor develops only in the Fino because of its low alcohol content.

Flor			No Flor

6—If the flor doesn't develop properly, a new style of Sherry called Amontillado is made. Now you have three styles of Sherry:

Fino		Amontillado	Oloroso

7—If a Fino is made and aged in the area of Sanlúcar, the flor develops much faster and the wine takes on a more delicate and lighter style. This wine will be called Manzanilla.

Resulting Sherries:

Fino	Manzanilla	Amontillado	Oloroso

What are the best vintages of Sherry?

If you expect a straight answer to this question, you're not reading me very well. I already told you there are no vintages in Sherry!

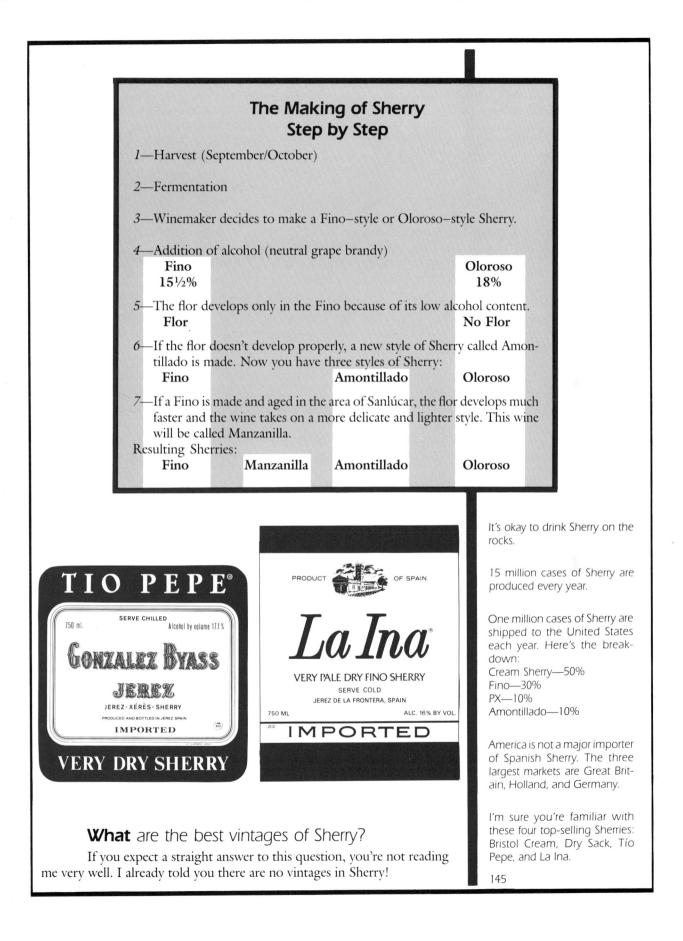

It's okay to drink Sherry on the rocks.

15 million cases of Sherry are produced every year.

One million cases of Sherry are shipped to the United States each year. Here's the breakdown:
Cream Sherry—50%
Fino—30%
PX—10%
Amontillado—10%

America is not a major importer of Spanish Sherry. The three largest markets are Great Britain, Holland, and Germany.

I'm sure you're familiar with these four top-selling Sherries: Bristol Cream, Dry Sack, Tío Pepe, and La Ina.

The grape variety is relatively unimportant when you're buying a Sherry and should not concern you. The producer is the key.

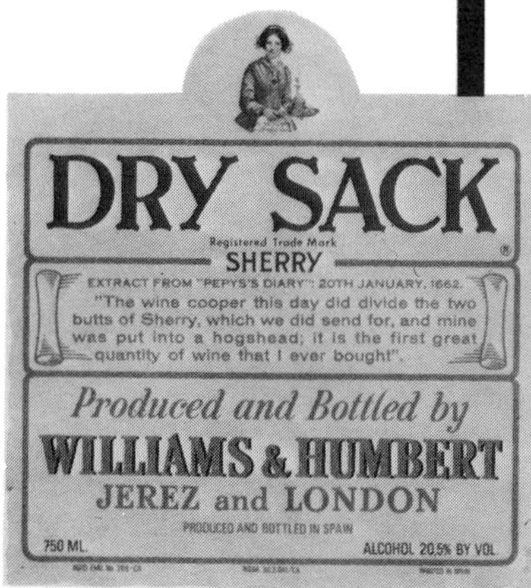

Fiction or non-fiction: Did you know about the mutiny on Columbus's ship? Do you have any idea what saved the day? The Sherry. Hearing rumors of mutiny, Columbus, a practical man, opened the best casks of Sherry. If he hadn't, we might not be here today. By discovering America, Columbus became the first importer of Sherry in the United States!

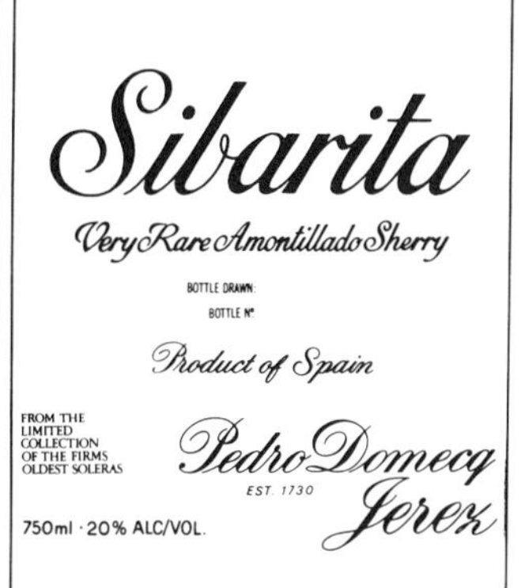

How do I buy Sherry?

Your best guide is the producer. It's the producer, after all, who buys the grapes and does the blending. Twenty firms account for 90 percent of Sherry's export sales. Only seven producers account for 60 percent of the export market:

1. González Byass
2. Croft
3. Pedro Domecq
4. Harvey's
5. Sandeman
6. Williams & Humbert
7. Savory and James

How long does Sherry last once it's been opened?

Sherry will last longer than a regular table wine, because of its higher alcoholic content, which acts as a preservative. But once Sherry is opened, it *will* lose its freshness. To drink Sherry at its best, you should consume the bottle within two weeks and keep the open bottle refrigerated. Cream Sherry will last longer—up to two months at room temperature.

WINE AND food

Muricio Gonzalez—He believes that one should always serve Fino well chilled. He enjoys having it as an apéritif with Spanish tapas (hors d'oeuvres), but he also likes to complement practically any fish meal with the wine. Some of his suggestions: clams, shellfish, lobster, prawns, langoustines, fish soup, or a light fish, such as salmon.

José Domecq—He suggests that very old and rare Sherry should be served with cheese. Fino and Manzanilla can be served as an apéritif or with light grilled or fried fish, or even smoked salmon. "You get the taste of the smoke better than if you have it with a white wine," says Mr. Domecq.

Amontillado is not to be consumed like a Fino. It should be served with light cheese, chorizo (sausage), ham, or shish kebab. It is a perfect complement to turtle soup or a consommé.

Dry Oloroso is not commonly available in the United States, but according to Mr. Domecq, it is known as a sporty drink in Spain—something to drink before hunting, riding, or sailing on a chilly morning.

With Cream Sherry, Mr. Domecq recommends cookies, pastries, and cakes. Pedro Ximénez, however, is better as a topping for vanilla ice cream or a dessert wine before coffee and brandy.

For further reading, *Sherry* by Julian Jeffs.

PORT

Port comes from the Douro region in northern Portugal. In fact, in recent years, to avoid the misuse of the name "Port" in other countries, the true Port from Portugal has been renamed "Porto" or "Oporto" (for the name of the Port from which it's shipped).

Just a reminder: neutral grape brandy is added to Port *during* fermentation, which stops the fermentation and leaves behind up to 8 percent residual sugar. This is why Port is on the sweet side.

There are two types of Port:

Wood Port—This type includes Ruby Port, which is dark and fruity, blended from young non-vintage wines (Cost: $); and Tawny Port, which is lighter and more delicate, blended from many vintages, aged in casks—sometimes up to 20 years (Cost: $$/$$$).

Vintage Port—this wine is aged two years in wood and will mature in the bottle with time (Cost: $$$$).

Port is a blend of more than six grapes.

In the 1800s, Port wine was always shipped from Portugal to England. Because of the long voyage, the shippers fortified the Port with alcohol to preserve it for the trip. This resulted in Port as we know it today.

Port is usually 20% alcohol. Sherry, by comparison, is usually around 18%.

As with Sherry, evaporation is a problem—some 15,000 bottles evaporate into the air every year.

Another less expensive method of making Tawny Port is to add white Port to a young Tawny Port. A *true* Tawny Port is always expensive. You get what you pay for.

The production of vintage Port is very small—it only equals 3% of the harvest.

Is every year a vintage year for Port?

No, it varies from shipper to shipper. And in some years, no vintage Port is made at all. For example, in 1963 and 1970, two of the better vintages for Port, most producers declared a vintage. On the other hand, in 1962 and 1972, only four firms declared a vintage.

In recent years, vintage Port has become an extremely popular investment for Americans.

On average, only three years in ten are declared vintage years.

Wood Port vs. Vintage Port

The biggest difference between wood Port (Ruby and Tawny) and vintage Port is this: the wood Port is ready to drink as soon as you buy it. It will not improve with age. The vintage Port, on the other hand, gets better as it matures in the bottle. A great vintage Port will be ready to drink 15–30 years after the vintage date, depending upon the quality of the vintage.

Oporto has 51 lodges: a "lodge" is the term used to describe a Port firm.

In a typical year, 60% of the Port is Tawny and Ruby; 30% is vintage character; 7% is old Tawny; and 3% is vintage.

In Hong Kong, you'll sometimes see a separate label on Port which explains that very old, wood-aged Port is thought to be an aphrodisiac.

In France, the major importer of Port, the wine is used mainly as an apéritif.

85–90% of the Port made in Portugal is for export.

How do I buy Port?

Once again, as with Sherry, the grape variety should not dictate your choice. Find the style and the blend that you prefer, but even more important, look for the most reliable producers. Of the Port available in the United States, the most important producers are the following:

- Cockburn
- Croft
- Dow
- A. A. Ferreira
- Fonseca
- W. & J. Graham
- Robertson's
- Sandeman
- Taylor Fladgate
- Warre & Co.
- Niepoort & Co. Ltd.
- Porto Noval
- Harvey's of Bristol

Best Bets for Vintages of Port

1963 1970 1977

Should vintage Port be decanted?

Yes, because you are likely to find sediment in the bottle. By making it a practice to decant vintage Port, you'll never be bothered by sediment.

How long will Port last once it's been opened?

Port has a tendency to last longer than ordinary table wine because of its higher alcoholic content. But if you want to drink Port at its prime, you should consume the open bottle within one week.

The British are known to be Port lovers. Traditionally, upon the birth of a child, parents buy a pipe (700 bottles) of Port to put away for the baby until its 21st birthday: not only the age of maturity of a child, but also that of a fine Port.

A NOTE ON OTHER WINE-PRODUCING REGIONS

Many countries and their wines have not been included in this book. This is not to say that the only fine wine production comes from the regions covered in the Windows on the World Wine School. Many excellent wine books are available that cover these countries in the detail they deserve.

I would recommend that you continue expanding on your knowledge and not overlook the wines of: Argentina, Australia, Austria, Chile, Greece, Hungary, Israel, Romania, South Africa, Switzerland, and Yugoslavia.

The author teaches a class at the Windows on the World Wine School.

ON TASTING WINE

You can read all the books written on wine (and there are plenty) to become more knowledgeable on the subject, but you should *taste* wines to truly enhance your understanding. Reading covers the more academic side of wine, while tasting is more enjoyable and practical. A little of each will do you the most good.

Believe me, *books* have been written just on how to taste wine. You are about to learn the necessary steps. You may wish to follow them with a glass of wine in hand.

Wine tasting can be broken down into five basic steps: Color, Swirl, Smell, Taste, and Savor.

1. **Color**—The best way to get an idea of the color of the wine is to get a white background—a napkin or a linen tablecloth—and hold the glass of wine in front of it. The range of colors that you may see depends, of course, on whether you're tasting a white or red wine. Here are the colors for both:

White Wine	Red Wine
pale yellow-green	purple
straw yellow	ruby
yellow-gold	red
gold	brick red
old gold	red-brown
yellow-brown	brown
maderized	
brown	

Color tells you a lot about the wine. For instance, white wines, as they get older, gain color. Red wines, on the other hand, as they get older, lose color.

Since we started with the white wines, I'll tell you three reasons why a white wine may have more color:

1. It's older.
2. *Different grape varieties give different color.* (For example, Chardonnay usually gives off a deeper color than Riesling.)
3. The wine was aged in wood.

In class, I always begin by asking my students what color the wine is. It's not unusual to hear that some believe the wine is pale yellow-green, while others say it's gold. Everyone begins with the same wine in front of him, but there are several different perceptions of color. So you can imagine what happens when we actually *taste* the wine!

2. **Swirl**—Why do we swirl the wine? To allow oxygen to get into it. I'm not sure if you're ready for this yet, but I'll give it to you straight: Swirling releases the esters, ethers, and aldehydes combined with oxygen to yield the bouquet of the wine. In other words, swirling aerates the wine and gives you the bouquet.

   Everyone does a great job swirling wine. You can do it any way you want—with your left hand, your right hand, with two fingers, behind your back. . . . But I must warn you right now: You will start swirling everything—your milk, soft drinks, your morning coffee. You're going to have some serious problems, but you'll get used to it.

3. **Smell**—Now that you've swirled the wine and released the bouquet, what does the wine smell like? What type of *nose* does it have? The "nose" is the word that wine tasters use to describe the bouquet and aroma of the wine. This is another very important step in the tasting process that people simply don't spend enough time on. The same goes for looking at the color.

   The idea behind pinpointing the nose of the wine is to get you to identify certain characteristics. The problem here is that many people in class want to know exactly what the wine smells like. Since I prefer not to use pretentious words, I may say the wine smells like a French white Burgundy. Still, I find this does not satisfy the majority of the class. They want to know more. I ask these people to describe what steak and onions smell like. They answer, "Like steak and onions." See what I mean? The same is true for tomato sauce or a pine tree forest. What do they smell like? Tomato sauce and a pine tree forest.

For those who remain unconvinced, I hand out a list of 500 different words commonly used to describe wine. Here is a small excerpt from that list:

acetic	earthy	nose
aftertaste	finish	nutty
aroma	flat	off
astringent	fresh	oxidized
austere	grapey	petillance
baked-burnt	green	short
balanced	hard	soft
big-full-heavy	hot	stalky
bitter	legs	sulphury
body	light	tart
bouquet	maderized	thin
character	mature	tired
corky	metallic	vanilla
delicate	mouldy	woody
	yeasty	young

Another question inevitably comes up. People often ask me, "What kind of wine do *you* like?" I'd have to say I like my wine bright, rich, mature, developed, seductive, and with nice legs.

Another interesting point is that you're more likely to recognize some of the defects of a wine through your sense of smell. Below is a list of some of the negative smells in wine:

The Most Common Negative Smells in Wine

Smell	**Why**
Vinegar	Too much acetic acid in wine
Sherry	Oxidation
Cork	Wine absorbs taste of defective cork
Sulphur (burnt matches)	Too much sulphur dioxide

Sulphur dioxide is used in many ways for winemaking. It kills bacteria in wine, prevents unwanted fermentation and acts as a preservative. However, a good wine should never have the smell of sulphur dioxide. This smell creates a burning and itching sensation in your nose.

4. **Taste**—To most people, tasting wine means taking a sip and swallowing immediately. This is not tasting. Tasting is something you do with your taste buds. And remember, you have taste buds all over your mouth. They're on both sides of the tongue, underneath, on the tip, and they extend to the back of your throat. If you do what most people do, you take a gulp of wine and bypass all of those important taste buds.

   There's an old saying in the wine industry: "Buy on apples; sell on cheese." Apples bring out any defects you may find in a wine, whereas cheese has a tendency to smooth over them, leaving you with a more pleasing taste sensation.

What *should you think about when tasting wine?*

Be aware of the most important sensations of taste and where they occur on your tongue and in your mouth.

The Many Tastes of Wine

Sweetness—Found on the tip of the tongue. If there is any sweetness in a wine whatsoever, you'll get it right away since the tip of your tongue is sensitive.

Fruit and Varietal Characteristics—Found in the middle of the tongue.

Acidity—Found at the sides of the tongue and cheek area. It is most commonly present in white wines.

Tannin—Found in the middle of the tongue. Tannin frequently exists in red wines or wood-aged white wines. It dries the palate to excess when the wines are too young.

Aftertaste—This is the overall taste that lingers after you taste the wine. How long does the taste linger? Usually a sign of a high-quality wine is a long, pleasing aftertaste—15 to 20 seconds after you've swallowed it.

Note: Everything we've discussed so far—the color, the swirling, the nose and the taste—happens within 30 seconds!

5. **Savor**—After you've had a chance to taste the wine, sit back for a few moments and savor it. Think about what you just experienced and ask yourself the following questions to help focus your impressions. Was the wine:
   - Light, medium, or full-bodied?
   - For a white wine: How was the acidity? Very little, just right, or too much?
   - For red wine: Is the tannin in the wine too strong or astringent? Is it pleasing? Or is it missing?
   - How long did the aftertaste last?
   - Most importantly, did you like the wine?
   - Is the wine worth the price to your taste?

This brings us to another important point. The first thing you should consider after you've tasted a wine is whether or not you like it. Is it your style?

You can compare tasting wine to browsing in an art gallery. You wander from room to room looking at the paintings. Your first impression tells whether you like one or not. Once you decide you like a piece of art, you want to know more: Who was the artist? What is the history behind the work? How was it done? And so it is with wine. Usually, once oenophiles discover a new wine that they like, they have to know all about it—the winemaker, the grapes, exactly where the crop was planted, the blend if any, and the history behind the wine.

How do you know if a wine is good or not?

The definition of a good wine is one that you enjoy. *Please do not let others dictate taste to you!*

When is a wine ready to drink?

This is one of the most frequently asked questions at the Windows on the World Wine School. The answer is very simple—when all components of the wine are in balance to your particular taste.

For further reading: Michael Broadbent's *Pocket Guide to Wine Tasting*.

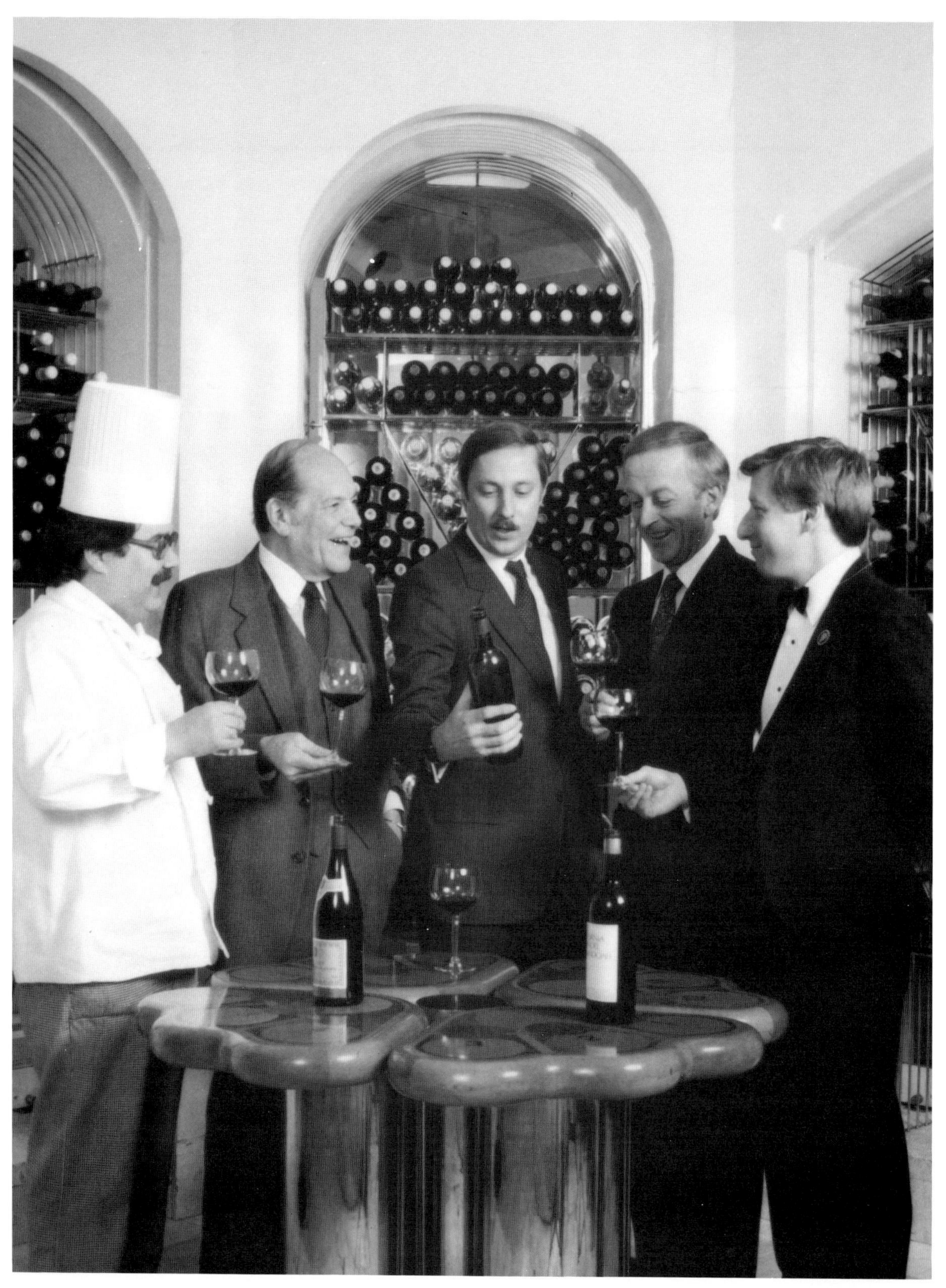

Chef Hermann Reiner, Alan Lewis, Kevin Zraly, Toni Aigner, and Barry Mills make selections for the wine list

CREATING AN EXEMPLARY WINE LIST

Anyone who is even marginally aware of market trends knows that the popularity of wine has increased dramatically. Wine lists are no longer the province of an elite group of high-ticket, white-tablecloth culinary temples. There are ever-increasing ranks of customers who actively seek to enjoy wine in restaurants of all price levels.

To attract these potential customers, many a restaurateur has toyed with the idea of revamping and expanding his wine list. Yet, when confronted with the stark reality of such a task, many panic and accept the judgment of others who have their own profit motives in mind. Once the restaurateur has acknowledged that it's time to start carrying more than house red, white, and rosé wines, he must lay the groundwork for building a list.

If you use the step-by-step method which follows, your wine list should complement your menu offerings, be attractively priced, offer an appealing selection, and be easy for the customer to select from and understand.

To illustrate: The hypothetical restaurant to which you've just taken the deed is a picturesque 100-seat establishment located in a moderately sized city. Your restaurant is open for both lunch and dinner and does not possess any definite ethnic identity, falling under that umbrella label of "continental."

You're looking for an average check of $25 per person (including wine). The menu features five appetizers, among them such classics as oysters on the half shell, shrimp cocktail, and duck liver terrine. Two soups are offered daily and there are ten different entrees, which reflect contemporary trends composed of three red meat, four fish, two poultry, and one pasta. Five desserts complete the menu card.

Here's a step-by-step procedure in question-and-answer format for building a wine list for your restaurant:

What is your competition?

Before you start to consider which châteaus to choose, or fret about whether to have 40 or 400 wines, take the time to investigate your market. Visit both the restaurants that attract the clientele you're aiming at (your target market) and the ones above and below your scale. Study how they merchandise wine, how well their staff serves it, and obtain a copy of their wine list—provided it's not chained to the sommelier's neck. Go during a busy dinner hour and observe how many bottles of wine are nestled in ice buckets or present on tables. Get a feeling of your competition's commitment to wine. See what is being done in your area, and what has yet to be done.

Can wine distributors offer help?

Contact the various suppliers in your area and explain to them what your objectives are. Ask them to suggest a hypothetical wine list—you're under no obligation to use it. Many wine distributors have specially trained people to work with restaurants on their wine lists. They can also suggest ways of merchandising and promotion. Use them as a resource.

What is your storage capacity?

Wine requires specific storage conditions: temperature of 55°F. (12.8°C.), away from direct sunlight and excessive vibrations. Your wine storage does not belong next to the dishwashing machine or the loading deck. How large a space do you have? Does it allow room for shelving? You'll want to store the bottles on their sides. How accessible is the wine to service personnel?

What are the preferences of your consumers?

Preliminary research reveals that in the United States, 75 percent of the wine consumed is domestic and 25 percent is imported. The consumer preferences of our target audience are predominantly for American and French wines. Given the present weakness of the French franc against the dollar, we decided to use the exchange rate to our advantage by purchasing a higher proportion of French wines than we might if the franc was stronger.

How long should your list be?

This is, in part, determined by storage space and capital investment. For our hypothetical restaurant, we decided to feature 60 wines on the list. Initially, this might seem like a lot for a 100-seat restaurant, but consider that those wines will be divided between sparkling, red, white, and rosé, and encompass the regions of France, the United States, Italy, Spain, and Germany. Sixty is almost the minimum number which will allow you the flexibility to offer both a range of types and tastes and wine for special occasions, as well as for casual quaffing. We want our customers to know that wine matters in our restaurant.

What proportion of red to white?

There is a decided consumer preference for white wines in the present market, and our wine list will reflect this. If our entrees were primarily red meats, we would ignore these figures and lean more heavily towards reds because of their suitability to the menu offerings. However, our hypothetical restaurant has only three red meat entrees out of ten, so the decision to feature more whites than reds is a sound one, based on both market trends and wine/food combinations.

How should prices be set?

Don't plan on paying your mortgage with profits from your wine list. Pricing is dictated according to your selections. We would like 60 percent of these wines to be moderately priced. Why? Because this is the price category in which the highest volume of sales will take place. For our purposes, mid-priced wines sell between $14 and $18. Therefore, we want 36 of our wines priced in this range. Of the remaining wines, 20 percent (12 wines) would be priced less than $14 and 20 percent more than $18.

The percentage of profit realized on wine is less than on cocktails. However, the dollar-value profit is greater since the total sale is much more. Too many restaurateurs have intimidated much of the potential wine market by stocking only very rare, expensive wines and pricing them into the stratosphere. You want a wine list that will enable all your customers to enjoy a bottle (or two) of wine with their meal, without having to float a bank loan. The bulk of your customers are looking for a good wine at a fair price—not a rare vintage at $400 a bottle.

What is your capital investment?

Determine, with your accountant, the amount of money that you will initially invest. Decide whether you want an inventory which will turn over in 30 to 60 days, or if you wish to make a long-term investment in cellaring wines. The majority of restaurants opt to make short-term wine investments.

What will it actually cost?

Once we've decided on the number of wines on the list, and the general pricing breakdown, it's an easy matter to determine what it will cost for one case of each wine. With some wines—the ones we anticipate will be very popular—our initial order will be for two cases, and on the more expensive wines, where sales may be sluggish, we will start off with a half case. Our 60-wine list will require an initial investment of approximately $5,000. Here's how we arrived at that ballpark figure:

Low-priced wines:
12 cases @ $48 per case $576.00
Medium-priced wines:
36 cases @ $96 per case $3,456.00
High-priced wines:
12 cases @ $120 per case $1,440.00
5,472.00

What categories of wine should be used?

Our wine list includes six sparkling wines (three French, two American, and one Spanish). There are 32 white ones, 20 red, and two rosé, for a grand total of 60. Here is one example of how the categories might be broken down. Of course, each restaurant should choose the wines according to availability and price.

White wines (32)

French Whites (12)
2 Mâcon Blanc
2 Chablis (1 Appellation Contrôlée, 1 Premier Cru)
1 Meursault
1 Puligny-Montrachet
1 Pouilly-Fuissé
1 Pouilly-Fumé or Sancerre
2 Alsatian (1 Riesling, 1 Gewürztraminer)
2 Bordeaux (1 Graves, 1 Sauternes)

American (12)
1 Riesling
1 Chenin Blanc
2 Sauvignon Blanc
8 Chardonnay

Italian (4)
1 Soave
1 Verdicchio
1 Orvieto
1 Pinot Grigio

German (4)
2 Rhein (1 Kabinett, 1 Spätlese)
1 Liebfraumilch
1 Mosel (Kabinett)

Red wines (20)

French (9)
1 Beaujolais
3 Burgundy (such as Nuits-St-Georges, Pommard, Volnay)
3 Bordeaux (different price categories)
2 Rhône Valley (1 Côtes du Rhône, 1 Chateauneuf-du-Pape or Hermitage)

American (8)
1 Merlot
1 Pinot Noir
2 Zinfandel
4 Cabernet Sauvignon

Italian (3)
1 Chianti
1 Bardolino or Valpolicella
1 Barolo

Rosé wines* (2)

1 French Tavel Rosé
1 American Rosé
*The rosés of Portugal are popular and might be considered for the list.

Should I buy wine without tasting it?

Tasting the wines for the list is of utmost importance. If you've decided to feature a Meursault, contact your distributors and ask to taste all the Meursaults that conform to your criteria of availability and price. Tasting the wines blind will help you make selections on the basis of quality rather than label. These tastings represent quite an investment of time. To choose a wine list of 60 wines, you could easily taste three times that many.

Once you've narrowed the field, try pairing the wines with your menu offerings. If possible, include your staff in these tastings. The more familiar they are with the wines on the list and the foods they complement, the better they'll be able to sell your selections.

Recheck the availability of your selected wines. Place your orders. Remember, you don't have to buy 25 cases of each wine—you might initially purchase just six bottles of the more expensive wines.

What goes on the wine list?

There are many different styles of wine lists. Some opt for long descriptions of the wine's characteristics and feature facts and maps of viticultural regions.

For our restaurant, we're going to adopt a very straightforward approach. The list is divided into categories by type and each type is divided into regions. The progression is: sparkling wine, white, red, and rosé.

Our French wines will be broken down into regions—Alsace, Burgundy, Bordeaux, and so on. Each entry on the wine list will give the following information:

Bin Number—This simplifies inventory and reordering, and assists both customer and staff with difficult pronunciation.
Name of Wine—Be precise.
Vintage—This is often omitted on wine lists by restaurateurs who want to be able to substitute whatever they can get. This practice is resented by anyone with a passing interest in wine. If the wine is non-vintage, the letters "NV" are used.
Shipper—This information is very important for French wines, particularly those from the Burgundy region.

The type, style, and color of the paper you choose for your wine list are personal decisions. However, double-check all spelling and prices before it is sent to the printer. Your customers will be sure to point out any errors.

Your restaurant is open—what's next?

This is a guideline to establishing an initial list. At Windows on the World, with our high volume, we are continually updating and revising the list to meet the requirements of our customers and the ever-changing wine market.

Once your list has been implemented, it is imperative that you track wine sales to determine how successful the list has been. Analyze your wine list with respect to the following factors:

- The number of bottles sold per customer (divide the number of covers by the number of bottles).
- How much white wine to red (by percentage)—you might find that you need more or less whites, more or less reds.
- The average price of a bottle of wine sold in the first three months.
- The ten most popular wines on the list.

Instruct your staff to report any requests for wines not on the list.

The steps involved in compiling our hypothetical list of 60 wines are the same steps that are used in compiling larger, more ambitious lists. Obviously, this list only highlights the major areas—60 wines barely scratch the surface of what is available. True, with this size restriction we are unable to give much depth of selection, but it is a list where the average customer would find something appealing.

If you have taken the time to read this section, you now have a good idea of the detail involved in creating a balanced wine list. For most restaurateurs, who have many other pressing concerns and responsibilities, the logistics of creating a wine list may seem Olympian. This checklist was offered to take some of the mystery out of this task.

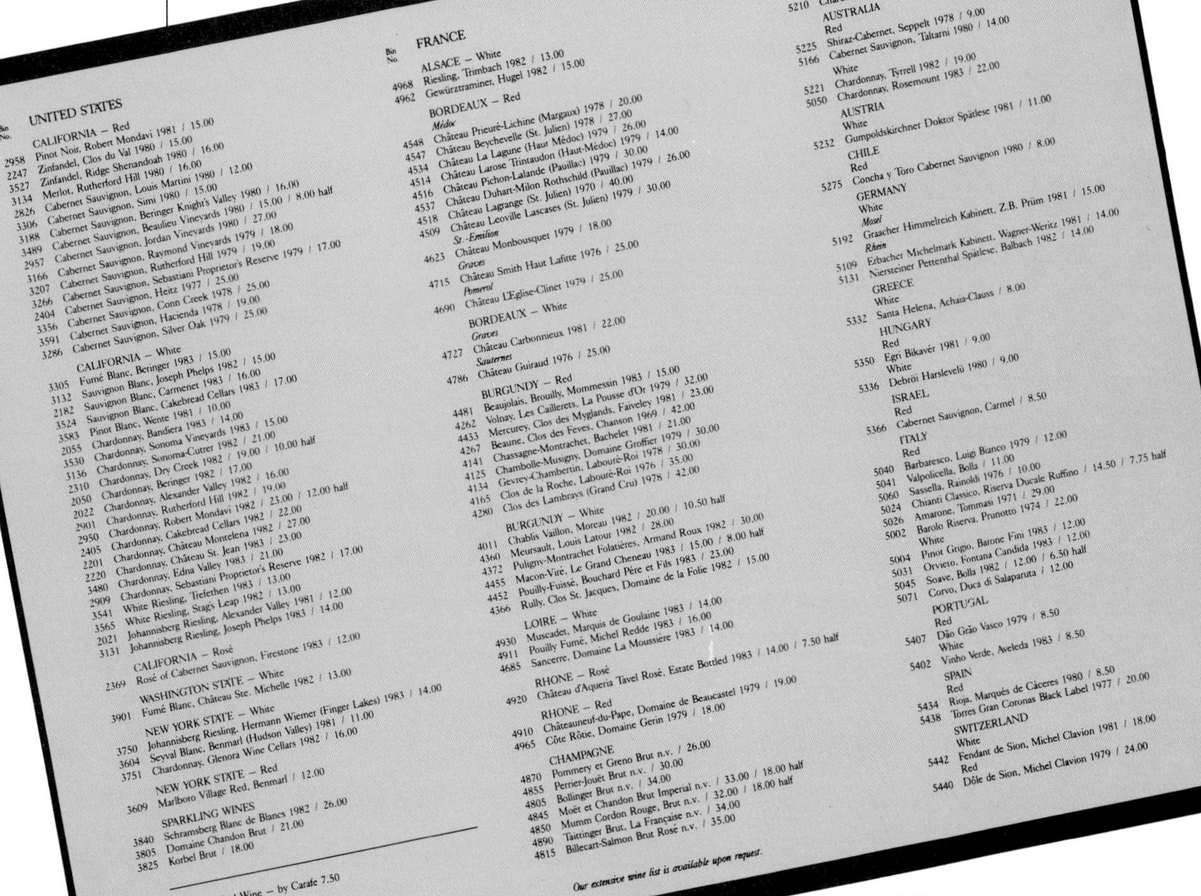

Bin No.

UNITED STATES

CALIFORNIA – Red
2958 Pinot Noir, Robert Mondavi 1981 / 15.00
2247 Zinfandel, Clos du Val 1980 / 15.00
3527 Zinfandel, Ridge Shenandoah 1980 / 16.00
3134 Merlot, Rutherford Hill 1980 / 16.00
2826 Cabernet Sauvignon, Louis Martini 1980 / 12.00
3306 Cabernet Sauvignon, Simi 1980 / 15.00
3188 Cabernet Sauvignon, Beringer Knight's Valley 1980 / 16.00
3489 Cabernet Sauvignon, Beaulieu Vineyards 1980 / 15.00 / 8.00 half
2957 Cabernet Sauvignon, Jordan Vineyards 1980 / 27.00
3166 Cabernet Sauvignon, Raymond Vineyards 1979 / 18.00
3207 Cabernet Sauvignon, Rutherford Hill 1979 / 19.00
3266 Cabernet Sauvignon, Sebastiani Proprietor's Reserve 1979 / 17.00
2404 Cabernet Sauvignon, Heitz 1977 / 25.00
3356 Cabernet Sauvignon, Conn Creek 1978 / 25.00
3591 Cabernet Sauvignon, Hacienda 1978 / 19.00
3286 Cabernet Sauvignon, Silver Oak 1979 / 25.00

CALIFORNIA – White
3305 Fumé Blanc, Beringer 1983 / 15.00
3132 Sauvignon Blanc, Joseph Phelps 1982 / 15.00
2182 Sauvignon Blanc, Carmenet 1983 / 16.00
3524 Sauvignon Blanc, Cakebread Cellars 1983 / 17.00
3583 Pinot Blanc, Wente 1981 / 10.00
2055 Chardonnay, Bandiera 1983 / 14.00
3530 Chardonnay, Sonoma Vineyards 1983 / 15.00
3136 Chardonnay, Sonoma-Cutrer 1982 / 21.00
2310 Chardonnay, Dry Creek 1982 / 19.00 / 10.00 half
2050 Chardonnay, Beringer 1982 / 17.00
2022 Chardonnay, Alexander Valley 1982 / 16.00
2901 Chardonnay, Rutherford Hill 1982 / 19.00
2950 Chardonnay, Robert Mondavi 1982 / 23.00 / 12.00 half
2405 Chardonnay, Cakebread Cellars 1982 / 22.00
2201 Chardonnay, Château Montelena 1982 / 27.00
2220 Chardonnay, Château St. Jean 1983 / 23.00
3480 Chardonnay, Edna Valley 1983 / 21.00
2909 Chardonnay, Sebastiani Proprietor's Reserve 1982 / 17.00
3541 White Riesling, Trefethen 1983 / 13.00
3565 White Riesling, Stag's Leap 1982 / 13.00
2021 Johannisberg Riesling, Alexander Valley 1981 / 12.00
3131 Johannisberg Riesling, Joseph Phelps 1983 / 14.00

CALIFORNIA – Rosé
2369 Rosé of Cabernet Sauvignon, Firestone 1983 / 12.00

WASHINGTON STATE – White
3901 Fumé Blanc, Château Ste. Michelle 1982 / 13.00

NEW YORK STATE – White
3750 Johannisberg Riesling, Hermann Wiemer (Finger Lakes) 1983 / 14.00
3604 Seyval Blanc, Benmarl (Hudson Valley) 1981 / 11.00
3751 Chardonnay, Glenora Wine Cellars 1982 / 16.00

NEW YORK STATE – Red
3609 Marlboro Village Red, Benmarl / 12.00

SPARKLING WINES
3840 Schramsberg Blanc de Blancs 1982 / 26.00
3805 Domaine Chandon Brut / 21.00
3825 Korbel Brut / 18.00

White and Red Wine – by Carafe 7.50

Bin No.

FRANCE

ALSACE – White
4968 Riesling, Trimbach 1982 / 13.00
4962 Gewürztraminer, Hugel 1982 / 15.00

BORDEAUX – Red
Médoc
4548 Château Prieuré-Lichine (Margaux) 1978 / 20.00
4547 Château Beychevelle (St. Julien) 1978 / 27.00
4534 Château La Lagune (Haut Médoc) 1979 / 26.00
4514 Château Larose Trintaudon (Haut-Médoc) 1979 / 14.00
4516 Château Pichon-Lalande (Pauillac) 1979 / 30.00
4537 Château Duhart-Milon Rothschild (Pauillac) 1979 / 26.00
4518 Château Lagrange (St. Julien) 1970 / 40.00
4509 Château Leoville Lascases (St. Julien) 1979 / 30.00
St.-Emilion
4623 Château Monbousquet 1979 / 18.00
Graves
4715 Château Smith Haut Lafitte 1976 / 25.00
Pomerol
4690 Château L'Eglise-Clinet 1979 / 25.00

BORDEAUX – White
Graves
4727 Château Carbonnieux 1981 / 22.00
Sauternes
4786 Château Guiraud 1976 / 25.00

BURGUNDY – Red
4481 Beaujolais, Brouilly, Mommessin 1983 / 15.00
4262 Volnay, Les Caillerets, La Pousse d'Or 1979 / 32.00
4433 Mercurey, Clos des Myglands, Faiveley 1981 / 23.00
4267 Beaune, Clos des Feves, Chanson 1969 / 42.00
4141 Chassagne-Montrachet, Bachelet 1981 / 21.00
4125 Chambolle-Musigny, Domaine Groffier 1979 / 30.00
4134 Gevrey-Chambertin, Labouré-Roi 1978 / 30.00
4165 Clos de la Roche, Labouré-Roi 1976 / 35.00
4280 Clos des Lambrays (Grand Cru) 1978 / 42.00

BURGUNDY – White
4011 Chablis Vaillon, Moreau 1982 / 20.00 / 10.50 half
4360 Meursault, Louis Latour 1982 / 28.00
4372 Puligny-Montrachet Folatières, Armand Roux 1982 / 30.00
4455 Macon-Viré, Le Grand Cheneau 1983 / 15.00 / 8.00 half
4452 Pouilly-Fuissé, Bouchard Pére et Fils 1983 / 23.00
4366 Rully, Clos St. Jacques, Domaine de la Folie 1982 / 15.00

LOIRE – White
4930 Muscadet, Marquis de Goulaine 1983 / 14.00
4911 Pouilly Fumé, Michel Redde 1983 / 16.00
4685 Sancerre, Domaine La Moussière 1983 / 14.00

RHONE – Rosé
4920 Château d'Aqueria Tavel Rosé, Estate Bottled 1983 / 14.00 / 7.50 half

RHONE – Red
4910 Châteauneuf-du-Pape, Domaine de Beaucastel 1979 / 19.00
4965 Côte Rôtie, Domaine Gerin 1979 / 18.00

CHAMPAGNE
4870 Pommery et Greno Brut n.v. / 26.00
4855 Perrier-Jouët Brut n.v. / 30.00
4805 Bollinger Brut n.v. / 34.00
4845 Moët et Chandon Brut Imperial n.v. / 33.00 / 18.00 half
4850 Mumm Cordon Rouge, Brut n.v. / 32.00 / 18.00 half
4890 Taittinger Brut, La Française n.v. / 34.00
4815 Billecart-Salmon Brut Rosé n.v. / 35.00

Our extensive wine list is available upon request.

Bin No.

ARGENTINA
White
5210 Chardonnay, Andean / 9.00

AUSTRALIA
Red
5225 Shiraz-Cabernet, Seppelt 1978 / 9.00
5166 Cabernet Sauvignon, Taltarni 1980 / 14.00
White
5221 Chardonnay, Tyrrell 1982 / 19.00
5050 Chardonnay, Rosemount 1983 / 22.00

AUSTRIA
White
5232 Gumpoldskirchner Doktor Spätlese 1981 / 11.00

CHILE
Red
5275 Concha y Toro Cabernet Sauvignon 1980 / 8.00

GERMANY
White
Mosel
5192 Graacher Himmelreich Kabinett, Z.B. Prüm 1981 / 15.00
Rhein
5109 Erbacher Michelmark Kabinett, Wagner-Weritz 1981 / 14.00
5131 Niersteiner Pettenthal Spätlese, Balbach 1982 / 14.00

GREECE
White
5332 Santa Helena, Achaia-Clauss / 8.00

HUNGARY
Red
5350 Egri Bikavér 1981 / 9.00
White
5336 Debröi Harslevelü 1980 / 9.00

ISRAEL
Red
5366 Cabernet Sauvignon, Carmel / 8.50

ITALY
Red
5040 Barbaresco, Luigi Bianco 1979 / 12.00
5041 Valpolicella, Bolla / 11.00
5060 Sassella, Rainoldi 1976 / 10.00
5024 Chianti Classico, Riserva Ducale Ruffino / 14.50 / 7.75 half
5026 Amarone, Tommasi 1971 / 29.00
5002 Barolo Riserva, Prunotto 1974 / 22.00
White
5004 Pinot Grigio, Barone Fini 1983 / 12.00
5031 Orvieto, Fontana Candida 1983 / 12.00
5045 Soave, Bolla 1982 / 12.00 / 6.50 half
5071 Corvo, Duca di Salaparuta / 12.00

PORTUGAL
Red
5407 Dão Grão Vasco 1979 / 8.50
White
5402 Vinho Verde, Aveleda 1983 / 8.50

SPAIN
Red
5434 Rioja, Marqués de Cáceres 1980 / 8.50
5438 Torres Gran Coronas Black Label 1977 / 20.00

SWITZERLAND
White
5442 Fendant de Sion, Michel Clavion 1981 / 18.00
Red
5440 Dôle de Sion, Michel Clavion 1979 / 24.00

The Cellar in the Sky at Windows on the World.

WINE IN RESTAURANTS—WHAT'S RITUAL AND WHAT'S REQUIRED

By Raymond Wellington

The wine boom of the 1970s and '80s has brought consumers a greater awareness of how wine is presented in American restaurants. Many people learn about wines by ordering them in restaurants, which offer them the opportunity to sample and experiment, not only with wine, but with wine and food combinations. Decisions about how to stock a home cellar are frequently reached in this way. In restaurants noted for their wine lists, there is often the added pleasure of drinking a wine that is no longer available in retail stores.

Unfortunately, many restaurants have turned the simple task of ordering wine into a seemingly complex ritual involving sommeliers, *tastevins*, and intimidating lists that resemble telephone books. Add to that words such as "breathing" and "decanting," and you suddenly have a complicated situation on your hands.

Ordering wine need not be an intimidating ordeal. In fact, some restaurants make it relatively simple by providing straightforward wine lists and waiters or captains who have been properly trained to make sensible suggestions. Others make it more difficult, but whether you're in a grand, full-service restaurant or your favorite bistro, there are some basics to keep in mind.

The first problem you'll encounter often is actually obtaining the wine list. It's mystifying how difficult that can be sometimes. A restaurant genuinely interested in selling wine provides their list right along with the menu. If the wine list doesn't appear, or if you want to start the meal with wine before seeing a menu, then immediately ask for the list. With a little luck, they'll have more than one or two copies on hand!

Raymond Wellington is the director of wine services for Inhilco Inc., which includes Windows on the World.

The Wine List

Regardless of format, there is certain information that any good wine list should provide. First and foremost is the complete name of the wine. For example, if a wine list simply lists "Chambolle-Musigny," it is incomplete. It also means that they're going to make you work a little bit to find out exactly what wines they actually have. The complete name of the wine should be something like "Chambolle-Musigny, Domaine Groffier 1979." As you have learned by now, there could be many different producers of Chambolle-Musigny and which one can make a world of difference. The vintage is also essential: There is a vast difference between, say, a 1977 Chambolle-Musigny and one from 1979. If a wine is listed without a producer, or without a vintage, then ask the waiter. If the waiter doesn't know, let him or her find out and perhaps bring a bottle to show you.

The majority of American restaurants do not have wine stewards or *sommeliers*, as they're sometimes called. In restaurants that are concerned with their wine selections and service, waiters and waitresses are often trained to be able to suggest wines. If a sommelier is available, however, it is usually worth taking advantage of his or her services.

The Sommelier

"Who is that man with the ashtray around his neck?" It is commonplace, if not downright fashionable, to deride the sommelier as condescending, pretentious, less knowledgeable than his guests, and sporting an odd costume adorned with keys, "ashtrays" on chains (the *tastevin*), and other seemingly mystical paraphernalia. This tarnished image of the sommelier has resulted, at least in part, from the practice of restaurateurs who have misunderstood the position and appointed someone unqualified for the job. As restaurant patrons become more informed about wine, owners are realizing the importance of having someone in the dining room who can knowledgeably discuss wine selections.

Often when the services of a sommelier are available, the only way to find out is to ask. He or she need not be someone "to be reckoned with," but may be the one person who can help orchestrate and enliven your entire meal. Using a competent sommelier offers two advantages: He or she has tasted the wines on the list more recently than you and also knows how the menu items you ordered are actually being prepared.

selecting a wine

Whether you're ordering from a sommelier or a waiter, there are a number of points to keep in mind. First, it's perfectly reasonable to keep the list and look it over for a few minutes before discussing your choices.

Secondly, if you want suggestions, give the sommelier or waiter something to work with. Do you have a particular region in mind? For example, if you've been dreaming about a fabulous California Chardonnay all week, say so!

Next consider the style of wine you would like. Do you or your guests want something light and direct or do you prefer more aggressive, heavier wines? What price range are you thinking of? There's nothing wrong with saying you want something under $25. You can also do this by pointing to a price on the list and saying you want something "along these lines."

If wines are suggested that are not on the list, the waiter or sommelier should tell you the price along with the vintage, just as waiters and captains quote the prices of daily specials. If they don't tell you, then ask; no one wants to risk apoplexy when the check arrives!

When ordering more than one wine, discuss when the wines are to be served. The best rule of thumb is to have them all brought—and even opened—as soon as you order them. This enables you to see that the correct wine is at the table, and you don't have to worry that the waiter will be busy when you want it.

opening the wine

How often does it happen that after arriving at your selections you wait and watch as the waiter fumbles with the cork—perhaps even breaking it—before successfully withdrawing it from the bottle? There is a right and a wrong way to open a bottle of wine, or at least one method that works better than others.

Of the many different kinds of corkscrews and cork-pullers available, two or three seem most efficient. One is referred to as the "Ah-So." This is a cork-puller with two thin prongs and a handle. You slip the prongs in between the bottle neck and the cork with a rocking motion. A gentle twist and pull withdraws the cork easily. Ubiquitous in California, the main drawback of this type of cork-puller is that it does not have a knife with which to cut the capsule first, and some people claim it can push the cork back into the bottle.

The most efficient and easiest tool to use is the pocket model of the Screwpull, a patented device that includes a knife and a very long screw. Simply by turning it in one continuous direction, the cork is extracted effortlessly. This is the best type of corkscrew for home use and because it is gentle, it is best for removing long, fragile corks from older wines.

The corkscrew most commonly used in restaurants is the "waiters' corkscrew." Small and flat, it contains a knife, screw, and lever, all of which fold neatly into the handle.

When opening a wine bottle, the first step is to remove the capsule. You can accomplish this best by cutting around the neck on the underside of the lip. Once you remove the capsule, wipe the top of the cork clean—often dust or mould adheres to the cork while the wine is still at the winery before the capsule is put on the bottle. In the next step, you insert the screw and turn it so that it goes as deeply as possible into the cork. Sometimes you'll need to raise the cork slightly and then turn the screw a bit further into it. This prevents breaking the cork in two.

The Tasting Ritual

Once you extract the cork, the "tasting ritual" begins. At this point the waiter should present the cork to the person who ordered the wine. Most people believe they're supposed to sniff the cork. This is really unnecessary, as it is the wine itself you want to smell. After all, a cork smells like a cork! The cork is presented so you can check its condition and authenticity. A moist cork is a good sign, a dry cork suggests there may have been a storage problem. If a cork is dried out, air may have gotten into the bottle and oxidized the wine. A dried-out cork could mean the wine has been stored upright rather than on its side.

Smelling and tasting are obviously the next two steps. At this point you are looking for flaws that render the wine unacceptable. When tasting wine, remember that anyone may be unsure after the first taste. Taste it again, take a moment and concentrate.

There are several valid reasons to reject a bottle of wine. For example, a bottle of wine might be "corky" or "maderized." It does not take great tasting experience to detect these flaws. Having the experience even once is usually enough to lock it in your taste memory. A "corky" bottle is one that smells strongly of mould: the result of a bad cork, not poor winemaking. A maderized wine has the distinct aroma of sweet Sherry or Madeira, hence the term. This is frequently the result of poor storage or exposure to heat.

A more experienced taster may detect excessive sulphur in the nose and perhaps the taste of a wine. Often this dissipates with a bit of swirling; if it does not, it may make the wine unpleasant and worthy of rejection.

Policies regarding rejected wine vary among restaurants. Some restaurants will take a bottle back without a question; others may take issue with a guest's complaint. It is extremely poor business for a restaurateur to put a customer on the spot and challenge his or her taste. If a very expensive wine, say over $50, is rejected, it is not uncommon for a restaurant owner or manager to come to the table and taste the wine.

Many places have no established policy, but handle each situation individually. At Windows on the World, incidentally, out of 10,000 bottles of wine sold in a month only about a dozen are sent back.

WINE GLASSES

Whether you're dining out or at home, the enjoyment of food and wine is enhanced by fine silver, china, linen, and, of course, glassware. Wine glasses that are artfully etched, rose-tinted or perhaps green-stemmed may be lovely to look at and handle, but they're not really appropriate for the service of fine wine. The color of wine is as much a part of its pleasure and appeal as its bouquet and flavor. Glasses which alter or obscure the color of wine detract from the wine itself. The most suitable wine glasses are those of clear glass with a bowl large enough to allow for swirling—that nervous habit which by now you have no doubt acquired!

The perfect size glass for a white or red wine is about ten ounces. To allow for swirling and the development of the wine's bouquet, a wine glass should not be filled more than halfway. Therefore, glasses that hold less than ten ounces are really too small. Although it's possible to find glasses as large as 20 or 24 ounces, these are unnecessary and often awkward to drink from.

A variety of shapes are available and personal preferences should guide you when selecting glasses for home use. Some shapes, however, are better suited for certain wines than for others. For example, a glass which closes in a bit at the top helps to concentrate the bouquet of a white wine and also helps it keep its chill. Larger, balloon-shaped glasses are more appropriate for red wines.

There are three popular styles of Champagne glasses. The most common and least desirable is the saucer-shaped *coupe*. Awkward to balance, these also tend to dissipate Champagne bubbles. If you consider how much effort has gone into getting those bubbles in the Champagne in the first place, you'll understand why the *coupe* glass is so inappropriate!

The most suitable Champagne glasses and the ones more and more restaurants are using are the tulip or Champagne flute. These narrow glasses hold between four and eight ounces, and they allow the bubbles to rise from a single point. The tulip shape also helps to concentrate the bouquet.

Port or Sherry is best served in smallish, narrow glasses with a straight chimney shape. Four to six ounces is the ideal size for this type.

The Decanting and Breathing Controversy

There is something romantic—if intimidating—conjured up by the image of a sommelier in black tie peering over a candle and solemnly pouring wine into a crystal decanter. There are good reasons for decanting a wine, although many restaurants go to an extreme: Either they decant far more wines than necessary, or they don't decant even those wines that require it. Where is the sensible ground in all of this and what is the best way to decant a bottle of wine?

There are two primary reasons for decanting wine: (1) to separate the wine from the sediment and (2) to aerate the wine. The rule of thumb we've established by experience at Windows on the World is this: Red wines ten years old or older need to be decanted. This is primarily because of sediment and is especially true of Bordeaux wines. However, many California Cabernet Sauvignons also begin to accumulate sediment after ten years. Burgundies tend to be more fragile, so care should be taken not to decant them too far in advance of when you want them served. In fact, many producers in the Burgundy region do not believe in decanting their wines at all, regardless of the sediment.

As far as aeration is concerned, no blanket rule applies to all red wines. Many theories have been put forth about the benefit to be derived from aerating or letting a wine "breathe" before serving it. Our experience at Windows on the World suggests that the vast majority of red wines do not improve with "breathing." There is no question that some wines do, but these are the exception and your own experience should serve as your guide. If you order a wine that you believe improves with a little bit of air, either have it decanted or at least have the wine poured into glasses that you can swirl rather than simply removing the cork and letting the bottle stand. This last option is at once the most common practice in restaurants and the least effective. Think about it: By simply removing the cork, how much air is actually in contact with the wine?

how to decant a bottle of wine

1. Completely remove the capsule from the neck of the bottle. This will enable you to see the wine clearly as it passes through the neck.
2. Light a candle. Most red wines are bottled in very dark green glass, making it difficult to see the wine pass through the neck of the bottle. A candle will give you the extra illumination you need. Anything else would do, but candles keep things simple.
3. Hold the decanter firmly in your left hand (if you are right-handed). A carafe or glass pitcher can also be used for this purpose.
4. Holding the wine bottle in your other hand, gently pour the wine into the decanter while holding both over the candle at such an angle that you can see the wine pass through the neck of the bottle.
5. Continue pouring in one uninterrupted motion until you begin to see the first signs of sediment.
6. Stop decanting once you begin to see sediment.

dining at the cellar in the sky

Whether you're in a restaurant or at home, it's often fun to plan a meal around a particular wine or a number of wines. Here are two menus from The Cellar in the Sky at Windows on the World, offering a dinner of seven courses designed around five different wines.

At the Cellar in the Sky, we like to begin dinner with a choice of apéritif: a glass of Champagne, a dry Sherry or a white wine Kir are appropriate. As most people like to progress from white to red, we then design a first course around a good California Chardonnay, white Burgundy, or a similar wine. With the main course, an appropriate red will complement duckling or veal or beef; lighter preparations generally require lighter-style wines. The progression then leads to cheeses that complement an older or more intense red wine.

THE
cellar
IN THE SKY

— Canapes —

— Summer Salad with Artichokes and Sweetbreads —

— Lobster Bisque —

THE CELLAR APERITIFS

— Filet of Sea Bass with Pepper Sabayon —

MEURSAULT LES GENEVRIERES, MOREY 1979

— Medallions of Beef with Sweet Garlic Sauce —

Confit of Zucchini and Tomatoes

SILVER OAK CABERNET SAUVIGNON 1978

— International Cheese Board —

BAROLO, VINICOLA PIEMONTESE 1970

— Gratin of Berries —

ELTVILLER LANGENSTÜCK AUSLESE 1976

COLOMBIAN COFFEE

— Petit Fours —

107th FLOOR/ONE WORLD TRADE CENTER/NEW YORK, N.Y. 10048/(212) 938-1111

Generally, we like to serve the dessert wine about ten minutes prior to the dessert itself. Experience has taught us that most desserts are considerably sweeter than dessert wines and tend to make the wines taste dry or unsuitable. Should you wish to serve a sweet wine with dessert, the most successful combinations are desserts based on a fruit, such as a pear or apricot tart, with a rich Sauternes, a German Beerenauslese, or a late harvest Riesling from California.

—**R.W.**

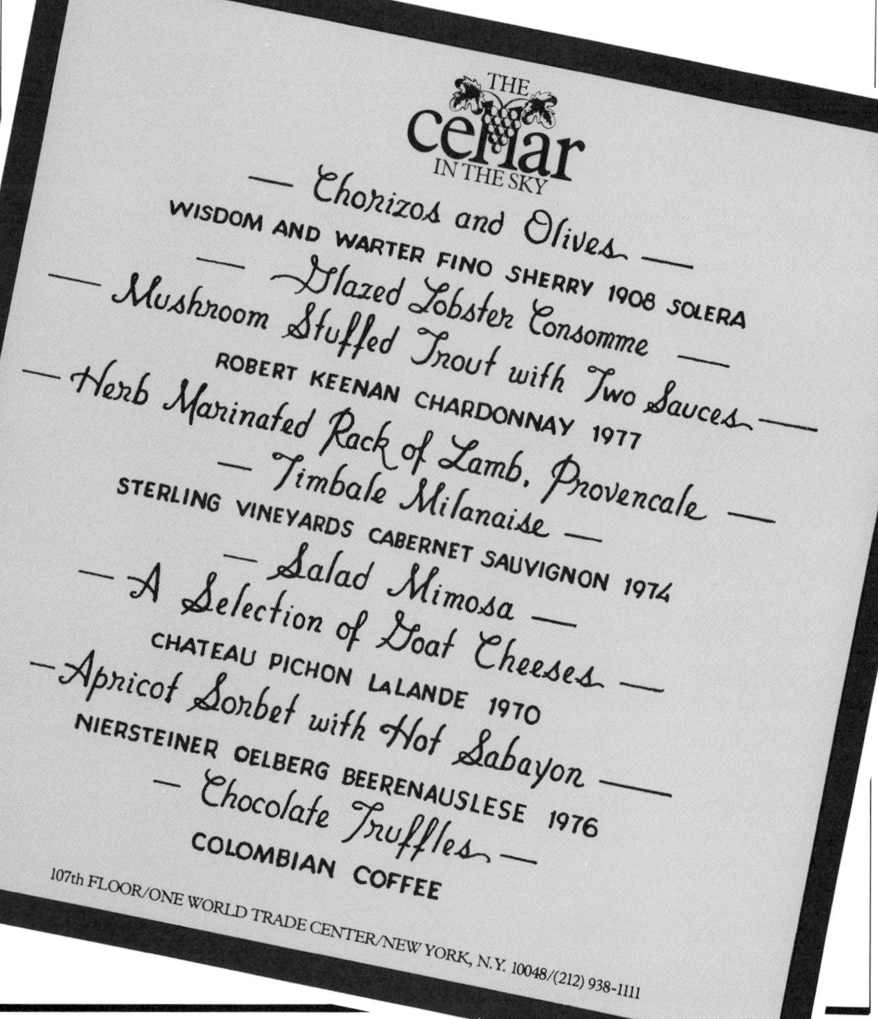

THE
Cellar
IN THE SKY

— Chorizos and Olives —
WISDOM AND WARTER FINO SHERRY 1908 SOLERA
— Glazed Lobster Consomme —
— Mushroom Stuffed Trout with Two Sauces —
ROBERT KEENAN CHARDONNAY 1977
— Herb Marinated Rack of Lamb, Provencale —
— Timbale Milanaise —
STERLING VINEYARDS CABERNET SAUVIGNON 1974
— Salad Mimosa —
— A Selection of Goat Cheeses —
CHATEAU PICHON LALANDE 1970
— Apricot Sorbet with Hot Sabayon —
NIERSTEINER OELBERG BEERENAUSLESE 1976
— Chocolate Truffles —
COLOMBIAN COFFEE

107th FLOOR/ONE WORLD TRADE CENTER/NEW YORK, N.Y. 10048/(212) 938-1111

AWARD-WINNING WINE LISTS

Excellent wine lists can be found at restaurants throughout the United States. The restaurants listed below were chosen by *The Wine Spectator*, the largest-selling wine newspaper in the United States, for having the best lists in the country.

CALIFORNIA

Ambrosia
695 Town Center Drive
Costa Mesa, California 92626
(714) 751-2829

La Bella Fontana
Beverly Wilshire Hotel
9500 Wilshire Boulevard
Beverly Hills, California 90212
(213) 275-4282

Blue Boar Inn
1713 Lombard Street
San Francisco, California 94123
(415) 567-8424

Carnelian Room
Bank of America Center
555 California Street
San Francisco, California 94104
(415) 433-7500

The Chronicle
897 Granite Drive
Pasadena, California 91101
(213) 792-1179

Doros
714 Montgomery Street
San Francisco, California 94111
(415) 367-6822

Elario's Summer House Inn
7955 La Jolla Shores Drive
La Jolla, California 92037
(619) 459-0541

Ernie's
847 Montgomery Street
San Francisco, California 94133
(415) 397-5969

Five Crowns
3801 East Coast Highway
Corona Del Mar, California 92625
(714) 760-0331

The French Room
Four Seasons Clift Hotel
Geary at Taylor Streets
San Francisco, California 94102
(415) 775-4700

Johnny's Restaurant
2250 East 17th Street
Santa Ana, California 92701
(714) 836-6722

Mr. Stox
1105 East Katella Avenue
Anaheim, California 92805
(714) 634-2994

Narsai's
385 Colusa Avenue
Kensington, California 94707
(415) 527-7900

La Rive Gauche
320 Tejon Place
Palos Verdes Estates, California 90274
(213) 378-0267

The Sardine Factory
701 Wave Street
Monterey, California 93940
(408) 373-3775

Scandia
9040 Sunset Boulevard
Los Angeles, California 90069
(213) 272-9521

Silverado Restaurant
1374 Lincoln Avenue
Calistoga, California 94515
(707) 942-6725

La Strega Ristorante
400 South Western Avenue
Los Angeles, California 90020
(213) 385-1546

Top o' the Cove
1216 Prospect
La Jolla, California 92037
(619) 454-7779

Valentino
3115 Pico Boulevard
Santa Monica, California 90405
(213) 283-0991

colorado

Flagstaff House Restaurant
Flagstaff Road
Boulder, Colorado 80302
(303) 442-4640

The Heritage Hotel
5150 South Quebec
Englewood, Colorado 80111
(303) 796-8966

district of columbia

Jean-Louis
The Watergate
2650 Virginia Avenue, N.W.
Washington D.C. 20037
(202) 298-4488

florida

Bern's Steak House
1208 South Howard Avenue
Tampa, Florida 33606
(813) 251-2421

The Breakers Hotel
1 South Country Road
Palm Beach, Florida 33480
(305) 655-6611

The Colony
1620 Gulf of Mexico
Longboat Key, Florida 33548
(813) 383-6464

The Down Under
3000 East Oakland Park Boulevard
Fort Lauderdale, Florida 33306
(305) 564-6984

The Forge
432 Arthur Godfrey Road
Miami Beach, Florida 33140
(305) 538-8533

Spinelli's Restaurant
1200 Pennsylvania Avenue
St. Cloud, Florida 32769
(305) 892-2435

ILLINOIS

The Dining Room
Ritz-Carlton Hotel
Water Tower Place
160 East Pearson
Chicago, Illinois 60611
(312) 266-1000

Italian Village Restaurant
71 West Monroe
Chicago, Illinois 60603
(312) 332-7005

The 95th Restaurant
The John Hancock Building
875 North Michigan Avenue
Chicago, Illinois 60611
(312) 787-9596

LOUISIANA

Brennan's Restaurant
417 Royal Street
New Orleans, Louisiana 70130
(504) 525-9711

MASSACHUSETTS

Anthony's Pier 4
140 Northern Avenue
Boston, Massachusetts 02210
(617) 482-6262

NEW YORK

The American Hotel
Main Street
Sag Harbor, New York 11963
(516) 725-3535

Lutèce
249 East 50th Street
New York, New York 10022
(212) 752-2225

Pierce's 1894 Restaurant
Oakwood & 14th Streets
Elmira Heights, New York 14903
(607) 734-2022

Sparks Steak House
210 East 46th Street
New York, New York 10017
(212) 687-4855

Windows on the World
One World Trade Center
107th Floor
New York, New York 10048
(212) 938-1111

OREGON

Salishan Lodge
Highway 101
Gleneden Beach, Oregon 97388
(503) 764-2371

VERMONT

The Hermitage
Coldbrook Road
Wilmington, Vermont 05363
(802) 464-3511

WASHINGTON

Rosellini's Other Place
319 Union Street
Seattle, Washington 98101
(206) 623-7340

Le Tastevin
19 West Harrison Street
Seattle, Washington 98119
(206) 283-0991

ENGLAND

Gidleigh Park
Chagford, Devon
England
(06473) 2225

FRANCE

Taillevent
15 rue Lamennais
Paris, France
563-39-94

ITALY

Enoteca Pinchiorri
Via Ghibelina, 87
Florence, Italy
055-24-27-77

Printed with permission from *The Wine Spectator*, 400 East 51st Street, New York, NY 10022.

Glossary

Acidity The amount of citric, tartaric, or malic acid in a wine.

Aligoté A white grape grown in the Burgundy region of France.

Amarone A type of Veronese wine made by a special process in which grapes are harvested late and allowed to raisinate; it has a high alcoholic content.

Amontillado A type of Sherry.

Anjou Rosé A rosé wine from the Loire Valley in France.

A.O.C. An abbreviation for Appellation d'Origine Contrôlée; the government agency that controls wine production in France.

A.P. number The official testing number displayed on a German wine label that shows the wine was tasted and passed government quality-control standards.

Aroma The smell of the grapes in a wine.

Barbaresco A full, red wine with a high alcoholic content from Piedmont, Italy.

Barbera A red grape grown in Piedmont, Italy.

Barolo A full, red wine with a high alcoholic content from Piedmont, Italy.

B.A.T.F. An abbreviation for Bureau of Alcohol, Tobacco, and Firearms; the government agency that controls wine production in the United States.

Beaujolais A light, fruity red Burgundy wine from the region of Beaujolais; in terms of quality, the basic Beaujolais.

Beaujolais Nouveau The "new" Beaujolais that is produced and delivered to your local retailer in a matter of weeks after the harvest.

Beaujolais Supérieur A Beaujolais wine that has more alcohol than regular Beaujolais.

Beaujolais-Villages A Beaujolais wine that comes from a blend from villages in the region; it is better quality than regular Beaujolais.

Beerenauslese A full, sweet white German wine made from the rich, ripe grapes affected by "noble rot."

Blanc de Blancs A white wine made from white grapes.

Blanc de Noir A white wine made from red grapes.

Botrytis cinerea ("Noble Rot") A mould that forms on the grapes that is necessary to make Sauternes, and the rich German wines (Beerenauslese and Trockenbeerenauslese).

Bouquet The smell of the wine.
Brix A measurement of the sugar level in a wine.
Brunello di Montalcino A high-quality red Italian wine from the Tuscany region.
Brut The driest-style Champagne.
Bung Cork.

Cabernet Franc A red grape of the Bordeaux region of France.
Cabernet Sauvignon The most important red grape grown in the world, which yields many of the great wines of Bordeaux and California.
Canaiolo A red grape grown in Italy.
Chablis The northernmost region in Burgundy that produces only white wine; a wine that comes from grapes grown anywhere in the Chablis district.
Chablis Grand Cru The highest classification of Chablis in terms of quality.
Chablis Premier Cru A good-quality Chablis that comes from a specific vineyard or a blend of vineyards.
Champagne The region in France that produces authentic Champagne.
Chaptalization The addition of sugar to the must (fresh grape juice) before fermentation.
Chardonnay The most important and expensive white grape grown primarily in the Burgundy and Champagne regions of France and California.
Charmat process A method sometimes used to produce sparkling wine; the second fermentation takes place in a large container instead of the individual bottle.
Château The "legal" definition is a house attached to a vineyard having a specific number of acres with winemaking and storage facilities on the property.
Château wine Usually of the best quality, this wine is the product of an individual château.
Chateauneuf-du-Pape A red wine from the southern Rhône Valley region of France; it means "new castle of the Pope."
Chenin Blanc A white grape grown in the Loire Valley region of France and California.
Chianti A basic red wine from the Tuscany region of Italy.
Chianti Classico One step above Chianti in terms of quality, this wine is from an inner district of Chianti.
Chianti Classico Riserva The best quality level of Italian Chianti; it is aged for a minimum of three years.

Cinsault A red grape from the Rhône Valley region of France.

Classified châteaus The châteaus in the Bordeaux region of France that are known to produce the best white wine.

Concord A red grape used to make some New York State wines.

Claret A dry red wine from the Bordeaux region of France.

Colheita The term meaning "vintage" in Portuguese.

Cosecha The term meaning "harvest" in Spanish.

Côte Rôtie A red wine from the northern Rhône Valley region of France.

Coupe A saucer-shaped glass sometimes used to drink Champagne; it is more appropriate for a fruit cup or sherbet.

Cream Sherry A type of Sherry made from a mixture of Pedro Ximénez and Oloroso.

Crozes-Hermitage A red wine from the northern Rhône Valley region.

Cru Growth or vineyard.

Cru Beaujolais The top grade of Beaujolais wine that comes from one of the nine highest-quality villages in Beaujolais.

Cru Bourgeois A subdivision of wines included on the Official Classification of 1855 in Bordeaux.

Dão A red or white Portuguese wine.

Decanting The process of pouring wine from its bottle to a carafe to separate the sediment from the wine.

Dégorgement One step of the Champagne-making process used to expel the sediment from the bottle.

Demi-sec The sweetest-style Champagne.

D.O.C. An abbreviation for Denominazione di Origine Controllata; the government agency that controls wine production in Italy.

D.O.C.G. An abbreviation for Denominazione di Origine Controllata Garantita; the Italian government allows this marking to appear only on the finest wines. The "G" stands for "Guaranteed."

Dolcetto A red wine from Piedmont, Italy, that is similar in style to a Beaujolais wine.

Dosage A combination of wine and cane sugar that is used in making Champagne.

Eau de vie A fruit brandy that comes in a variety of flavors.

Edelfäule (*See also Botrytis cinerea and "Noble Rot"*) A German name for the mould that forms on the grape vines when the conditions permit it.

Erzeugerabfüllung A German word for an estate-bottled wine.

Estate-bottled Wine that is made, produced, and bottled by the owner.

Extra dry Less dry than brut Champagne.

Fermentation The process by which grape juice is made into wine.
Fiaschi Straw-covered Chianti bottles.
Fino A type of Sherry.
First growth The highest-quality wine in the Classification of 1855 in Bordeaux.
Flor A type of yeast that develops in some Sherry production.
Fortified wine A wine that has additional neutral grape brandy that raises the alcohol content, such as Port and Sherry.
French Colombard A white grape grown in California and used to make jug wines.

Gamay A red grape used to make Beaujolais wine.
Gamay Beaujolais A red grape grown in California.
Garnacha A red grape grown in Spain that is related to the Grenache grape of the Rhône Valley of France.
Garrafeira A Portuguese word that signifies higher quality and longer aging.
Gewürztraminer The "spicy" white grape grown in Alsace, California, and Germany.
Graves A basic dry wine from the Bordeaux region of France.
Graves Supérieures A dry or semi-sweet white wine from the Bordeaux region of France; a step above a regional Graves wine.
Grand Cru A wine that comes from an excellent vineyard, which has the best soil and slope conditions in Burgundy; one step above a Premier Cru.
Gran Reserva A Spanish wine that had extra aging.
Grenache A red grape of the Rhône Valley region of France.

Hectare A metric measure that equals 2.471 acres.
Hectoliter A metric measure that equals 26.42 U.S. gallons.
Halb-trocken The German term meaning "semi-dry."
Hermitage A red wine from the northern Rhône Valley region of France.

Jug wine A simple drinking wine.

Kabinett A light, semi-dry white German wine.

Landwein A German table wine; one step above Tafelwein.
Liebfraumilch An easy-to-drink white German wine; it literally means "milk of the Blessed Mother."
Lodge The English term for a Port firm.

Long-vatted A term for a wine fermented with the grape skins for a long period of time to acquire a rich red color.

Luxury Champagne The highest-quality French Champagne.

Mâcon Blanc The most basic white wine from the Mâconnais region of France.

Mâcon Supérieur A white wine from the Mâconnais region; one step above the regional Mâcon Blanc in quality.

Mâcon-Villages A white wine from a specific village indicated on the label; one step above the Mâcon Supérieur in quality.

Malvasia A white grape grown in Italy

Manzanilla A type of Sherry.

Mechanical harvester A machine used on flat vineyards that shakes the vines to harvest the grapes.

Merlot The red "softening" grape grown primarily in the Bordeaux region of France.

Méthode Champenoise The method by which Champagne is made.

Microclimate A term that refers to an area that has a climate within a climate. While one area may be generally warm, it may have a cooler "microclimate" or region.

Mosel A region in Germany that produces a light-style white wine.

Mousseux The term for all French sparkling wines that are not produced in Champagne.

Müller-Thurgau A cross between the Riesling and the Silvaner grapes of Germany.

Muscadet A light, dry wine from the Loire Valley of France.

Must Grape juice.

Nebbiolo A red grape grown in Piedmont, Italy, which produces some of the finest Italian wine.

"Noble Rot" (*See Botrytis cinerea*)

Non-vintage Champagne Champagne made from a blend of vintages (more than one year's crop); it is more typical of the house style than vintage Champagne.

Nose The term used to describe the bouquet and aroma of wine.

Official Classification of 1855 A classification drawn up by wine brokers of the best Médoc wines of that time.

Pale Cream Sherry A type of Sherry made from Pedro Ximénez and Fino Sherry.

Palomino A grape used to make Spanish Sherry.
Petit Chablis Ordinary French Chablis wine.
Petite Château Lesser-known châteaus that produce good-quality wines for reasonable prices.
Petite Sirah A red grape grown in California.
Phylloxera A grape louse that kills the vines.
Pinot Blanc A white grape grown in Alsace.
Pinot Meunier A red grape grown in the Champagne region of France.
Pinot Noir A fragile red grape that is difficult to grow; it is found in the Burgundy and Champagne regions of France and California.
Pouilly-Fuissé The highest quality white Mâconnais wine.
Pouilly-Fumé A dry white wine from the Loire Valley region of France.
Pouilly-Vinzelles A dry white Mâconnais wine.
Premier Cru A wine that comes from a specific vineyard in Burgundy, France, which has special characteristics and bears that name.
Proprietary wine A wine that is given a name like any other product and marketed as such, i.e., Riunite, Mouton-Cadet.
PX An abbreviation for Pedro Ximénez Sherry.

Qualitätswein A German term meaning "quality wine."
Qualitätswein mit Prädikat A quality German wine with distinction.

Remueur A French term for "riddler," the person in a Champagne house who turns the bottles each day.
Reserva A term that means a wine has extra aging; it is found on Spanish, Portuguese, and Italian wine labels.
Reserve A term sometimes found on American wine labels. Although it has no legal significance, it is usually a better-quality wine.
Residual sugar An indication of how dry or sweet a wine is.
Riddling One step of the Champagne-making process in which the bottles are turned gradually each day until they are almost upside down with the sediment resting at the neck of the bottle.
Riesling A white grape grown in Alsace, Germany, and California.
Ruby Port A dark and fruity wine blended from non-vintage wines.

Sancerre A dry white wine from the Loire Valley region of France.
Sangiovese A red grape grown in Tuscany, Italy.
Sauternes A sweet white wine from the Bordeaux region of France.
Sauvignon Blanc A white grape grown primarily in the Loire Valley, Graves, and Sauternes regions of France, Washington State, and California.

Sec A sweet style of Champagne.

Sekt A German sparkling wine.

Sémillon A white grape found in the Graves and Sauternes regions of France.

Short-vatted A term for a wine fermented with the grape skins for only a short time.

Silvaner A white grape grown in Germany and Alsace.

Solera system A process used to systematically blend various vintages of Sherry.

Sommelier The French term for cellarmaster, or wine steward.

Spätlese A white German wine made from grapes picked later than the normal harvest.

Spumante An Italian sparkling wine.

Stainless-steel tank A container used to ferment some wines because of its capability for temperature control; it helps maintain fruitiness, especially in white wines.

St-Véran A white Mâconnais wine one step above Mâcon-Villages in quality.

Style The characteristics of the grapes and the wine.

Sulphur dioxide A substance used in winemaking as a preservative.

Süss-Reserve The unfermented grape juice added to German wine after fermentation to give more sweetness.

Syrah A red grape grown in the Rhône Valley region of France.

Tafelwein A German table wine.

Tannin A natural compound that comes from the skins, stems, and pips of the grapes and also from the wood that wine is aged in.

Tavel A rosé wine from the southern Rhône Valley region of France.

Tawny Port A Port that is lighter, softer, and aged longer than Ruby Port.

T.B.A. An abbreviation for the German wine Trockenbeerenauslese.

Tempranillo A red grape grown in Spain.

Thompson seedless A white grape grown in California and used to make jug wines.

Trebbiano A white grape grown in Italy.

Trocken The German term for "dry."

Trockenbeerenauslese The richest and sweetest wine made in Germany from the most mature grapes via the process of "Noble Rot."

Varietal wine A wine that is labelled with the predominant grape used to produce the wine, i.e., a wine from Chardonnay (predominantly) would be labelled "Chardonnay."

V.D.Q.S. An abbreviation for Vins Delimités de Qualité Supérieure; a classification of French wine, one step below A.O.C.

Veronese wine The wines from Veneto, Italy; Valpolicella, Bardolino, Soave, and Amarone.

Village wine A wine that comes from a particular village in Burgundy.

Vin de Pays A French classification of wine one step below V.D.Q.S.

Vinho Verde A white Portuguese wine.

Vino Nobile di Montepulciano A high-quality red wine from Tuscany.

Vins de Table Ordinary French table wine.

Vintage The year the grapes are harvested.

Vintage Champagne Champagne made from 100 percent of a particular vintage.

Vitis labrusca A native grape species in America.

Vitis vinifera A European grape species used to make European and California wine.

Vouvray The white "chameleon" wine from the Loire Valley region of France; it can be dry, semi-sweet, or sweet.

Wood Port Ruby and Tawny Port; they are ready to drink as soon as you buy them.

Zinfandel A red grape grown in California.

index

Rosemary Beale

Edwin C. Horner

Barry Mills

LUIS LATORA

Renato Ratti

Marvin R. Shanken

F Bouchard

Rodney D. Strong

Raymond Wellington

James Trezise

Louis P. Martini

Mike Stephens